FIRST EDITION

SUPERVISION:
A PROFESSIONAL'S PERSPECTIVE

By David Tipton

cognella® | ACADEMIC PUBLISHING

Bassim Hamadeh, CEO and Publisher

Kassie Graves, Director of Acquisitions and Sales

Jamie Giganti, Senior Managing Editor

Miguel Macias, Senior Graphic Designer

John Remington, Senior Field Acquisitions Editor

Monika Dziamka, Project Editor

Brian Fahey, Licensing Associate

Karen Wiley, Production Editor

Joyce Lue, Interior Designer

ISBN: 978-1-63487-781-7(pbk) / 978-1-63487-782-4 (br)

CONTENTS

PREFACE

This is a book about supervision and management for those who don't want to be supervisors or managers. It is a book for those confronted with the professional obligation to supervise and manage a staff and other professionals. The primary audience is those trained in what are considered the traditional professions of health care, law, education, architecture, engineering, and so on. It is also for those trained for some activity not thought of as a traditional profession but that requires either formal or informal training to enter, such as an executive chef, police captain, hotel manager, surveyor, social worker, and so on. The objective is to provide such individuals the mental models, frameworks, theories, ideas, and skills necessary to be proficient at the task of supervision to a *professional standard*.

There are innumerable reasons why a student selects a major and thus an occupational track. Those reasons may include parental influence, the job itself, economic benefits, quality of work life, or prestige associated with the job. No matter how much students research, some aspects of the job only emerge once they enter the field. Students choose career paths to design great buildings, write winning briefs, or deliver first-rate health care. Dealing with a recalcitrant administrative assistant who keeps providing substandard work or showing up late was not part of the dream. Had students been interested in supervision and management as a primary activity, the assumption is that they would have gone to business school. It is unlikely when making their career choice that professional students were aware that they were also making a decision to become a supervisor.

Professionals are obligated to meet certain standards related to the technical aspects of their profession. In many professions, support staff do the actual work, and the professional simply supervises the activity to ensure that standards are met. Just as the technical aspects of the job require a professional perspective, the supervisory aspects of the job also require a professional perspective. This is the key point. A professional is required to be excellent in the technical aspects of the job and the supervisory aspects. To reiterate, professionalism is the standard for both the technical and the supervisory aspects of the job.

The purpose of this book is not to summarize and convey the extensive literature on supervision and management from all its perspectives. Nor is the purpose to burden students with unnecessary details in informationally dense chapters. The world's information resides twenty-four hours a day on the Internet. The purpose is to deliver information that is simple, clear, and sufficient to the task of developing supervisors who are competent to meet their professional obligations.

The standards of simplicity, clarity, and sufficiency guide the writing style and the structure of the chapters. At the end of the course, students should come away with a set of ideas and mental models that will enable them to succeed in their supervisory role.

Most professional students focus their academic interest and energies on acquiring the technical skills to graduate, obtain licensure, and get a first position. A course on supervision is likely to sink to the bottom of their priority list. Students will filter the required readings and information through a very narrow tolerance for what is too much. They will question why they need to know this or be forced to memorize this. The classic student refrain for assimilating information and attention is: "Is this going to be on the test"? or "Just tell me what I need to know." The information included in the text is what students need to know, and it will be on the test. The actual test, however, is the reality of practice.

The first two chapters, on thinking and professionalism, establish a foundation for all subsequent chapters. The easiest way to influence people is to change their mental models, the way they think. Unlike some aspects of human behavior, mental models are relatively easy to surface and isolate. There is long history of this in cognitive psychology and therapy; the treatment of depression, for example, is based on this approach. The chapter on professionalism establishes a standard for assessing supervisory behavior and an ideal to aspire to. The next chapter, on management, provides in a very condensed format a view of classical management ideas and includes many of the topics that would be in a principles of management course, but targeted for this audience.

The next section deals with issues related to people, specifically supervising yourself, supervising people as individuals, and supervising people in teams. Following this the focus is on organizational issues: leadership, culture and politics, innovation and change. Finally, the "things" to be supervised—operations, quality and inventory; marketing and customer service; money, accounting, finance, planning, and budgets; law, ethics, and stakeholders—are discussed. The chapter sequence is presented below.

SECTION I: THE FOUNDATION

Chapter 1: Thinking
Chapter 2: Professionalism
Chapter 3: Management Overview

In Dickens's *A Christmas Carol*, the ghost Jacob Marley talks to his former business partner Ebenezer Scrooge. When Scrooge claims he was an honest man of business, Marley's reply is, "Mankind was my business. The common welfare was my business; charity, mercy, forbearance, benevolence, were all my business. The dealings of my trade were but a drop of water in the comprehensive ocean of my business!" It is my view that organizations of the type most likely to be termed professional, and their supervision and management, if done right, *if done professionally*, are for the service of the patient, the client, the community, and the staff. Hopefully, by linking professionalism to supervision, this message is conveyed explicitly and implicitly in the text, and students will recognize that *mankind is their business*.

SECTION I
THE FOUNDATION

The section provides the foundation for the rest of the book. It delivers the ideas, theories, and mental models that are the intellectual constellation that guides all subsequent chapters.

Chapter 1: Thinking

This is a chapter about thinking as applied to management and supervision. The key aspect is that belief systems about the work of management and supervision are important, in that they impact behaviors. These beliefs are aggregated into mental models. Beliefs with intention are considered mindsets. The chapter discusses certain ways of thinking that are important for managers and supervisors and presents several thinking tools.

Chapter 2: Professionalism

This chapter lays out a content and process model of professionalism. The content aspect of the model of professionalism includes the elements of accountability, altruism, duty, honor, integrity, excellence, and respect for others. The process aspect of the model includes professional sensitivity, motivation, judgment, and action. Whether management is a profession is discussed.

Chapter 3: Management Overview

This chapter presents an overview of the basics of management to include a definition and a discussion of the purpose of a business. It considers the context of management and various perspectives. Management functions, competencies and roles are presented. The management functions of planning, organizing, leading, and controlling are expanded on. Finally, a picture of a well-managed organization is presented.

1 THINKING

ALEX

For Alex, life has been great for the past two years. No tests to worry about or reports to write. Having passed the board, Alex had settled in at his new job, a job that he really liked. He liked all the people with one or two exceptions, but while not friendly, the relationships were still cordial. The only less-than-perfect aspect of his life was the problems in his personal relationship. His long-time girlfriend of the past seven years, having just graduated, had moved out. They were now arguing over who got what and who got the dog. He had not seen it coming.

At lunchtime yesterday, the director of the department stopped by and asked to meet with him today at 2:00 p.m. At the meeting Alex found out that the director was diagnosed with cancer and was scheduled for surgery and chemotherapy to begin next week. Alex was to be the interim director for the department, beginning next week.

On his way home and now, sitting in front of the TV listening to the presidential debates, Alex's mind began to wander, skipping from point to point. As he began to pay attention to the sounds in his head, this is what was playing:

I really don't want to do this.

What if I'm no good at it?

Will the staff still like me and invite me for Friday drinks if I do this?

I don't know anything about being a supervisor.

What was it they said in class about management?

I really want to keep the dog. ... I found her and named her.

My mother always said above all be nice. ... Can I do that and still be in charge?

This means I'm in control; I can do what I want.

Some of the people from the other departments really hate their supervisors.

I'm going to tighten things up in the department.

What is it, exactly, that a supervisor does? Most of them just seem to sit in their offices and go to meetings.

Are they going to pay me more?

What if I'm no good at it? I've never failed anything.

And, on and on the thoughts kept playing in Alex's head.

"The goal of effective living is to think effectively; to know when we have crazy ideas."

(Friday 1999, 15)

As a child, having done something foolish, one familiar response you were likely to hear from a parent was, "What were you thinking?"

LEARNING OBJECTIVES

- Discuss mental models and supervision and management.
- Discuss mindsets and supervision and management.
- Demonstrate how to construct a mind map.
- Discuss the thinking skills of mindfulness and reflection.
- Describe and list the thinking tools in the chapter.

BELIEFS

It matters what assumptions supervisors/managers hold, what they believe, and how they organize their beliefs about themselves and the task of management. It's a simple point, but a powerful one—that assumptions and beliefs dictate behavior. It is acknowledged that beliefs alone do not control behavior and that human behavior is more complicated; that genetics, the subconscious, personality, and the environment are also drivers of human behavior. But unlike genetics, the subconscious, personality, the environment, and the beliefs that humans hold embodied in mental models, and mindsets are relatively accessible, controllable, and pliable. For these reasons, instilling and altering mental models, beliefs, and mindsets is a powerful management device. The job as a supervisor or manager is to get people to believe they can change the world, because as Steve Jobs observed, "Because the ones who are crazy enough to think that they can change the world, are the ones who do" (https://en.wikiquote.org/wiki/Apple_Inc.). Realistically, the supervisor's job is to get people to believe that out of respect for their colleagues, they should return e-mails in a timely fashion and that quality matters and they should take an extra second to double-check their work.

WAYS OF THINKING

Each of us knows what thinking is. It is what goes on inside our head when we try to solve problems. People who think better are deemed to be more intelligent. Supervisors and managers who think better are more effective. There are all types of thinking: clinical, rational, faulty, delusional, systems, realistic, creative, strategic, linear, abstract, theoretical, disciplined, and magical. There are as many types of thinking as there are problems to be solved.

"The chief executive of a major Canadian company complained recently that he can't get his engineers to think like managers. … What does it mean to think like a manager?" (Gosling and Mintzberg 2003, 1). Mintzberg goes on to write about five ways managers interpret and deal with the world around them. He calls these five ways the aspects of the managerial mind, and they are equivalent to an attitude, a frame of mind, or a perspective on how to think. The five ways to think are:

- The reflective mind, managing self: The reflective mind is about digesting, reflecting on, and relating to patterns; and synthesizing events and happenings. It is about attaching meaning to circumstance, without which it is mindless. Reflection is looking inward so that you can look out and see the familiar in a new way.
- The analytic mind, managing organizations: The analytic mind involves breaking larger units into smaller segments. It is about decomposing complex phenomena into component parts. Effective analysis seeks to avoid the obvious and superficial linkages and probe for the essential relationships and linkages. It also involves incorporating soft data such as the values that underlie organizational choices. True analysis does not simplify complexity but enhances the organization's ability to act in the midst of the complexity.
- The worldly mind, managing context: A worldly mind is not the same as globalization. Globalization seeks to make the world similar, to encourage homogeneity of perspective. A worldly mind is about moving in both practical and sophisticated ways

to experience other worlds, other people's circumstances. To manage context is to manage at the edges, where the organization and all the worlds that surround it join.

- The collaborative mind, managing relationships: The collaborative mind focuses not on managing people but on managing the relationship. It is about embedding yourself in a network, for the most part, of equal actors. Rather than leading heroically, it is about the Japanese idea of leading from the background, so that the sun may shine on all.

- The action mind, managing change: The action mind is about mobilizing energy, emotions, and aspirations around those things that need to be changed while maintaining the continuity of those things that do not need changing. Action must be coupled with reflection or it is thoughtless. Action is a learning process.

(Mintzberg, in his article uses the term mindsets. *This designation is not derived from any psychological or physiological definition or formulation. He uses the extension set to mean settle on these perspectives, recognize the merit of these five ways. He warns against using the extension to mean "set," as in frozen, or "cured," as concrete might. To avoid confusion with our use of the term mindset, we use the generic term* mind *to describe each of the five. The substance of his discussion is not altered by this substitution and acknowledges Mintzberg as the source for this section.)*

Howard Gardner (2008), in his book *5 Minds for the Future*, provides several examples of thinking that are of use to the manager. They include:

- The synthesizing mind: The synthesizing mind takes elements from disparate sources and weaves them into a coherent whole. The synthesizing mind sees the big picture. A narrative, or story, is an attempt at synthesizing multiple strands. The understanding of how synthesis occurs is limited, but learning to view issues from multiple perspectives is helpful. Synthesizers can take in vast amounts of information and then declutter such that only what is essential remains.

- An ethical mind: An ethical mind requires the ability to think abstractly about whether one is fulfilling his or her assigned obligations; in this case, as relates to work. An ethical mind is bound by the following standards: Is the work produced ethical in quality? Are the implications for the wider community an issue? Is the work being done meaningful, challenging, and engaging?

Though the term *mind* is not used, there is a practical type of thinking that benefits a supervisor.

- This way of thinking is termed *constructive* (Epstein 1998), *tacit* (Sternberg 1999), or *practical* (Albrecht 2007; Sternberg et al. 2000). This is the kind of thinking that is applied, focused on specific day-to-day problems, and acquired unknowingly from experience. Taken together, these ways of thinking approximate the idea of common sense. It's great to think analytically or synthetically, but it is also helpful for supervisors to know how the copy machine works or the best time to approach a superior.

A way of thinking about the future that is helpful to supervisors and managers is strategic thinking.

- Strategic thinking involves viewing the obvious factors in the right perspective without being dissuaded by emotion or fad in an attempt to position a company in front of the inevitable future.

Sometimes supervisors and managers need to go with their "gut," what they feel the right choice is. In fact, they are engaging in intuitive thinking.

- In contrast to analytical thinking, thinking that is unconscious and rapid is intuitive. Much high-level thinking is intuitive, operating like the autopilot in a jetliner without conscious involvement or attention.

A kind of thinking that is used when there really is no precedent for a situation and a solution is termed *judgment*.

- Judgment is the ability to infer, estimate, and predict the character of unknown events. Judgment is the thinking process used when you don't have all the information. Beginning a recommendation with a phrase such as "My best guess" is an indicator of judgment.

Sometimes supervisors/managers need to be wise in their thinking.

- The key aspect of wisdom is the idea of balancing competing interests. This definition rests on the idea of an understanding of the essence of the human condition and the conduct of a good life. Wisdom includes knowledge about the uncertainties of the world. Those who are wise have a rich factual knowledge about life, a rich procedural knowledge about life, an understanding of the issues related to each stage of life, an understanding of life's priorities and what is valuable, and an understanding that life is uncertain. Wisdom is an understanding of what is important.

Ways of thinking can be considered the operating systems for the mind of the supervisor and manager. The effective supervisor or manager is astute enough to recognize that certain types of thinking are more useful for certain situations than others. Astute supervisors and managers recognize that the core of a complicated problem, for example, is really an ethical dilemma, and this way of thinking is spotlighted. For a supervisor/manager to think about which type of thinking is most appropriate is to engage in metacognition—thinking about thinking.

This is a chapter about thinking. Stupidity is the result of not thinking. Excessive adherence to rules and protocols in the face of the evidence is stupidity. Stupidity is the "learned corruption of learning" (Welles 1991, 1). It is a legitimate subject of study within psychology (Sternberg 2002). Stupidity is the "unquestioning acceptance of any one set of constraints or axioms that algorithmically 'determine' the problem-solving steps one needs to take in order to produce the desired behavior" (Moldoveanu and Langer 2002, 229). Sometimes, supervisors and managers are stupid in that they don't "think" their problems through. Chico Marx in the movie *Duck Soup* captured this idea when he said, "Well, who are you going to believe, me or your own eyes?" https://en.wikiquote.org/wiki/Duck_Soup Stupidity is a result of thinking becoming frozen.

MANAGEMENT MYTHS

Besides not thinking, sometimes supervisors and managers, particularly those who are new, hold some beliefs about their situation that are flawed. For example, (1) I have the power to implement my ideas and do want I want, (2) I am in control now, (3) I need to build strong individual relationships, and (4) the job is to make operations run smoothly. The reality is different. In order, formal power may have been bestowed by the organization, but effective power must be earned by demonstrating technical and human competence. The power to hire, fire, and promote may ensure compliance, but effective supervisor/managers build commitment to the organization's goals. Strong individual relationships are beneficial, but the real job is to build and develop an effective department or team. Finally, making the operations run smoothly is just a beginning; making it better is the real objective. To reiterate, beliefs are important, and if they are flawed, performance suffers (adapted from Hill 2007).

CHANGING MINDS

People change their minds all the time. Sometimes it is a gradual process, and other times it is instantaneous. The mechanism for that process is detailed in the book *Changing Minds* by Howard Gardner (2006). People change their minds by (1) using reason and a rational approach of identifying relevant factors, weighing each, and making an assessment that there is a superior way to believe than a currently held belief; (2) conducting formal or informal research and concluding that a change of mind is in order; (3) feeling that an alternative belief is better; (4) being able to express the changed perspective in multiple forms—linguistic, numerical, or graphic—that reinforce each expression; (5) being able to reward the new way of thinking; and (6) experiencing real-world events that enhance or retard the movement to a changed mind.

MENTAL MODELS

A mental model is an organizing cognitive structure that characterizes aspects of the external world; for example, in this context, what supervisor/managers actually do. Mental models are our internal blueprints of what is real in the world. They are an aggregate of what we believe is real and true. For a supervisor/manager, is the task to inspire and facilitate or command and control? Do manager/supervisors believe they have a chance to make people's lives better, or do they believe that profit is the sole metric? Does staff believe their job is to process orders or satisfy and delight a customer? Do employees believe they own 50 percent of their relationship with their boss, or do they believe they are powerless?

According to Douglas McGregor in his 1960 book *The Human Side of Enterprise*, those who adhere to theory X management believe that employees

- dislike working;
- avoid responsibility and need to be directed;
- have to be controlled, forced, and threatened to deliver what's needed;
- need to be supervised at every step, with controls put in place; and
- need to be enticed to produce results; otherwise they have no ambition or incentive to work.

Those who believe in theory Y management believe that employees

- take responsibility and are motivated to fulfil the goals they are given,
- seek and accept responsibility and do not need much direction, and
- consider work as a natural part of life and solve work problems imaginatively.

A theory X *belief* results in organizations that are centralized and tightly controlled, while a theory Y *belief* results in an organization that is decentralized and participative.

Thus, supervisors' and managers' beliefs about their job aggregated into their personal mental model is a powerful element in determining the process and quality of work life and performance. Mental models are therefore important.

Everyone has some idea or mental picture of what managers or supervisors are supposed to look like, how they are supposed to act, and how they should handle the job. This picture likely originates from how one's family was "managed," who was in control, and how decisions were made. Everyone has seen movies and television programs of managers, supervisors, and leaders. Biographies of presidents and other famous leaders are also influential. Jobs held, sports teams, clubs, and organizations of which we were members also influence beliefs about supervision and management. Stories about supervision and management count also. On and on, a gradual picture of what constitutes management and supervision develops. For many, promoted to supervision and management, it is this picture of management that initially influences their style and their behavior. While elements of this mental picture are undoubtedly correct, it is likely that some elements are missing, others are naive, and others are patently dysfunctional. The purpose of the text is to provide those who would be managers a more sophisticated, nuanced, and complete mental blueprint of what management is. It is then management's task to instill and convey to staff mental models and blueprints of how to do their job. In short, management's task is to manage mental models. As Peter Senge writes, "But what is most important to grasp is that mental models are *active*—they shape how we act" (1990, 175). Senge also writes that the traditional view of organizational life is managing, organizing, and controlling, whereas vision, values, and mental models constitute a new approach.

MINDSETS

Mindsets are viewed as beliefs related to management coupled with an intention to act. In a sense mindsets are beliefs operationalized. For example, at the schema level our personal belief that all humans deserve respect translates at the managerial mental model level to respecting individuals is the best way to motivate and at the mindset level to a statement such as, "Clients first, paperwork second." Mindsets are what managers try to inculcate and develop in their staff. They are brief declarations of how work is to be done and of what expectations are. A mindset for a transfer company of "every package every day" establishes the expectation that every package scheduled for delivery on a given day is to be delivered, no matter how long it takes. In the military the mindset of "no one left behind" establishes expectations and makes clear what the requirement is. Managers manage their schema and mental models; they manage the mindsets of others.

A residue is something that remains after the main element is gone. In this case a mindset is what remains of a person as a supervisor. Residue is the result of inculcating certain beliefs into staff such that when left to their own devices they will know how to act. Mindset is the default code for any situation. A mindset of "clients first" leaves little doubt about how to behave. It is the idea of belief linked with intention to act that distinguishes mindset. Effective management at the mindset level of analysis is about developing a collective mind, a way of thinking that engages everyone in the organization.

THINKING TOOLS

Mind Maps

Each subsequent chapter begins with an exercise in mind mapping. To doodle absent-mindedly on a piece of paper is to construct a type of mind map. A mind map, or cognitive map, is a technique for making the internal cognitive terrain of individuals visual. Mind maps incorporate both visual and linguistic elements. They capture concepts and their relationship to one another, both the direction of causality and intensity. They are descriptions of what an individual knows or believes about a topic; for example, conflict management. They are both descriptive and integrative in that they present a holistic representation of an individual's understanding of a subject. As an assessment device they are idiosyncratic. Elucidated cognitive maps serve as anchors from which new concepts and ideas can radiate; those ideas coming in this case from classroom instruction, readings, and exercises. Through instruction, idiosyncratic mind maps converge on a collective diagrammatic representation. In other words, at the beginning of a topic in a class of thirty students there will be thirty versions; following instruction there should be consistency and similarity across the thirty mind maps, though not necessarily exactness. The various linkages, if expressed verbally, represent the beliefs one holds about a subject. In a mind map, I might link generational differences with conflict; thus, the belief expressed verbally is, "Different generations have trouble getting along at work." (The exercise section provides instruction on completing a mind map.)

Mindfulness

Mindfulness is paying attention on purpose. It is the activity of observing what we experience, including feelings, perceptions, thoughts, and behaviors. A critical aspect of this observation is that it is nonjudgmental and there is no reaction to our observations. Embedded in the idea of mindfulness is the ability to recognize patterns of automatic emotional responses. Being aware of these responses, we are then poised to alter them. Being able to identify our thoughts is a necessary first step to examining our beliefs about any particular subject and also any personal schemas we might hold. There are five facets to mindfulness: (1) the ability to describe our internal experiences in words; (2) the ability to act with awareness; (3) nonjudging, or the absence of positive or negative appraisal; (4) nonreactivity, or permitting feelings and thoughts without an automatic response; and (5) observation, or remaining conscious of experience, even if painful. Engaging in mindfulness allows acceptance of who we are and what we think and feel. Mindfulness enhances our awareness of everyday life, influencing well-being. It allows us to see our thoughts as distinct phenomena not requiring a particular response. Therefore, we can more easily regulate our emotions and behaviors. Mindfulness helps us clarify our values and act in accordance with those values. Being nonjudgmental, we no longer have to condemn ourselves for the thoughts and feelings that all humans experience. Mindfulness also alters structural and functional patterns in the brain, enhancing our cognitive and emotional processing.

Learning from Experience: Reflective Thinking

In writing on whether management is a profession or a craft, Mintzberg states, "You end up with a job that is above all a *practice*, learned through experience and rooted in context" (2013, 9). Thus, the process of how one learns from experience as a manager is crucial. That process involves the following four stages:

- Concrete experience (feeling): learning from specific experiences and relating to people

- Reflective observation (watching): observing before making a judgment; looking for the meaning of things
- Abstract conceptualization (thinking): logical analysis of ideas
- Active experimentation (doing): ability to get things done by influencing people (Kolb 2015)

Something happens to a manager at work; say he gets into an argument with an associate (concrete experience). He retires to his office and reviews why this happened (reflective observation). As a result of this reflection, he concludes that the best way to avoid and handle conflict is to listen first, rather than try dominate the conversation from the beginning (abstract conceptualization changes). He then tests this new conceptualization in practice. In the language of this chapter, the manager alters his belief system, or mental model, about dealing with conflict and thus changes his behavior.

In altering a belief system, the ability to reflect is critical. Without reflection, activities are just the flotsam and jetsam of everyday life. They are without meaning, relevance, or the power to influence. Asking yourself why something happened and what it meant is the essence of reflection and is to look for causation and importance. Again, in the language of this chapter, reflection is ultimately about surfacing particular beliefs and then testing to determine whether the beliefs are appropriate. Determining whether a particular belief is appropriate hinges on the following standards. Do the beliefs meet the test of everyday common sense? Is there empirical evidence for the validity of this belief someplace? And, most important, is it functional? Does it work? If not, then a change is in order.

Case Analysis

A time-honored way to think through a problem is the case analysis approach. The mechanics of this process are as follows:

Step 1:   Identify the problem.
Step 2:   Assess by collecting history and physical data.
Step 3:   Formulate competing hypotheses, diagnoses, alternatives, and so on.
Step 4:   Gather additional information and conduct research in support of each hypothesis, diagnosis, alternative, and so on.
Step 5:   Select a specific hypothesis, diagnosis, or alternative as correct.
Step 6:   Develop a plan of action.
Step 7:   Implement and evaluate choice.

Tips on case analysis:

1. Read through the case quickly to get a general impression of the problem. Highlight any points that jump out. Begin to formulate the problem.
2. To focus attention, use the following devices:

    a. Consider all factors (CAF): Ask yourself if all the important factors have been considered.

    b. Other people's views (OPV): How would another clinician look at this same problem? Is there an alternative view of the problem?

    c. Plus, minus, interesting (PMI): Which facts support your hypothesis, which facts do not, and which facts are interesting but irrelevant?

3. In making the decision, use the following aids:

    a. Clarify what the purpose of the decision is, and in working through the choices remain focused on this purpose.

    b. What are the short-term and long-term consequences of the choices?

    c. If you approached the problem from another person's point of view, what would the decision be?

    d. Is it possible to look at the problem from a different perspective?

    e. Does the proposed choice violate or support my values? (adapted from de Bono 1994).

Six Thinking Hats

Edward de Bono developed the Six Thinking Hats method. It is a way of looking at a problem from multiple perspectives, but only one at a time. Simplifying the thinking about problems eliminates confusion and helps clarify potential choices. With the Six Thinking Hats method, only one thing is done at a time.

White Hat thinking: White Hat thinking mimics a computer. A computer is neutral. It does not interpret nor offer shades of meaning. It is an instrument that deals in facts and information. White Hat thinking is objective and analytical. White Hat thinking separates information into tiers: that which is proved and absolutely true and that which is believed to be true, but not yet verified. White Hat thinking excludes intuition, hunches, and choices based on experience.

Red Hat thinking: Red Hat thinking is about emotion and feeling. It is the opposite of White Hat thinking. Ultimately, all decisions are emotional. White Hat (analytical) thinking provides a thinking map. In the end, our values and emotions determine the route we take. There is no need to justify an emotion; we just feel that way. Red Hat thinking accounts for intuition and hunches. Red Hat thinking also accounts for deep emotions that might color our choices, such as fear, anger, and jealousy, as well as transient emotions that occur while working through the problem.

Black Hat thinking: Black Hat thinking is the hat of caution. It is not balanced. It is a conscious attempt to consider everything that might go wrong. Black Hat thinking is risk assessment, an assessment of the future consequences of a decision taken. Black Hat thinking is the most important hat. Its overuse must be guarded against. It is easier to be negative than constructive.

Yellow Hat thinking: Yellow Hat thinking is the opposite of Black Hat thinking; it is positive and optimistic without being delusional or being a Pollyanna. Yellow Hat thinking is a search for value and benefit in our actions that is grounded in logic and analysis. Yellow Hat thinking is about visions and dreams.

Green Hat thinking: Green Hat thinking is about new ideas, perceptions, change, and creativity. Green Hat thinking attempts to go beyond the known and the obvious in pursuit of a new and better way of doing things.

Blue Hat thinking: Blue Hat thinking is about control and orchestrating which type of thinking is appropriate at what stage of the process. It is thinking about the type of thinking a problem requires. Blue Hat thinking says we have spent enough time examining the negative aspects of this problem, it is now time to examine the benefits to be gained from our choice (adapted from de Bono 1999).

YOUR THINKING IS A CHOICE

The Greek philosopher Epictetus wrote, "People are disturbed not by things, but by the view which they take of them" (http://www.wisdomquotes.com/quote/epictetus-6.html). Or, as Abraham Lincoln observed, "Most folks are usually about as happy as they make their minds up to be" (https://www.brainyquote.com/quotes/quotes/a/abrahamlin100845.html). Things happen to people, and it is their choice how they think and react. One can choose to think about a personal failure as an insurmountable tragedy or an opportunity to grow. One can choose to think of one's staff as assets to be exploited or people to be developed. It is a choice.

SUMMARY

The key idea in this chapter was that belief impacts behavior. Individual beliefs are aggregated into mental models that are representations of an aspect of reality. When beliefs are linked to intention, they are termed mindsets. The supervisor's or manager's task is to leave specific beliefs and mindsets in the mind of staff as a residue of his or her efforts. It is also important to recognize that each of us is in control of how and what we think. Gandhi's quote below is an apt summarization of this chapter.

> "Your beliefs become your thoughts,
> Your thoughts become your words,
> Your words become your actions,
> Your actions become your habits,
> Your habits become your values,
> Your values become your destiny."

(http://www.goodreads.com/quotes/50584-your-beliefs-become-your-thoughts-your-thoughts-become-your-words)

—Mahatma Gandhi

EXERCISES

Summarizing

Write a one-page executive summary of the chapter.

Discuss with your classmates how you would teach this material.

Write a two-page case from your experience on this topic that would be instructional for other students.

Develop a mental model for this chapter based on the mind mapping technique.

What's Important to You in the Chapter?

With several of your classmates, discuss the most important ideas from the chapter. Which ideas do you think will be most useful to you in your career? Which ideas do you think you will remember in six months?

What Do the Practitioners/Others Say?

Discuss with your colleagues or someone at work any of the ideas in the chapter. Alternatively, read an article from any source on thinking and be prepared to summarize its message.

Mind Mapping

In developing a mind map, it is best to begin in the center of the page. Then, array any terms and ideas that come to mind randomly around the central concept. Link those elements using the convention below. Practice mind mapping using the idea of *superior grades* as the central element.

Straight solid line	a direct relationship between two elements
Broken line	an uncertain relationship
Single-headed arrow	direction of causality
Double-headed arrow	reciprocal causality
Thickness, darkness of lines	intensity of relationships

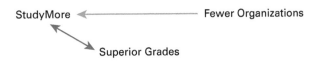

Learning History

As a method for reflection about an event, simply write what happened, including the people, the venue, what was said, and how it turned out. However, only use the right side of the paper to write this narrative. In other words, tell the story. On the other side of the page, analyze what was going on. What emotions were involved, and what were you thinking at the time of the event. Did it change over the course of the event? Is there a repetitive theme? If the event didn't work out as hoped, why not? What could have been done differently? The idea is to isolate the critical variables that determined the outcome of the event, usually the emotions and thoughts involved.

Try this for some event you had difficulty with.

Three-Minute Thinking

Set a timer for three minutes. On a piece of paper, record each thought that pops into your brain. Just capture the key word. For example, for "I'm hungry for a snack," write "hungry." Count the number of thoughts over the three minutes.

Opposing Ideas

F. Scott Fitzgerald said, "The test of a first-rate intelligence is the ability to hold two opposed ideas in mind at the same time and still retain the ability to function" (https://www. brainyquote.com/quotes/quotes/f/fscottfit100572.html).

How does one reconcile the obligation to think both analytically and synthetically as described above?

Mental Models

The classic supervision/management functions are to plan, organize, lead, and *control*. How would your behavior change if you believed the functions were to plan, organize, lead, and *facilitate*?

If necessary, research the distinction between control and facilitation in dealing with people.

Thoughts

If you were in Alex's position about to assume a supervisory role, what thoughts would be going through your head? How would you handle this situation?

REFERENCES AND WORKS CONSULTED

Albrecht, K. 2007. *Practical Thinking*. San Francisco: Jossey-Bass.

Ardelt, M. 2004. "Wisdom as Expert Knowledge System: A Critical Review of a Contemporary Operationalization of an Ancient Concept." *Human Development* 47: 257–85.

Argyris, C., and D.A. Schon. 1974. *Theory in Practice*. San Francisco: Jossey-Bass.

Baltes, P.B., and U.M. Staudinger. 2000. "Wisdom: A Metaheuristic (Pragmatic) to Orchestrate Mind and Virtue toward Excellence." *American Psychologist* 55: 122–36.

Carroll, M. 2007. *The Mindful Leader*. Boston: Trumpeter.

Craig, M. 2000. *Thinking Visually*. New York: Continuum.

Dane, E., and M.G. Pratt. 2009. "Conceptualizing and Measuring Intuition: A Review of Recent Trends." *International Review of Industrial and Organizational Psychology* 24: 1–40.

de Bono, E. 1994. *DeBono's Thinking Course*. New York: Facts On File.

de Bono, E. 1999. *Six Thinking Hats*. New York: Back Bay.

Dweck, C.S. 2006. *Mindset*. New York: Ballantine.

Epstein, S. 1998. *Constructive Thinking*. Westport, CT: Praeger.

Friday, P.J. 1999. *Friday's Laws*. Pittsburgh: Bradley Oak.

Gardner, H. 2006. *Changing Minds*. Boston: Harvard Business School Press.

Gardner, H. 2008. *5 Minds for the Future*. Boston: Harvard Business School Press.

Garten, J.E. 2001. *The Mind of the C.E.O.* New York: Basic.

Gonzalez, M. 2012. *Mindful Leadership*. Mississauga, ON: Wiley.

Gosling, J., and H. Mintzberg. 2003. "The Five Minds of a Manager." *Harvard Business Review* (November): 1–9.

Gostick, A., and C. Elton. 2012. *All In*. New York: Free Press.

Greenhalgh, T. 2002. "Intuition and Evidence—Uneasy Bedfellows." *British Journal of General Practice* 52 (478): 394–400.

Hams, B. 2012. *Ownership Thinking*. New York: McGraw-Hill.

Hill, L.A. 2007. "Becoming the Boss." *Harvard Business Review* (January): 1–9.

https://en.wikiquote.org/wiki/Apple_Inc.

https://en.wikiquote.org/wiki/Duck_Soup

http://www.wisdomquotes.com/quote/epictetus-6.html

https://www.brainyquote.com/quotes/quotes/a/abrahamlin100845.html

http://www.goodreads.com/quotes/50584-your-beliefs-become-your-thoughts-your-thoughts-become-your-words

Ibarra, H. 2015. *Act like a Leader Think like a Leader*. Boston: Harvard Business Review Press.

Kahney, L. 2008. *Inside Steve's Brain*. New York: Penguin.

Kets de Vries, M.F.R. 1999. "Transforming the Mind-Set of the Organization: A Clinical Perspective." *Administration and Society* 6: 640–75.

King, L., and J.V. Appleton. 1997. "Intuition: A Critical Review of the Research and Rhetoric." *Journal of Advanced Nursing* 26: 194–202.

Kleiner, A., and G. Roth. 1997. "How to Make Experience Your Company's Best Teacher." *Harvard Business Review* (September–October): 172–77.

Kolb, D.A. 2015. *Experiential Learning*. Upper Saddle River, NJ: Pearson Education.

Langer, E.J. 2014. *Mindfulness*. Philadelphia: DaCapo.

Martin, R. 2007. "How Successful Leaders Think." *Harvard Business Review* (June): 75–81.

McGregor, D. 1960. *The Human Side of Enterprise*. New York: McGrawHill.

Mento, A.J., P. Maartinelli, and R.M. Jones. 1999. "Mind Mapping in Executive Education: Applications and Outcomes." *Journal of Management Development* 18 (4): 390–416.

Mezirow, J. 1990. *Fostering Critical Reflection in Adulthood*. San Francisco: Jossey-Bass.

Mintzberg, H. 2013. *Simply Managing*. San Francisco: Berrett-Koehler.

Mockler, R.J., and D.G. Dologite. 1999. "Learning How to Learn: Nurturing Professional Growth through Cognitive Mapping." *New England Journal of Entrepreneurship* 2 (2): 65–79.

Moldoveanu, M., and E. Langer. 2002. "When 'Stupid' Is Smarter than We Are." In *Why Smart People Can Be So Stupid*, edited by R.J. Sternberg. New Haven, CT: Yale University Press.

Olson, A.K., and B.K. Simerson. 2015. *Leading with Strategic Thinking*. Hoboken, NJ: Wiley.

Pollock, J.M., J.L. Burnette, and C.L. Hoyt. 2012. "Self-Efficacy in the Face of Threats to Entrepreneurial Success: Mind-Sets Matter." *Basic and Applied Social Psychology* 34: 287–94.

Quirk, M. 2006. *Intuition and Metacognition in Medical Education*. New York: Spring.

Rouse, W.B., and N.M. Morris. 1986. "On Looking into the Black Box: Prospects and Limits in the Search for Mental Models." *Psychological Bulletin* 100 (3): 349–63.

Schaeken, W., A. Vandierendonck, W. Schroyens, and G. d'Ydewall, eds. 2014. *The Mental Models Theory of Reasoning*. New York: Psychology Press.

Schon, D.A. 1987. *Educating the Reflective Practitioner*. London: Jossey-Bass.

Senge, P.M. 1990. *The Fifth Discipline*. New York: Doubleday.

Sternberg, R. 1998. "A Balance Theory of Wisdom." *Review of General Psychology* 2 (4): 347–65.

Sternberg, R.J., ed. 2002. *Why Smart People Can Be So Stupid*. New Haven, CT: Yale University Press.

Sternberg, R.J., G.B. Forsythe, J. Hedlund, J.A. Horvath, R.K. Wagner, W.M. Williams, S.A. Snook, and E.L. Grigorenko. 2000. *Practical Intelligence in Everyday Life*. New York: Cambridge University Press.

Sternberg, R.J., and J.A. Horvath, eds. 1999. *Tacit Knowledge in Professional Practice*. New York: Routledge.

Tversky, A., and D. Khaneman. 1974. "Judgment under Uncertainty: Heuristics and Biases." *Science* 185: 1124–31.

Van Vreeswijk, M., J. Broerson, and G. Schurink. 2014. *Mindfulness and Schema Therapy*. West Sussex, UK: Wiley.

Wagner, R.K., and R.J. Sternberg. 1985. "Practical Intelligence in Real-World Pursuits: The Role of Tacit Knowledge." *Journal of Personality and Psychology* 49 (2): 436–58.

Wagner, R.K., and R.J. Sternberg. 1987. "Tacit Knowledge in Managerial Success." *Journal of Business and Psychology* 1 (4): 301–12.

Weick, K.E., and K.H. Roberts. 1993. "Collective Mind in Organizations: Heedful Interrelating on Flight Decks." *Administrative Science Quarterly* 38: 357–81.

Welles, J.F. 1991. *The Story of Stupidity*. Orient, NY: Mount Pleasant.

2 PROFESSIONALISM

THE MEETING

Even Alex knew the meeting was a disaster. In his first meeting with the staff, everything had gone wrong. It was his intention to just lay out several ideas in an informal manner for improving the department. He had scribbled a few ideas on the back of a piece of paper and thought he would wing it. Several of the ideas to be presented were derived from informal lunch conversations with the staff. Alex thought these would be readily accepted and everyone would be on board with the changes. It didn't turn out that way. The first proposal evoked universal disdain, and nothing was resolved. The second proposal was flat-out rejected. One of the senior professional staff stood up, said if the proposal were instituted he wouldn't comply and would start to look for a new job, and then left the room. From this point the meeting lost its focus and degenerated into an open and rambling complaint session. It was hardly an auspicious beginning.

Driving home, Alex was upset. Nothing like that had ever happened before. He ruminated on the drive home.

I thought these were my friends.

I thought they liked me; I want them to like me.

I can't believe someone walked out.

Why would anyone quit their job over this?

I can't believe how bad I was, what a failure I am.

I'll never last.

I just missed my turn.

This is the third candy bar I've had on the way home.

Why am I biting my nails?

I'm going to get fired.

Alex called his mother on the cell phone. His mother was a long-time and experienced corporate executive and detailed the situation. She reassured Alex that these things happen. She also mildly chastised Alex for blaming the staff and complaining that he had not been taught this in school. She told Alex that it was his job to get this transition and these meetings right. In a very nice way Alex's mother told him it was time to grow up. It was time to be a professional. Alex's mother reiterated, the only criteria that matters is performance.

MENTAL MODELS

In the center of the space below, write the word *professionalism*. Next, write the words that come to mind when you think of either this activity or this type of person. Do not edit your thoughts or collaborate with anyone. There is no right or wrong answer.

If things are related, connect them with an arrow. If the relationship is reciprocal (they both affect each other), put arrows at both ends of the line. If one relationship is stronger than another, make the arrow darker and thicker.

The goal is to capture your mental model of what you believe about professionalism. This is the starting point for the discussion on professionalism.

LEARNING OBJECTIVES

- Discuss the definition of a *profession* and *professionalism*.
- Describe the content aspects of professionalism: altruism, accountability, excellence, duty, honor and integrity, and respect for others.
- Discuss the process aspects of professionalism: sensitivity, judgment, motivation, and action.
- Discuss whether management is a profession.
- Discuss the link between professionalism and supervision.

This chapter details a content and process model of professionalism. This model establishes the standards to be used as a supervisor. Moving through the text and discussing the subsequent chapters, the unspoken subtext is that supervision is a professional activity. As such, there is a professional standard to be met. This chapter establishes what that standard is.

A Profession

A profession is an occupation characterized by the following aspects:

- Body of knowledge and skills
- Monopoly on that knowledge and skills
- Formal education
- Code of ethics/behavior
- Social contract with society to do good
- Autonomy
- Self-regulation
- Licensing

The classical professions are law, medicine, and the clergy, of which university teaching is a variant. There are newer professions, such as dentistry, architecture, accounting, and engineering; other professions are termed emergent and are exemplified by pharmacy, nursing, chiropractic, public school teaching, and librarianship, among others. Still, numerous occupations claim professional status without necessarily meeting all of the above standards. Finally, many occupations claim to deliver professional-level work. Therefore, they are exhibiting a professional ethos, meaning that professional beliefs and ideals shape their work.

Professionalism

Professionalism is a complex pattern of values, attitudes, behaviors, cognitions, and emotions. Despite all the writing on the subject, professionalism is an elusive topic. While it can be broken down into its component elements, professionalism is somewhat fuzzy. Professionalism is much like leadership in that it can be deconstructed into its component elements; and in doing so the essence is lost. Only contextually, in its idiosyncratic expression, can the true essence of professionalism be captured. Professionalism is an expression of character. Professionalism transcends the outward markers. It is not acting professional—it is being professional. Professionalism is framed by a commitment to the highest standards of excellence, a commitment to the interest of others, and a commitment to the needs of the community.

THE PROFESSIONALISM MODEL: CONTENT

The content model of professionalism for this text is derived from the American Board of Internal Medicine's Project Professionalism and includes the following aspects:

Altruism: A formal definition of *altruism* is "intentional and voluntary actions that aim to enhance the welfare of another person in the absence of any quid pro quo external rewards" (Steinberg 2010, 249). Altruistic behavior is motivated by a desire to alleviate another's pain and suffering. Altruism is characterized by seeking to increase the welfare of another person rather than oneself; it is voluntary; the intention is to help another; and no external reward is expected. In many instances altruism contains an element of personal risk; for example, running into a burning building to save someone else's child. However, altruism can be found in the simplest of gestures; for example, just taking a few moments to comfort someone in distress.

There is a dysfunctional aspect of altruism that is termed pathological. It is characterized as hyperempathy. Pathological altruism is irrational and has negative consequences for the other and for the self. Codependency and even suicide martyrdom are misguided attempts to help someone.

Accountability: "Accountability generally refers to the obligation of one party to be held responsible for its actions by another interested party" (Emanuel 1996, 240). Accountability is the willingness to accept responsibility for one's actions. Accountability consists of the people accountable to one another, the areas of accountability, and the process by which people are held accountable. While individuals should be held accountable, if acting in good faith, with due diligence, and in a professional manner, they are not blameworthy. The world of professionals does not deal in certainty. Negative and undesired outcomes are the fabric of professional life.

Excellence: Excellence is exceeding expectations, being superior, being at the pinnacle, and pursuing perfection. Excellence is captured in the idea that amateurs practice to get it right, and professionals practice so they can't get it wrong.

There is little argument that excellence should be pursued, but to what end? In the pursuit of excellence, the individual may be motivated by two different goals. The first goal is a performance goal—a performance goal is about winning positive accolades and avoiding negative condemnations. This approach is about appearing smart. The second goal is the focus on mastery of the task, of increasing one's competence. The second goal is a learning goal. With this approach, setbacks are seen as opportunities for learning, rather than insurmountable obstacles (Dweck 2006). It is excellence as mastery that is the standard.

Duty: Codes of ethics specify the obligations and responsibilities of a professional. It is the professional's duty to meet those obligations and responsibilities.

Honor and integrity: Honor and integrity are the consistent regard for the highest standards of behavior and the refusal to violate one's personal and professional codes. Honor and integrity imply being fair, being truthful, keeping one's word, meeting commitments, and being straightforward. A person who is dutiful, is honorable, and resonates with integrity is virtuous, and that virtue is grounded in a personality anchored to his or her character. Duty, honor, and integrity bind the professional to an obligation for exemplary conduct.

Respect for others: There are different types of respect. One type of respect is based on an appraisal of an individual's worth. For example, we appraise someone as being a good person or a fine practitioner. As a result, we believe the person is worthy of respect on this dimension. Appraisal respect is based on a comparison. As such, some people may be deemed not worthy of respect. A second type of respect is based on recognition of an individual's personhood. In other words, every person is entitled to respect, no matter their status, condition, or accomplishments. With this respect there is no comparison, no appraisal. This type of respect is due to all people, and due to them equally. In short, an unconditional valuing of each person is the aspiration.

THE PROFESSIONALISM MODEL: PROCESS

One cannot separate professionalism from the individual who exemplifies it, just as one cannot separate the dancer from the dance. Concentrating on the individual as a factor leads to consideration of the individual psychology of professionalism, the process by which individuals assess, choose, and implement professional behaviors.

Professionalism is a system of right and wrong conduct nuanced to a specific context—in this case, work. Kultgen writes, "I shall argue that professionalism should be conceived in such a way that it is limited to moral conduct and elicits moral conduct, and that morality should be conceived in such a way as to require professionalism" (1988, 1). Campbell discusses the idea of "morally professional and professionally moral" (1996, 73). The point is that the ideal professional is a moral person and that moral behavior and professional behavior are similar. As such, moral psychology can serve as a template for the psychology of professionalism.

The model used to link moral and professional is derived from Rest and Narvaez, eds. (1994), and is composed of four elements: professional sensitivity, professional judgment, professional motivation, and professional action. In describing professional psychology as a process, the word *professional* is used as a direct substitute for the word *moral* that appears in the original articles.

PROFESSIONAL SENSITIVITY

Professional sensitivity is a complex phenomenon of perception and interpretation of situations requiring a professional response that considers what is possible, what is required, who will be affected, and how they will react. Professional sensitivity involves the ability to see the larger context of a situation. Recognizing professional issues from the mass of environmental cues impinging on a professional requires selective attention, encoding, and recall of professionally related stimuli. Perception of professional issues is semiconscious or unconscious.

PROFESSIONAL JUDGMENT

Human decisions can be guided by logic (the pursuit of truth, maintaining consistency across beliefs, and solving syllogisms); probability (performing inductive inferences, dealing with samples of information involving error rather than full information that is error free); and heuristics (rules of thumb that are fast, frugal, satisfice rather than optimize, and use limited amounts of information). For a practitioner, professional judgment (decision making) is about choosing a preferred course of action, often "on the fly." Decisions made on the fly are not likely to be conscious, controllable, effortful, or exclusively rational. Rather, professional judgments often appear effortlessly in consciousness in a process that is inaccessible to the decision maker, does not require attentional resources, is context specific, is driven by dual-processing cognitive and affective systems, and described as a social intuitionist perspective (Haidt 2001). In other words, professional judgment is intuitive and subconscious.

Professional judgments are not easy; often competing interests are at play. Judgments in this context require wisdom. Wisdom may be defined as "the application of tacit knowledge as mediated by values toward the goal of achieving a common good (a) through a balance among multiple intrapersonal, interpersonal, and extrapersonal interests" (Sternberg 1998, 353). An alternative definition of wisdom is "expertise in the fundamental pragmatics of life" (Baltes and Staudinger 2000, 124). This definition rests on the idea of an understanding of the essence of the human condition and the conduct of a good life. Wisdom addresses important and difficult questions and strategies about the conduct of the meaning of life and the uncertainties of the world. Wisdom represents knowledge used for the good or well-being of oneself and that of others. Wisdom is easily recognized when manifested, although difficult to achieve or specify.

PROFESSIONAL MOTIVATION

Motivation is the link between judgment and action. It is the link between deciding what is preferred and enacting that choice. Motivation is a process that initiates and guides goal-oriented behavior. Motivation arouses an individual to act toward and sustains an individual in the pursuit of goals. Motivation results from the interaction of internal and external, conscious and unconscious factors that stimulate desire and energy to accomplish a goal. According to Rest (1984), moral motivation is selecting from competing values and deciding to act according to one's moral ideal. Professional motivation is the driving force for selecting a professional course of action. Professional motivation is the individual's desire to place professional values ahead of other competing values; for example, money, career, family, or pleasure. Professional motivation is the driving force for professional behavior.

Theories to explain why people might act professionally include the following:

- Those who choose to act professionally, and groups that choose to act professionally, both prosper and survive in the economic and political environment where professional privilege can be revoked.
- The uncomfortable and debilitating power of shame, fear, and guilt serve as powerful controlling mechanisms.
- Individuals learn to act professionally by modeling the behaviors and attitudes of admired mentors and professionals that are reinforced by the environment.
- People act professionally due to allegiance to a higher power.
- People act professionally having been socialized into a profession and a caring community.
- People act professionally to maintain their sense of identity and personal integrity.
- People act professionally through education that broadens their perspective and mitigates individual prejudices (adapted from Narvaez and Rest 1995).

Professional motivation is assumed to be linked to professional judgment, the ability to prioritize a course of action as being preferable. Having determined one course of action to be preferable, the individual is then motivated to enact that choice. The argument is that it is irrational for an individual to declare a choice preferable and then not act on that choice. However, individuals often act as happy victimizers, those who know the rules but do not act accordingly and feel happy about their gains at the expense of another (Minnameier 2010).

PROFESSIONAL ACTION

Recognizing a professional dilemma, valuing professionalism as a personal core value, and being able to determine a preferred professional choice are nothing without the ability, skills, and tacit knowledge to implement those choices. It is one thing to know that a department head or senior clinician is making a mistake, quite something else to take that person on and to know how to do it. Numerous skills and personal characteristics could be utilized in implementing a single professional choice. In all cases it is the courage to act that is required. "Courage entails the exercise of will to accomplish goals in the face of opposition, either external or internal" (Peterson and Seligman 2004, 199). Courage is multifaceted. It can be a virtue, a state of mind, an attitude, an emotion, a force, or an action (Yang, Milliren, and Blagen 2010). Courage is not the absence of fear but the ability to function in spite of fear. Courage can also be thought of as bravery, perseverance in pursuit of goals, authenticity and honesty, and vigor and enthusiasm. Courage is the use of willpower to support one's beliefs; it is the psychological muscle that powers moral choice. Courage is the mental strength that allows one to persevere in the presence of adversity. It takes courage to confront a grieving family following a mistake that killed a family member; courage to confront a powerful clinician who may be slipping into senility; and courage to risk your job to expose a financial scandal within an organization. Courage may require an overt act or require doing nothing in the face of pressure. Individual courage is relatively stable but malleable. Aristotle believed courage was a habit that formed through repetition. Professionalism without the courage to act is an academic exercise; it is wishful thinking.

It is not suggested that the psychological aspects of professionalism, when applied, occur in the order detailed above. Rather, like all human behaviors, they are an ensemble of cognitions, emotions, and choices that act in some ill-defined manner to evoke a professional response.

Table 2.1 displays the content and process aspects of professionalism along each axis. Doing so allows one to apply each of the process aspects of professionalism to the content aspects of professionalism; for example, to consider the motivation to act with integrity. Further, as we move through the chapters, this analysis can be applied to specific supervisory issues. What is my motivation to act with integrity in hiring staff? And, most important, to reflect on whether I have conducted myself according to the professional standard?

Table 2.1. Content and process aspects of professionalism

Content/Process	Sensitivity	Motivation	Judgment	Action
Accountability				
Altruism				
Duty				

Honor				
Integrity		Hiring staff		
Excellence				
Respect for others				

To understand this matrix, consider as a student what is your motivation regarding the element of accountability in dealing with professors and your performance, or how does your sense of duty impact your judgment regarding class preparation.

SUPERVISION AND PROFESSIONALISM AS A STANDARD

Khurana and Nohria argue that "it's time to make management a true profession" (2008, 1). They go so far as to offer a Hippocratic oath for managers, mimicking the oath taken by physicians. In contrast, Richard Barker contends that "no, management is not a profession" (2010, 1), since it is not possible to come to an agreement on what a manager needs to know. Finally, Mintzberg (2013) argues that management is a practice that can only be learned through experience, as the problems managers deal with are complicated and intractable, requiring the exercise of soft skills, intuition, and judgment. Unlike the true professions, the required body of knowledge to be a manager cannot be codified. Also, many successful managers have no formal education.

Whether supervision and management is a profession does not preclude using the attributes of the professionalism model offered here as standards for managerial and supervisory behavior. In other words, in dealing with subordinate staff, respect for others is the standard by which all interactions will be judged. Or that a pursuit of excellence in management technique is an obligatory standard for any professional, whatever the discipline; just as the pursuit of excellence in the technical aspects of the profession is the standard. This approach is justified because the quality of technical services delivered will be improved by a more coherent, functioning organization, department, and collaborative staff. In other words, the better the supervision, the better the professional service.

Read the following case

*Two-month old Jose Eric Martinez was brought to the outpatient clinic of Hermann Hospital of Houston and diagnosed as having a ventricular defect, a hole in his heart. Typically, these holes close as the baby matures; if they do not, routine surgery is indicated. In the meantime, to alleviate the symptoms of congestive heart failure, digoxin was prescribed. The attending physician discussed the order with the resident and determined that the correct dose was .09 **milligrams** to be administered intravenously. The resident inadvertently ordered 0.9 **milligrams**, ten times the correct dose.*

The medication order was faxed to the pharmacy, with a follow-up original to arrive later. The pharmacist thought the dose was too high, paged the resident, and separated the order for further attention, placing it on the pharmacy coffeepot, the unofficial important pile. The resident had left for the day and did not receive the page. The technician filled the order with 0.9 milligrams of digoxin from the follow-up original; the pharmacist verified that the dosage on the prescription matched the dosage in the vial, having forgotten that he had originally questioned the order, and the order was sent to the nursing unit. (Belkin 1997)

The nurse received the medication and was concerned that it was wrong. She asked the resident on call, different from the original resident, to check the dose. The resident checked the math, came up with .09 milligrams, looked at the chart, saw "0" and "9," but missed the decimal point error. Following procedure, the nurse asked a second nurse to confirm that the order in the chart was the same as the label on the vial. It was. Within twenty minutes, ten times the correct dose was administered. Two-month old Jose Eric Martinez died.

A superficial analysis might conclude that the professionals involved in this situation just didn't pay attention, that it was an individual failure. A more appropriate conclusion is that the error was due to faulty system design and poor communication. As such, the standard for excellence in supervision was breeched. Though not in this case, oftentimes in hospitals communication and respect across departments is problematic. Again, the professional standard was breeched.

As the book unfolds and various topics related to supervision and management are presented, the point that the standard for supervisory activity is professionalism, as conveyed in this model, will continue to be emphasized.

MODELS, MARKERS, AND MINDSETS

This chapter has detailed a model of professionalism composed of the following elements: accountability, altruism, duty, honor, integrity, excellence, and respect for others. Establishing such a model is only a first step in making the concepts real and influential, both for yourself and for others. To make these concepts real, how do the elements in the model for professionalism translate into practice? To do this, the first step is to establish markers for each of the elements of the model. A marker for respect for others can be as simple as learning people's names or returning e-mails within a reasonable period. The marker of respect may vary by position in the organization. For managers and supervisors, respect might entail not going around the established lines of authority, while for staff it might mean not taking excessive and prolonged breaks. If professionalism is to be a force in an organization, markers need to be established. In addition, supervisors might develop markers specific only to their department.

In chapter 1 the idea of residue was established as a goal of supervision and management. The residue of supervisory efforts is a belief and understanding in the mind of staff of what to do and what the expectations are when left alone. The residue is a belief about how to act that is linked to intention termed a mindset. As suggested before, in the military as a sign of respect for comrades and their sacrifices, the mindset of "no one left behind" is the residue of training. There is no doubt with this mindset of what the expectation is or of what to do. Mindsets are introduced, reiterated, enforced, and reinforced until they become second nature and thinking is not required. This is the task of the supervisor/ manager—establishing concrete markers for behavior and the mindsets to insure that those markers are honored; in this case, as related to professionalism. It is a four-step process: (1) establish the model (beliefs), (2) define the specific behaviors (markers), (3) develop the mindsets to support the markers, and (4) reinforce these mindsets.

SUMMARY

This chapter provided a content and process model for professionalism. It began with definitions of a profession and professionalism. The issue of whether management is a profession was considered. A four-step model for ensuring professional behavior was described. The idea that supervision and management are subject to the same professional standards as the technical aspects of the job was proposed.

EXERCISES

Summarizing
Write a one-page executive summary of the chapter.
Discuss with your classmates how you would teach this material.
Write a two-page case from your experience on this topic that would be instructional for other students.
Develop a mental model for this chapter based on the mind mapping technique.

What's Important to You in the Chapter?
With several of your classmates, discuss the most important ideas from the chapter. Which ideas do you think will be most useful to you in your career? Which ideas do you think you will remember in six months?

What Do the Practitioners/Others Say?
Discuss with your colleagues or someone at work any of the ideas in the chapter. Alternatively, read an article from any source on professionalism and be prepared to summarize its message.

Professions

Go to the Board of Professional Registration for your state. Determine which occupations require licensure. Do they all meet the test of a profession? (The exact title in your state may vary, but a quick Internet search should yield the appropriate agency.)

Assessment

On the professionalism elements of accountability, altruism, duty, honor, integrity, excellence, and respect for others, rate yourself compared to your classmates. For example, on accountability I would rate myself in the upper 10 percent, and so forth.

Markers and Mindsets

For the content elements of the professionalism model, for your circumstances now as a student, define the specific markers for each element and an associated mindset statement. For example, for accountability, I do not "lawyer up" for a few more points on an exam. The mindset might be: Work = Results.

Element	Marker	Mindset
Accountability		
Altruism		
Duty		
Honor		
Integrity		
Excellence		
Respect for others		

Accountability

Take a moment to consider if the following statements describe you.
I believe I am in control of my circumstances.
I believe that others are in control of my circumstances.
It is easy for me to accept blame and admit mistakes.
I believe it is up to me to make myself happy.
I tend to feel sorry for myself.
I believe I am in control of my feelings.
I tend to meet all my obligations on time.

In group projects I do my fair share.

I believe I am in control of my physical health.

I believe I am in control of my stress levels.

Based on your responses to the exercises, write a one-paragraph description of yourself as it relates to accountability.

With several of your classmates, discuss specific behaviors that indicate whether a student is acting accountable for his or her actions or that a practicing professional is acting accountable for his or her actions.

Altruism

With several of your classmates, discuss whether you believe potential students should be required to demonstrate altruistic attitudes, values, and behaviors for acceptance into your program. If so, how would you assess this?

Write a one-paragraph summary of your discussion.

Duty, Honor, and Integrity

"I am loath to close. We are not enemies, but friends. We must not be enemies. Though passion may have strained it must not break our bonds of affection. The mystic chords of memory, stretching from every battlefield and patriot grave to every living heart and hearthstone all over this broad land, will yet swell the chorus of the Union, when again touched, as surely they will be, by the better angels of our nature" (https://en.wikipedia.org/wiki/Abraham_Lincoln%27s_first_inaugural_address).

—Abraham Lincoln, first inaugural address, March 4, 1861

Faced with secession and the splitting of the Union, Lincoln closed his first inaugural address with the quote above. His appeal to prevent this dissolution rested on a belief in the "better angels of our nature," the best part of what it means to be human. He believed that ultimately, this aspect of humanity would assert itself. Do you agree that there is a better part of human nature?

Do you believe it is better to die rich as a result of having stretched the obligations of duty, honor, and integrity (but not being illegal) or less affluent and having adhered strictly to the obligations of duty, honor, and integrity?

Excellence

Given the appropriate attitude, commitment, and work, do you believe people can accomplish anything they want?

Review a time in your life and a circumstance where you pursued excellence; how did it turn out? What did you learn?

Respect for Others

Have you ever made fun of someone at work, said something hurtful, cursed at someone, been rude to someone, or gossiped about someone? If you answered yes to any of these, how did this make you feel? How did you handle it? How would you feel if someone did the same thing to you?

James Bond Stockdale

On September 9, 1965, James Bond Stockdale ejected from his A-4 airplane over North Vietnam. On landing with a badly broken leg, he was gang tackled and pummeled by the local villagers. He was then moved to the Hanoi Hilton, where he remained a prisoner for seven and a half years. As senior officer he clandestinely organized the eventual four hundred officers under his command. He was guided by the American Fighting Man's Code of Conduct, Article 4: "If I become a prisoner of war, I will keep faith with my fellow prisoners. I will give no information or take part in any action which might be harmful to my comrades. If I am senior I will take command. If not, I will obey the lawful orders of those appointed over me and back them up in every way." Based on this code, Stockdale created a code of conduct that governed prison behavior. He was routinely tortured and beaten. About to be paraded in public, he disfigured himself to avoid being used as propaganda.

In prison, Stockdale tested the ideas and beliefs of the Stoic philosophers, who counseled that each person is responsible for his or her own judgments (beliefs) and brings about his or her own good fortune, bad fortune, happiness, or wretchedness. Suffering to the Stoics was "remorse at destroying yourself" (Stockdale 1993, 5). According to the Stoics, individuals have to recognize the things that are up to them and the things that are not, the things that are in their power and the things that are not. "If you want to protect yourself from 'fear and guilt,' … you have to get rid of your instincts to compromise, to meet people halfway. You have to learn to stand aloof, never give openings for deals, never level with your adversaries" (Stockdale 1993, 11).

On entering the prison, each prisoner was made to "take the ropes" and then moved to total isolation for a month or so. Prisoners "confessed" their crimes under this duress. Finally meeting their comrades, they whispered of their betrayal, of their unworthiness. Stockdale realized that a broken back, a broken leg, and torture were nothing as to the pain associated with betraying and destroying the self-respecting man within. In other words, the physical pain was nothing compared to the pain associated with not doing one's duty. The linchpin of Stoic thought, Stockdale writes, is "that the thing that brings down a man is not *pain* but *shame*!" (1993, 19).

Near the end of their tenure in prison, and on being returned to the general population from isolation, a fellow officer passed to Stockdale on rough paper written with rat dropping ink the last verse of Ernest Henley's poem *Invictus*.

It matters not how strait the gate,

How charged with punishment the scroll,

I am the master of my fate:

I am the captain of my soul. (Stockdale, 1993)

Stockdale writes that the only way to tranquility, fearlessness, and personal freedom is to accept the fact that you must take responsibility for your actions. "You've got to get it straight. You are in charge of you" (Stockdale 1993, 19).

With several of your classmates, discuss the relevance of this section to the topic of professionalism and your conduct in school regarding your performance.

Take a few moments to Google James Bond Stockdale for further background.

Thick Face, Black Heart

Thick face, black heart is about action and effectiveness, says Chin-Ning Chu (1992) in her book of the same title. Thick face, black heart is an inward state that is required for words and actions to be effective. Thick face, black heart is a theory about behavior. It is a belief system.

Thick face derives from the Asian idea of face. It is a concern for the way other people think about you and how they treat you. Now, consider the Western idea of a thick skin. Thick face is a blending of both perspectives, resulting in the idea of creating a shield to protect ourselves and our self-esteem from the negative evaluations of others. Those with thick face dismiss self-doubt generated by the externally imposed beliefs about ourselves and our worthiness. People with thick face don't care what others think about them and will endure and ignore their criticisms.

Black heart is the ability to take action without regard for the consequences. In pre-anesthesia medicine, the surgeon who was the quickest and most ruthless in performing an amputation was practicing good medicine. Black-hearted people resist being swayed by short-sighted compassion. Black-hearted people focus on goals, not costs. To win a war, a general knows some must die so others might live; or in downsizing a company, some must go that others might prosper:

At the crudest level, thick face, black heart has no moral underpinnings and is absolutely ruthless. It is a superficial interpretation of the ideas of thick face, black heart. A second level of thick face, black heart is a search for the proper way to utilize this concept and an understanding and discovery that the mind is the root of success or failure, honor or dishonor. The first two phases merge into a final stage of dispassion and detachment in the pursuit of accomplishment. Now there is an indifference to the cost, the pain associated with doing the job. Doing the job is the only objective. A good person's actions are not always gentle; they may be seen as ruthless or cold. Think of the idea of tough love. Ruthlessness is not necessarily evil (adapted from Chu 1992).

With several of your classmates, discuss the applicability of this idea to the discussion of professionalism. Does this concept say that you have the right to hurt people? How does it square with the idea of altruism?

Thoughts

If you were in Alex's position and your first meeting as a supervisor had been a disaster, what thoughts would be going through your head? How would you handle this situation?

REFERENCES AND WORKS CONSULTED

Baltes, P.B., and U.M. Staudinger. 2000. "Wisdom: A Metaheuristic (Pragmatic) to Orchestrate Mind and Virtue toward Excellence." *American Psychologist* 55: 122–36.

Barker, R. 2010. "No, Management Is Not a Profession." *Harvard Business Review* (July–August): 52–60.

Belkin, L. 1997. "How Can We Save the Next Victim?" *New York Times*, June 15.

Beu, D., and M.R. Buckley. 2001. "The Hypothesized Relationship between Accountability and Ethical Behavior." *Journal of Business Ethics* 34: 57–73.

Campbell, E. 1996. "The Moral Core of Professionalism as a Teachable Ideal and a Matter of Character: The Moral Base for Teacher Professionalism by Hugh Socket." *Curriculum Inquiry* 26 (1): 71–80.

Chu, Chin-Ning. 1992. *Thick Face, Black Heart.* Beaverton, OR: AMC Publishing.

Cruess, S.R., S. Johnston, and R.L. Cruess. 2004. "'Profession': A Working Definition for Medical Educators." *Teaching and Learning in Medicine* 16 (1): 74–76.

Dweck, C.S. 2006. *Mindset.* New York: Ballantine.

Emanuel, L.L. 1996. "A Professional Response to Demands for Accountability: Practical Recommendations Regarding Ethical Aspects of Patient Care." *Annals of Internal Medicine* 124: 240–49.

Gigerenzer, G. 2008. "Moral Intuition = Fast and Frugal Heuristics?" In vol. 2 of *Moral Psychology*, edited by W. Sinnott-Armstrong. Cambridge, MA: MIT Press.

Haidt, J. 2001. "The Emotional Dog and Its Rational Tail: A Social Intuitionist Approach to Moral Judgment." *Psychological Review* 108 (4): 814–34.

https://en.wikipedia.org/wiki/Abraham_Lincoln%27s_first_inaugural_address

Huddle, T.S. 2005. "Viewpoint: Teaching Professionalism: Is Medical Morality a Competency?" *Academic Medicine* 80 (10): 885–91.

Kabbesa-Abramson, R. 2012. "Legitimacy, Shared Ethos and Public Management." *Society and Business Review* 7 (3): 289–98.

Khurana, R., and N. Nohria. 2008. "It's Time to Make Management a Profession." *Harvard Business Review* (October): 1–8.

Kultgen, J. 1998. *Ethics and Professionalism*. Philadelphia: University of Pennsylvania Press.

McDonald, S. 2011. "New Frontiers in Neuropsychological Assessment: Assessing Social Perception Using a Standardized Instrument, the Awareness of Social Inference Test." *Australian Psychiatry* 47: 39–48.

Minnameier, G. 2010. "The Problem of Moral Motivation and the Happy Victimizer Phenomenon: Killing Two Birds with One Stone." In *Children's Moral Emotions and Moral Cognition: Developmental and Educational Perspectives: New Directions for Child and Adolescent Development*, edited by B. Latzko and T. Malti, 55–75. San Francisco: Jossey-Bass.

Mintzberg, H. 2013. *Simply Managing*. San Francisco: Berrett-Koehler.

Oakley, B., A. Knafo, G. Madhavan, and D.S. Wilson, eds. 2012. *Pathological Altruism*. Oxford, UK: Oxford University Press.

Peterson, C., and M.E.P. Seligman. 2004. *Character Strengths and Virtues*. Oxford, UK: Oxford University Press.

Rest, J.R. 1982. "A Psychologist Looks at the Teaching of Ethics." *Hastings Center Report* 12 (1): 29–36.

Rest, J.R. 1984. "The Major Components of Morality." In *Morality, Moral Behavior, and Moral Development*, edited by W.M. Kurtinez and J.L. Gewirtz, 24–38. New York: Wiley.

Rest, J.R. and D. Narvaez. 1994. "Background: Theory and Research." In *Moral Development in the Professions*, 1–26. Hillsdale, NJ: Erlbaum.

Steinberg, D. 2010. "Altruism in Medicine: Its Definition, Nature, and Dilemmas." *Cambridge Quarterly of Healthcare Ethics* 19: 249–57.

Sternberg, R. 1998. "A Balance Theory of Wisdom." *Review of General Psychology* 2 (4): 347–65.

Stockdale, James B. 1993. *Courage Under Fire: Testing Epictetus's Doctrines in a Laboratory of Human Behavior*. Stanford, CA: Hoover Institution on War, Revolution and Peace.

Wiersma, B. 2011. *The Power of Professionalism*. Los Altos, CA: Ravel Media.

Yang, J., A. Milliren, and M. Blagen. 2010. *The Psychology of Courage*. New York: Routledge.

3 MANAGEMENT OVERVIEW

ALEX

By custom all newly appointed department heads were invited to the monthly executive committee meeting. The object was to introduce new department heads and familiarize them with who was on the committee and help them understand the types of issues they would deal with and how the meetings were conducted. Though there was a formal agenda, Alex was surprised at how informal the meeting was. The people on the committee all looked intimidating, but they all seemed nice and were genuinely glad to meet Alex. Several briefly reminisced about when they were a new, young department head and their progression to the executive group. Alex did feel as if each member were measuring him for future possibilities. Without exception, all the members were MBAs, CPAs, attorneys, or had a master's degree in their specialty.

The subjects on the agenda were interesting, moving from the broad, long-term strategic issues to the quality of the vegetables in the cafeteria. What was clear to Alex was that this group of people had a different way of thinking about problems and used a different vocabulary in their discussions. *SWOT analysis*, *retained earnings*, *stakeholders*, *matrix*, *envisioning*, *contingency*, *leadership*, and so on were sprinkled throughout the discussion. Alex was interest but did not always follow the discussions or understand what the issues were. Alex enjoyed the meeting but was now walking back to the department thinking to himself.

I wonder how much money those people make.

What about the socks on the marketing head—lime green? What's up with that?

What's a SWOT; what's a matrix?

Maybe I should go to night school.

Will they pay?

Wait a minute, you don't even know if you like being department head.

I would really like to move back home; dad looks like he is starting to decline.

I can't believe the refs missed that call last night in the last ten seconds.

I wish I could get over this cold.

I wonder how much money they really do make?

I can't believe how long it took me to get to work today.

What would I do if I had as much money as I think they make?

MENTAL MODELS

In the center of the space below, write the words *manager* and *management*. Next, write the words that come to mind when you think of either this activity or this type of person. Do not edit your thoughts or collaborate with anyone. There is no right or wrong answer.

If things are related, connect them with an arrow. If the relationship is reciprocal (they both affect each other), put arrows at both ends of the line. If one relationship is stronger than another, make the arrow darker and thicker.

The goal is to capture your mental model of what you believe about managers and management. This is the starting point for the discussion on supervision.

LEARNING OBJECTIVES

- Discuss the purpose of a business.
- Describe the value chain.
- Discuss the various perspectives on management.
- Describe the typical management hierarchy.
- Discuss the management functions, competencies, and roles.
- Describe what a well-managed organization looks like.

This chapter provides an overview of the topic of management. Its goal is to provide a constellation of ideas, an intellectual universe of concepts and theories related to management in a condensed format, but one that is sufficient to ground the discussion of supervision that is the focus of the latter part of the book.

Supervisors are managers. More specifically, they are frontline managers working day to day with other professionals and support staff to deliver the goods and services of the business. Unlike middle and top management, supervisors are in the "thick of it." Some supervisors have the task of generating their own output of goods and services while simultaneously ensuring the output of the department. The foundational activity of supervision is managing other people.

DEFINITION OF MANAGEMENT

The definition of management is simple and straightforward; it is the process of accomplishing objectives with and through people. Good management is characterized as *efficient*, using the least amount of resources and inputs per unit of output, and *effective*, actually attaining declared goals.

THE PURPOSE OF A BUSINESS

Macro Level

There are two schools of thought on the purpose of a business. The first school believes that the sole purpose of a business is to maximize shareholder value. The idea is that the shareholders own the company, and therefore management's job is to maximize profits. The second school believes that there are others, termed stakeholders, who have an interest in the performance of a corporation. Five groups make up the typical list of stakeholders. The groups are shareholders, managers, employees, customers, and the local community.

While shareholders may invest cash, the other stakeholders make investments in other ways in the corporation, and they are entitled to consideration in the management of the company.

Micro Level

Any business has the same three goals that it must accomplish to survive. They are as follows:

- The business must deliver the products and services that solve the consumer's problems.
- The business must deliver these products and services with a level of customer service that meets consumers' expectations.
- The business must generate sufficient revenues, margins, cash flow, and profits to meet current obligations and fund future growth.

The minimal standard for meeting these goals is this: The business must be as good as the competition. The business must match the industry standard for performance on all three measures. It is an all-or-none proposition. Being good on any two of the three goals is not enough. If the object was to meet only one goal, or meeting each goal in succession, it would be relatively easy. These goals must be met in the short run and over time.

There is no maximum standard for performance; the bar is constantly being raised. New competitors will always emerge; consumer expectations, once met, will always rise. The pursuit of these goals is simultaneous and in real time. It is always a question of balance. F. Scott Fitzgerald wrote that "the test of a first rate intelligence is the ability to hold two opposed ideas in the mind at the same time, and still retain the ability to function" ("The Crack-Up", Esquire Magazine (February 1936). The ability of a first-rate supervisor/manager is to hold all three goals in the mind at the same time and still function.

THE VALUE CHAIN

Michael Porter (1985) developed the idea of the value chain as a way to understand the activities and systems that characterize most business units. The model holds for both manufacturing and service firms. The model consists of the primary activities related to transforming inputs into outputs and includes inbound logistics, operations, outbound logistics, sales and marketing, and servicing. Four activities are required to support this process: procurement, product and technology development, human resource management, and administrative and financial infrastructure. The benefit in this model is that is gives a simplified blueprint of often complicated systems and organizations. While some organizations may not conform precisely to this model, it is nevertheless useful and captures the activities and relationships of most organizations.

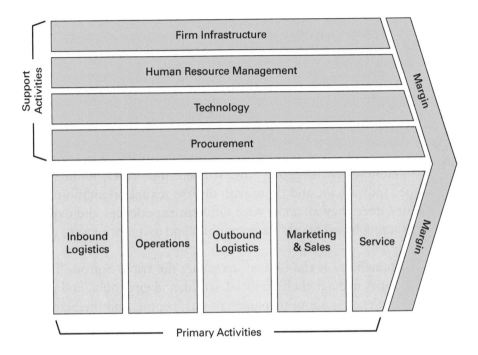

Fig. 3.1. Michael Porter's value chain

CONTEXT OF MANAGEMENT

Good management is both effective and efficient. The environment that managers operate in significantly impacts this requirement. One way to think about this problem is to understand that managers do not operate in a closed system. What happens in the world impacts their job. The economic crisis of 2008 impacted the construction, real estate, automobile, and banking industries directly and many other industries indirectly through a ripple, multiplier effect. In other words, managers can't close the door on external problems and still hope to meet their objectives. Significant factors impacting managers include the following:

- Globalization is the idea that as technology improves and spreads and national constraints are lifted, the world continues to integrate. Products are sourced from all over the world, money and ideas move at the speed of electronic impulses, and once unfamiliar people and cultures become commonplace. There are very few products and services that are immune to this pressure. Competition is not in the next county, but the next continent.
- Technology is any device, tool, equipment, or operating method that enhances work. Technology makes what once was an industry standard obsolete. Ask yourself, when

was the last time you used a phone connected to a landline? Technology changes how organizations are structured, how people are motivated, where they work from, and how they interact.

- E-business is buying and selling online. In the summer of 2015, Amazon passed Walmart as the largest retailer on the planet. Consider how people buy music today. Telemedicine is an emerging issue in health care. The point is that bricks and mortar and proximity are being negated as a competitive advantage.

- Workforce diversity is inescapable. Where the workforce was once primarily white males, it is almost anything but now. Women, minorities, immigrants, the elderly, handicapped individuals, and those with diverse sexual orientations are now all part of the labor force. They all come with different experiences and expectations. Methods of interacting based on old demographics and assumptions are not likely to be as effective.

- Business sustainability is the idea of managing the triple bottom line—a process by which companies manage their financial, social, and environmental risks, obligations, and opportunities. It is about managing profits, people, and the planet.

PERSPECTIVES ON MANAGEMENT

Management is a complicated human activity. Like most such activities, it can be viewed from multiple frames of references. The dominant views of management include the following:

- **Scientific management** is the idea that work and jobs can be studied utilizing the scientific method to determine the best way to do something. For example, in assembling any product, there is an optimal sequence that will minimize costs and increase quality. This perspective is most applicable at the lower levels of the organization.

- **Administrative management** attempts to discover and define universal principles of general management. This perspective is for the upper levels of the organization. Universal principles of management include division of labor, a hierarchy of authority, formal selection for advancement, formal rules and regulations, unity of command, unity of direction, centralization, order, and equity.

- **Human resources management** recognizes the centrality of the human being in accomplishing the organization's objectives. This perspective seeks to understand basic human behavior and psychology related to motivation and work. This approach relies on informal notions about humans and work as well as rigorous, empirically based conclusions about this topic. This perspective is appropriate across all levels of the organization.

- **Quantitative management** seeks to use statistics, computers, simulations, and models to improve the efficiency and effectiveness of management. This approach is appropriate across all levels of the organization.

HIERARCHY

The administrative structure of most businesses is arrayed in hierarchies that define the following:

- The chain of command; that is, who reports to whom
- The individuals delegated to accomplish certain tasks and given the authority and responsibility to accomplish organizational goals and objectives
- The span of control; the number of people one supervises
- The unity of command; the idea that an individual reports to only one person

Two other attributes related to the hierarchy of organizations are relevant to supervisors: centralization, the degree to which decisions are concentrated in the core, or higher levels, of the organization; and formalization, the degree to which affairs are conducted via written instructions and strict adherence to declared policies. Organizations that are decentralized will give more latitude to supervisors to make decisions, and organizations that are informal rely more on word-of-mouth communication and ad hoc responses to situations.

A typical hierarchical structure consists of top management, middle management, frontline supervisors, and staff or employees. Each element of the hierarchy has different responsibilities and concerns.

- Top-level managers are concerned with the overall operation of the business. They set the strategic direction for the business and establish the culture and policies for the business. They spend a significant amount of time dealing with outside stakeholders of the business. Executive-level top managers coordinate departments, establish budgets, and appoint and promote midlevel managers. Top-level managers are concerned with the direction of the industry, the nature of competition, and changes in consumer demand.
- Middle-level managers are accountable to top management and serve as liaisons between top management and frontline supervisors. They provide guidance to frontline supervisors. They make sure that top management's directives and policies are implemented and monitored. Their job is heavily dependent on their human relations skills.
- Frontline supervisors are responsible for seeing that the work gets done. Often they also engage in that work while supervising others. They are responsible for motivating and disciplining staff and employees on a day-to-day basis.

- Employees and staff are responsible for actually executing the work of the organization.

MANAGEMENT FUNCTIONS

Four functions are associated with the process of management. Those functions are as follows:

- Planning—establishing an organization's goals and strategy and developing the plans to make it happen
- Organizing—allocating resources and assigning individuals and groups to accomplish goals, along with devising the structure and hierarchy to meet those goals
- Controlling—monitoring performance and correcting for deviances in performance
- Leading—influencing and inspiring people to accomplish organizational goals

MANAGEMENT COMPETENCIES

Effective supervisors and managers have or develop certain competencies. They are as follows:

- Technical: the specialized expertise associated with the job. A supervising engineer clearly needs to be proficient in the required mathematics to function.
- Interpersonal: the skills and ability to get along with yourself and other people. It includes motivating, leading, and inspiring others to accomplish their required tasks in pursuit of larger goals.
- Conceptual: the ability to understand and analyze larger issues confronting the business. It involves understanding the financial, economic, and political world. It also requires an understanding of the processes and linkages of the complex systems that make up an organization.

MANAGEMENT ROLES

Besides the four functions of a manager and the three competencies detailed above, managers have certain roles to play. Henry Mintzberg (1971) described ten roles for managers, separated into three categories, as follows:

- Interpersonal
  - Figurehead: serve as the symbolic head
  - Leader: motivate and inspire people

    o Liaison: maintain inside and outside networks and contacts
- Informational
  - o Monitor: seek information inside and outside the company related to performance
  - o Disseminator: transmit information to relevant parties
  - o Spokesperson: represent organization to outside parties
- Decisional
  - o Entrepreneur: search for new ventures and opportunities
  - o Disturbance handler: serve as mediator for unexpected events
  - o Resource allocator: decide who gets resources
  - o Negotiator: advocate for organization

GOAL SETTING

A critical task for management is to establish goals for the organization and specific departments. In a traditional goal-setting approach, goals flow down from the top. Top management sees the "big picture" then sets goals for the entire organization. As the goal-setting process moves down the hierarchy, the goals become more specific and detailed. An alternative approach to goal setting is management by objectives. In this approach, goals are mutually agreed upon and then used to evaluate performance. The process of setting goals involves (1) reviewing the organization's mission statement, (2) evaluating available resources to make sure the goals are challenging but reasonable, (3) arriving at goals through a single individual or in conjunction with others, (4) writing down and communicating goals to all who need to know, and (5) reviewing goals periodically to determine if they are being met. Well-written goals should

- be phrased in terms of outcomes
- be measurable and quantifiable
- have a time frame
- be challenging but attainable
- be communicated

PLANNING

A plan is a road map or blueprint for accomplishing a set of objectives and meeting a goal. In general, the planning process results in a tangible document, with the obvious exception of informal planning. The fact that something is planned does not mean that it is going to happen. In fact, more often than not, there is considerable variation in the actual outcomes from the planned outcomes. This is not a measure of poor planning; rather, it reflects the reality of a world that is competitive, complex, often inscrutable, and constantly changing. The English writer G.K. Chesterton recognized this when he wrote:

> The real trouble with this world of ours is not that it is an unreasonable world, nor even that it is a reasonable one. The commonest kind of trouble is that it is nearly reasonable, but not quite. Life is not an illogicality; yet it is a trap for logicians. It looks just a little more mathematical and regular than it is; its exactitude is obvious, but its inexactitude is hidden; its wildness lies in wait (https://www.bestquotecollection.com/quote/gilbert-k-chesterton/321255).

Even though actual outcomes may vary from planned outcomes, the activity of planning; the thinking associated with planning; and the clarification of goals, objectives, parameters, methods, resources, individuals, and time frames is not a waste of time.

Types of Plans

- **Formal vs. informal:** The formal planning process is characterized as articulated, explicit, systematic, and comprehensive and is more typically associated with larger organizations. In contrast, informal plans are not written down, may not be articulated, and often reside solely in the brain of the planner. Small and entrepreneurial businesses typically engage in informal planning. Informal does not necessarily imply substandard or not well thought out.
- **Strategic vs. operational:** Strategic plans encompass longer time frames, generally around five years; deal with the overall direction of the business; contain the declared mission, goals and objectives of the business; and attempt to anticipate changes in customer demand, competitor moves, and industry-wide trends and disruptions and then position the business accordingly. Operational plans contain the details for accomplishing strategic objectives and may be daily, weekly, or monthly but usually are for less than one year and relate to specific departments. A strategic plan is a view from a thousand feet, while an operational plan is for the "boots on the ground."
- **Long term vs. short term:** Long-term plans are for more than five years, while anything less than a year is considered a short-term plan.
- **Directional vs. specific:** Directional plans indicate a course of action without elaborating specific goals. For example, cut costs in the next six months is a directional plan, while indicating cutting costs by 4 percent in the next six months is a specific plan.
- **Standing plans vs. single-use plans:** Standing plans provide the supervisor the policies, procedures, and rules for handling situations that are repetitive; for example, a plan for progressively disciplining employees. Single-use plans are for one-time, or infrequently occurring, projects and situations; for example, the plan to build a new distribution center, which happens every twenty-five years.
- **Business plans:** A business plan is a formal statement of the goals of the business, contains reasons why they are attainable, and details the specific steps in attaining

those goals. Business plans are most typically prepared for outside audiences, banks, investors, and so on, though they may also be prepared for in-house use. Business plans typically are written to contain the following elements:

- o Cover page and table of contents
- o Executive summary
- o Mission statement
- Business description
- Business environment analysis
- SWOT analysis
- Industry background
- Competitor analysis
- Market analysis
- Marketing plan
- Operations plan
- Management summary
- Financial plan
- Attachments and milestones

The value in planning, besides setting directions and methods, is that of coordination across departments and between individuals aimed at increasing the efficiency of the organization. It should be intuitive, if one department is focused on cutting costs while another is pouring funds into new product development, that problems will arise.

ORGANIZING

Think of a preschool class of three- to four-year-olds left to their devices. It is not hard to imagine the chaos. Now consider when the teacher arrives. Soon there are groups, there is order, there is direction, and there is a systematic approach to accomplishing the day's objectives. This is not to imply that employees are three- to four-year-olds, but conjuring the images of unsupervised three- to four-year-olds in a room illustrates the power of supervision and organizing—and the consequences of a lack of it. Organizing is the attempt to use time, resources, and people in the most efficient and effective way.

The process of organizing proceeds through these steps:

1. What needs to be done?
2. Narrow the tasks that need to be done to that which a single person can do; this is a job.
3. Group together the related jobs and sequence them in a logical manner, resulting in a department.
4. Establish the relationship and sequencing between departments.

Organizational Structures

Certain organizational structures that have stood the test of time are traditional approaches to organizing. These approaches are termed mechanistic in that there are rigid hierarchical relationships, fixed duties, high formalization, formalized communication, and centralized decision making.

- **Functional:** Tasks are grouped according to operating functions; for example, production, sales, and accounting.
- **Divisions or product:** Tasks are grouped according to the requirements to produce a specific product. An architectural firm may have divisions for commercial, industrial, and residential designs.
- **Customer:** Tasks are grouped around the needs of a specific customer.
- **Geographic:** Groupings are based on geographic considerations; for example, East Coast, Midwest, Rocky Mountain, and Pacific.

In contrast, some organizational structures are termed organic and are characterized by vertical and horizontal collaboration, adaptable duties, low formalization, informal communication, and decentralized decision making. Such structures are thought of as more contemporary, reflecting the dynamics of today's environment.

- **Simple:** Simple structures are characterized as having almost no structure and are typically flat, informal, and decentralized. A small business where a single owner/ manager controls and manages the frontline staff is an example.
- **Matrix:** A hybrid approach to organizing most often used for projects and one-of-a-kind operations. In this format there is operational oversight from two perspectives; for example, functional and project.
- **Network:** A small centralized organization relies on other, contracted organizations to perform the basic business functions; for example, hiring outside accounting and manufacturing firms to provide these services.
- **Task force:** This is a temporary structure to accomplish a specific project or task.
- **Team based:** This is a structure that consists entirely of work groups and teams.
- **Boundaryless:** This structure is based on the elimination of both internal and external boundaries or constraints, such as a virtual organization.

Any and all organizational structures have strengths and are deficient in certain aspects. In other words, there is no one size fits all. Structuring an organization is contingent on several factors. Those factors are the strategy of the organization, the size of the organization, and the technology employed in delivering goods and services to the marketplace.

Job Design and Description

Organizations are charged with completing innumerable tasks. If organizations are to be effective and efficient, these tasks should be bundled in a way that accommodates the skills and abilities of employees, the technology utilized, and the announced objectives. The way in which these tasks are bundled is an exercise in job design. Generally, the rubric for effective job design is the specialization of labor and the narrowing of tasks and focus.

Teams

Some jobs are best handled by a team, rather than an individual. Two types of teams are most common. An integrated work team, given multiple tasks, will have a supervisor assigned who is responsible for accomplishing the tasks. Self-managed work teams typically have more discretion than an integrated team in that they are given a goal, and how it is accomplished is up to them. They may select their own members and police one another's performance. In these teams the supervisor is less important than in an integrated work team.

LEADERSHIP

Management and leadership are not the same thing. The distinction is that generally, management is more concerned with the specifics of accomplishing objectives efficiently and effectively. Management is about *how*. Leadership is more about *why* and *where*. Leadership is more ephemeral and is about inspiration, vision, and motivation. Leaders have the ability to influence others to follow them. The presumption in this context is that leaders influence others to follow them to accomplish, in general, the organization's espoused goals and objectives, and specifically, the formal and informal goals and objectives of the department. In an attempt to understand how influence is exercised by leaders, several theories and perspectives have been advanced. Those theories and perspectives include the following:

- **Trait theories** suggest that there is something special about leaders that sets them apart and causes others to follow them. Specific traits associated with leaders include drive, self-confidence, honesty and integrity, intelligence, the desire to lead, and job-relevant knowledge. However, no distinct set of traits has been found that will always separate leaders from nonleaders.
- **Behavior theories**, like trait theories, seek to separate leaders from nonleaders based on specific behaviors. The behaviors typically considered in this approach divide into two categories. The first is behaviors associated with accomplishing the task, while the second is behaviors that focus on the employee and take a personal interest in the employee. As with trait theories, no pattern or combination of behaviors was found to distinguish the effective from noneffective leader.

- **Contingency theories** add the idea that the situation or context matters and that a given type of leadership behavior is more appropriate for a one circumstance than another. Leadership behaviors range from autocratic and dictatorial to participative and democratic. A workable framework for contingency and leadership is that it is the interplay between leader characteristics and subordinate characteristics along with the situational characteristics that influence the choice of leadership styles.
- **Charismatic theories** suggest that certain leaders produce high performance, as those working for such leaders exert extra effort and work harder than they would for others. Charismatic leaders tend to have a strong personal commitment to a goal, be unconventional and assertive, and have a compelling vision that they could communicate—think Steve Jobs. Charismatic leaders are more likely to emerge in politics or religion than business. Charismatic leaders focused on radical change may become a liability if the situation does not warrant it.
- **Transactional theories** suggest that leaders motivate their followers in the direction of established goals and inspire their followers to transcend their self-interest for the good of an organization, often resulting in profound changes.

CONTROLLING

In an organization, as in life, talk is cheap. It is what you are prepared to enforce and reinforce that tells what is considered important. All the effort to plan, organize, and lead is wasted if control and the assurance that the objectives and the standard are being adhered to is lacking. To control is to monitor. The control process involves measuring performance, comparing to a standard, and then taking corrective action.

Control is impossible without up-to-date and appropriate information. Information about performance can be acquired from personal observation, statistical analysis, oral reports, or written reports. The key aspect of control is to measure the appropriate information. It is a fact of organizational life that what is measured is what is attended to by managers and staff, as bonuses and promotions are often tied to those metrics. Some activities are difficult to measure, but most can be broken down to discrete aspects that can be quantified. In comparing performance, it is key to recognize that all management activities vary; the question is, what is the acceptable range? In other words, what magnitude of variance signals significant and uncorrectable drift? The response by management to a variance in performance can be to get back on track immediately. Alternatively, basic corrective action seeks to find the root cause, or source, of the variation and correct this element. Basic corrective action focuses on the underlying processes and systems as the source of variation. Finally, in some circumstances, the standard may have been inappropriate, requiring that the standard be changed.

Supervisors and managers engage in three types of control. The first is feed-forward control; the attempt to anticipate problems and correct them before they happen. The second is concurrent control, which takes place while the event happens and is usually in the form of direct supervision. The third type of control is feedback control, which occurs after the activity has taken place.

Five aspects of organizations require control: people, finances, operations, information, and overall organizational performance. People are controlled via training, mentoring, direct supervision, performance appraisal, selection, and rewards. The budget is the nexus of financial control. Controlling operations is to control the various activities required to produce the organization's goods or services. In today's environment information is controlled via technology in a management information system. Overall organizational performance is measured relative to the announced goals for the organization and whether the demands of key organizational constituencies or stakeholders are satisfied.

DECISIONS

Managers can't escape doing two things. One is managing people, and the other is making decisions. Both are the essence of their job. In this section a classic view of decision making is presented based on a rational and analytical way of making decisions. The steps to rational and analytical decision making include the following:

1. Identify a problem—any discrepancy between the desirable and the actual.
2. Collect relevant information—what facts and data are relevant to this decision?
3. Develop alternatives—generating all possible options.
4. Evaluate each alternative—what are the strengths and weaknesses of each choice, costs and benefits, time to implement, and so on?
5. Select the best alternative—derived from evaluation of the choices.
6. Implement the choice—allocate resources and assign those responsible.
7. Follow up and evaluate—did the decision work?

WHAT DOES A WELL-MANAGED ORGANIZATION LOOK LIKE?

In the definition above, good management is characterized as being both efficient and effective. A more detailed picture of what good management is and what constitutes a well-managed organization is possible. Attributes associated with good management and high-performing organizations include the following:

- Sufficient skilled, managerial talent
- Sufficient skilled, adaptive workers

- Employees with realistic expectations of what they will get and what they must give
- High levels of trust
- Open communication
- Minimal reliance on rules and procedures
- Effective information systems
- Ability to innovate and change
- Leaders with a sense of urgency and direction
- Future leaders identified and in the pipeline
- Middle managers who embrace and translate strategy
- Wide spans of control with minimal number of layers in the hierarchy
- Structure reflects strategy
- Individual capabilities matched to tasks
- Culture reflects strategy
- Engagement is cultivated and measured (adapted from Bhalla et al. 2011; Collins and Devanna 1994)

SUMMARY

Though condensed, the topics discussed above are those taught in a traditional management course. Most of these concepts and ideas were derived from experience in managing large, industrial firms. In a sense it is a classic view of management. It is also idealized. On the page, management is neat and tidy, boxes and lines and descriptions defining everything, goals clearly articulated, plans and timelines disseminated and understood by everyone. In reality, management is a full-contact, blood sport. It is messy. It is a human activity. So why spend time assimilating this somewhat unrealistic view of management? Think of how the manual indicated you are supposed to drive and how you drove while taking your driver's test. You have to know and understand the ideal before you can navigate the realities and messiness of actual day-to-day driving. For the most part management and supervision are about ambiguity. As a future supervisor, you need a mental picture of the ideal, of the aspiration, as an anchor to know whether you are off base and more importantly whether you are so far off base that you become ineffective.

Management/supervision is a mixture of three elements. The first is scientific and involves logic and analysis of a situation. It is deductive, derived from general concepts and then applied to the specific. It is concerned with replicability. It is the perspective of this chapter. Management/supervision is also an art. It is about imagination, novelty, and creative insights—it is about a vision. It is inductive, moving from the specific to the general. Finally, management/supervision is a craft. It is based on experience, trial and error, and utility—being practical, getting the job done. Art and craft without the science leads to disorganized managing. Craft and science without the creative vision of art lead to dispirited managing.

And art and science without the craft lead to disconnected management. Management/supervision are about bringing order out of ambiguity; therefore, all three perspectives described in this paragraph are required; it is the proportion of each that is dictated by the situation and is left to the effective manager/supervisor to utilize. Never forget, as a human activity management/supervision is messy. To get it right, to meet the professional standard, is hard work. But as a professional you have no choice; it is your professional obligation (adapted from Mintzberg 2005).

EXERCISES

Summarizing

Write a one-page executive summary of the chapter.

Discuss with your classmates how you would teach this material.

Write a two-page case from your experience on this topic that would be instructional for other students.

Develop a mental model for this chapter based on the mind mapping technique.

What's Important to You in the Chapter?

With several of your classmates, discuss the most important ideas from the chapter. Which ideas do you think will be most useful to you in your career? Which ideas do you think you will remember in six months?

What Do the Practitioners/Others Say?

Discuss with your colleagues or someone at work any of the ideas in the chapter. Alternatively, read an article from any source on management/supervision and be prepared to summarize its message.

Questions

1. What is the difference between supervision and surveillance?
2. What would you expect of someone who is an effective supervisor?
3. Do you believe supervision and management can be learned? What would be the best way to do this?
4. Wait a week and repeat the mental model exercise that begins the chapter. It is best to do it without consulting your notes. Note the changes, if any.
5. Take some of the ideas and themes of this chapter and condense into a poster; in other words, can you visually represent the ideas in the chapter in an appealing way?

6. Comment on the idea that management is just common sense.
7. Do you believe that management is a combination of science, art, and craft? Does one approach make more sense to you?
8. Identify a trend in your industry/profession that has the potential to alter the nature of supervision and work within your career.

The Future

As the influence of large industrial firms has waned and other types of businesses and organizations have emerged as key features in both the United States and global economy, new ideas regarding managers and management have emerged. The following few pages present some, though by no means all, of those ideas. The point is to recognize that management is a dynamic human activity that is being worked out in real time. In another hundred years some of the ideas presented here as new may be viewed as "classics," while other new ideas percolate, form, and are tested in whatever economy exists at the time. Do these "new" ideas seem reasonable to you? Will they be effective over the long term?

Self-Managing Organizations

In a *Harvard Business Review* article, Gary Hamel declared, "first, let's fire all the managers" (2011, 1). Hamel asserts that a hierarchy of managers imposes a burdensome tax on an organization. He also claims that as the number of managers increases, the likelihood of large calamitous decisions increases, and as the hierarchy lengthens, response to issues also lengthens. And finally, he believes that hierarchies of managers disempower lower-level managers.

Hamel describes an alternative approach embodied by $700 million, four-hundred-employee Morningstar Corporation, the world's largest tomato processor. At Morningstar no one has a boss, employees negotiate responsibilities with their peers, everyone can spend the company's money, each individual is responsible for acquiring the tools needed to do his or her work, there are no titles and no promotions, and compensation decisions are peer based.

In essence, Hamel is suggesting the classic bureaucracy and structure of most organizations be dismantled and replaced with a self-managing organization.

The Power of Metrics

In July 2015 Amazon became the most valuable retailer in the United States, eclipsing longtime leader Walmart. The reason for this can be attributed to the culture that Jeff Bezos, founder and CEO of Amazon, has established. That culture is characterized by an obsession with the customer and is embodied in fourteen rules provided to all employees on laminated cards. It is a culture of "purposeful Darwinism" in which winners prosper and losers get fired or leave in an annual culling. A 2013 survey by PayScale put the median tenure at Amazon at one year. Those who make it at Amazon are characterized as "Amabots."

To create this colossus, Bezos early on recognized the power of metrics, or measuring everything. The company runs a continuous performance algorithm on its staff. To prod employees, Amazon has a perpetual flow of real-time, ultra-detailed metrics. Regular team review meetings are driven by printouts fifty to sixty pages long, detailing teams' performance. In addition, there are detailed metrics on everything Amazon's customers do and on pages that do not load quickly enough. Amazon is a place where overachievers go to feel bad. Meetings are combative.

This has resulted in a workplace where people don't sleep for four days straight, where people work eighty-five hours a week, where according to the article, people have been given negative performance reviews because their work output suffered due to miscarriage, illness, or dying family members (Kantor and Streitfeld, 2015).

The Future of Work

In his book *The Future of Work*, Thomas Malone (2004) argues that new information technologies are causing a revolution in how we work. Technology now makes it possible for workers to be physically distant yet still interact. In this scenario technology allows for many of the advantages of a large organization, like economies of scale and knowledge, without sacrificing the human benefits of working in a small organization, like freedom, creativity, innovation, and motivation.

The organizations of the future will be described as self-organizing, self-managed, empowered, emergent, democratic, participative, people centered, and peer-to-peer. The term Malone prefers is *decentralized*. Decentralized, to Malone, means letting people make the decisions that matter to them. The net result is that we will move away from the classic view (described in the chapter) of command and control to coordinate and cultivate. Coordinate and cultivate that the power embodied in the hierarchy is diminished while participative democracy will flourish.

Thoughts

If you were in Alex's position and had just come from the executive meeting, what thoughts would be going through your head?

REFERENCES AND WORKS CONSULTED

Bhalla, V., J.-M. Caye, A. Dyer, L. Dymond, Y. Morieux, and P. Orlander. 2011. *High-Performance Organizations: The Secrets of Their Success*. Boston: Boston Consulting Group.

Busse, R. 2014. "Comprehensive Leadership Review-Literature, Theories and Research." *Advances in Management* 7 (5): 52–66.

Carroll, S.J., and D.J. Gillen. 1987. "Are the Classical Management Functions Useful in Describing Managerial Work?" *Academy of Management Review* 12 (1): 38–51.

Collins, E.G.C., and M.A. Devanna. 1994. *The New Portable MBA*. New York: Wiley.

Etzioni, A. 2014. "The Corporation as a Community: Stakeholder Theory; Corporations as Communities." In *Business Ethics*, 2nd ed., edited by M. Boylan. Malden, MA: Wiley.

Freeman, R.E. 2010. *Strategic Management: A Stakeholder Approach*. New York: Cambridge University Press.

Hales, C.P. 1986. "What Do Managers Do? A Critical Review of the Evidence." *Journal of Management Studies* 23 (1): 88–115.

Hamel, G. 2011. "First, Let's Fire All the Managers." *Harvard Business Review* (December): 48–60.

Harrison, J.S., and A.C. Wicks. 2013. "Stakeholder Theory, Value, and Firm Performance." *Business Ethics Quarterly* 23 (1): 97–124.

https://www.bestquotecollection.com/quote/gilbert-k-chesterton/321255

Hout, T.M. 1999. "Are Managers Obsolete?" *Harvard Business Review* (March–April): 161–68.

Kanter, R.M. 1989. "The New Managerial Work." *Harvard Business Review* (November–December): 85–92.

Kantor, J., and D. Streitfeld. 2015. "Amazon's Thrilling, Bruising Workplace." *New York Times*, August 16, p. A1.

Katz, R.L. 1974. "Skills of an Effective Administrator." *Harvard Business Review* (September–October): 90–102.

Kiechell, W., III. 2012. "The Management Century." *Harvard Business Review* (November): 63–75.

Kraut, A. I., P.D. Pedigo, D.D. McKenna, and M.D. Dunnette. 1989. "The Role of the Manager: What's Really Important in Different Management Jobs." *Academy of Management Executive* 3 (4): 122–29.

Lloyd, C., and J. Payne. 2014. "'It's All Hands-On, Even for Management': Managerial Work in the UK Café Sector." *Human Relations* 67 (4): 465–88.

Malone, T.W. 2004. *The Future of Work*. Boston: Harvard Business School Press.

McGivern, G., G. Currie, E. Ferlie, L. Fitzgerald, and J. Waring. 2015. "Hybrid Manager-Professionals' Identity Work: The Maintenance and Hybridization of Medical Professionalism in Management Context." *Public Administration* 93 (2): 412–32.

Mintzberg, H. 1971. "Managerial Work: Analysis from Observation." *Management Science* 18 (2): B97–B110.

Mintzberg, H. 1975. "The Manager's Job: Folklore and Fact." *Harvard Business Review* 53 (4) (March–April): 49–61

Mintzberg, H. 2005. *Managers Not MBAs*. San Francisco: Berrett-Koehler.

Pearlstein, S. 2014. *Social Capital, Corporate Purpose and the Revival of American Capitalism*. Washington, DC: Center for Effective Public Management at Brookings.

Porter, M.E. 1985. *Competitive Advantage*. New York: Free Press.

Wren, D. 2005. *The History of Management Thought*. Danvers, MA: Wiley.

Zaleznik, A. 1992. "Managers and Leaders: Are They Different?" *Harvard Business Review* (March–April): 2–11.

SECTION I
THE FOUNDATION

BEST IDEAS

Best ideas are defined as those ideas from the chapters in this section that you believe will be the most influential in your practice and that you will retain over time. Take a few moments to compile your ten best ideas. Consider these as the residue of the effort and time put into these readings and discussion. In other words, what did you learn?

IDEA ONE

IDEA TWO

IDEA THREE

IDEA FOUR

IDEA FIVE

IDEA SIX

IDEA SEVEN

IDEA EIGHT

IDEA NINE

IDEA TEN

SECTION II
| PEOPLE |

The first section laid the intellectual framework for the book. This section focuses on supervising and managing people; specifically yourself, people as individuals, and people in teams.

CHAPTER 4: SUPERVISION: A PEOPLE BUSINESS

This chapter discusses the people aspect of supervision. It discusses the relationship a supervisor has with those above, lateral, and below them. It talks about how to establish trust and your credibility, how to connect and set the mood at work, how to influence and persuade when your authority is limited. It discusses the relevance of emotional intelligence to supervision.

CHAPTER 5: SUPERVISING YOURSELF

This chapter begins with a discussion of self-awareness and its relationship to supervision and management. It then discusses personal schema, personality, personal values and emotional intelligence as issues for increasing self-awareness. It concludes by discussing issues and techniques to enhance self-supervision.

CHAPTER 6: SUPERVISING TEAMS

Chapter 6 considers the process of team development by discussing the stages of development, team roles, emotional intelligence and teams, conflict and negotiation, and multi-cultural and diverse teams. It also discusses the supervisor's role in this process and the establishment of team norms.

4 SUPERVISION: A PEOPLE BUSINESS

ALEX

Alex watched him relate to people. He was warm without being too familiar. Colleagues from decades ago kept in touch with him via Twitter and Facebook. He always smiled and seemed to be interested in everyone. When he talked with someone, he was focused on just them. But he wasn't friends with everyone. It was clear he had boundaries. He also had several colleagues, with whom it was clear he was distant and aloof. Alex finally had the opportunity to share a lunch with him and asked what his secret was to his relationship skills. His reply was simple and straightforward. First, I like myself. I spend a lot of time making sure my personal issues don't transfer to others. I believe everyone matters, that they are important. I look for the good in everyone, until they prove otherwise. Relationships, in general, matter more than issues. Finally, people at work are professional colleagues, not necessarily friends. Finishing his lunch, he wished Alex well and said to stop in to see him anytime. Alex thought.

That's the secret?

I don't like that many people that much.

Sometimes people are so stupid.

Sometimes people are so boring.

I think issues are more important; I don't get that.

I really had fun last night; I really like to dance.

Why would he take time to talk to me? I'm not in his department.

I wonder what happened between him and the ones that he is distant with. It should be a good story. I'll ask around, someone will know.

That's the secret?

I know I'm never going to like Jack; he has been spreading rumors about me.

I just want them to like me.

That's the secret?

MENTAL MODELS

In the center of the space below, write the word *supervisor*. Next, write the words that come to mind when you think of either this activity or this type of person. Do not edit your thoughts or collaborate with anyone. There is no right or wrong answer.

If things are related, connect them with an arrow. If the relationship is reciprocal (they both affect each other) put arrows at both ends of the line. If one relationship is stronger than another, make the arrow darker and thicker.

The goal is to capture your mental model of what you believe about supervision and supervisors. This is the starting point for the discussion on supervision.

LEARNING OBJECTIVES

- Discuss the realities of work.
- Discuss the misconceptions that managers have.
- Describe what inner work life is.
- Discuss how to set the mood at work.
- Discuss how to establish trust and credibility.
- Discuss the idea of reciprocity at work.
- Describe appreciative inquiry at work.
- Understand the value of civility, empathy, trust, transference, inner work life, mood, appreciative inquiry, and connecting to relationship management.
- Discuss how to manage your boss and other professionals.
- Understand the impact of diversity on supervision.

THE WORLD OF WORK

Knowing and doing are not the same thing. Being able to analyze a case, identify a problem, or recite a correct answer is not the same as being able to effectively supervise. Having a mental model (map) is not it either. The map is not the terrain. Oftentimes people will say that supervision and management are just common sense. If that were the case, there would be significantly more well-run organizations. Being able to discuss how to supervise is not the same as actually supervising. Think of the advice on trying to lose a few pounds—just eat less and exercise more. One stroll through any suburban mall will show you that losing a few pounds is not easy. Saying "communicate effectively" is easy; communicating in real time, buffeted by the day's pressures and distractions, is not. The conclusion is to never confuse simple with easy, particularly with regard to supervision.

Because of their position in the hierarchy, supervisors spend most of their time interacting with people one-on-one or in small groups in a single department. Engineering managers report that people management and people problems are the most frequent issues they deal with (Bennett 1996, 17). What makes this so hard? Because, as the historian Barbara Tuchman notes in *Practicing History,* "The human being is unreliable as a scientific factor" (1981, 255). People are unpredictable. Much of what you need to know about them is hidden, both from you and from themselves. Successful supervisory action one day results in different and unwanted responses the next. Though there may be consistency in dealing with people, there is not certainty. Supervision requires being comfortable with ambiguity, uncertainty, and risk. It is delegating authority and responsibility. It is building teams. None of these have concrete markers and perfected protocols. Sometimes supervision requires an eye, a feel, intuition, judgment, experience, and attention to your gut. Sometimes you have to know when to break the rules or when to establish a whole new set of rules. Supervision has elements of science, craft, and art.

To be a supervisor is to always be in the middle. The pull will be in opposite directions. The job is to satisfy upper management while maintaining harmony and productivity within the department. The supervisor's thinking must range from the very specific—what time does everyone need to eat lunch—to the broad and long-term objectives of the corporation, as well as how the two are related. From the world of physics, it is the dilemma of rationalizing the very large (relativity) with the very small (quantum mechanics). Being in the middle, being the supervisor, is probably the most difficult job in the organization. As supervisor you are the guardian of the long term in the face of short-term demands; you are the conscience of the department in meeting its obligations to the client, the other departments, and the organization as a whole.

In the final analysis you will be evaluated on results. Therefore, despite what you read or believe constitutes good management, or what good supervisors are supposed to do, the only effective guide is: Do what works. Supervisors work with individuals and take small groups and direct, govern, control, steer, persuade, convince, induce, prevail upon, talk into, seduce, entice, coerce, administer, allure, beguile, force, strong-arm, manipulate, compel, pressure, lead, excite, egg on, challenge, galvanize, motivate, goad, and inspire to accomplish the goals and objectives of the department. It is up to you to decide which of these approaches will work with that person on that day to solve that problem. If what you are doing is not working, get rid of it. The object is to win the game. The *Star Wars* character Yoda got this message right: "Do. Or do not. There is no try" (http://www.starwars.com/news/the-starwars-com-10-best-yoda-quotes).

MISCONCEPTIONS

Individuals who find themselves in a supervisory role often begin with some misconceptions of what the job is like. People, when dissatisfied with things at work, whisper to themselves, "If I were in charge, things would be different." It is likely things might be different, but not likely they would be better. The transition to supervision is not easy and is complicated by certain beliefs that supervisors may hold about their role that are not true. Some examples include the following:

- New supervisors tend to believe their power is based on the formal authority associated with their position. This is far from true, especially when dealing with talented, educated subordinates. Just because a supervisor gives direction, it does not mean people will comply. New supervisors need to understand that influence over subordinates derives from subordinates being willing to trust and the respect they have earned.

- As to be expected, when first taking a job, supervisors want to do well and to meet expectations. To that end, they believe they need to micromanage and overcontrol. In place of their personal control of the situation, supervisors need to build commitment by subordinates to organization goals. Compliance is not the desired objective; initiative is. Initiative is only possible if a supervisor is willing to delegate.
- Supervisors believe their job is to build strong individual relationships. There is nothing wrong with that idea; but their real job is to build a strong, functioning team. Only the team can accomplish mandated objectives.
- Supervisors believe their job is to ensure things run smoothly, that there are no glitches in operations. Of itself, this is a difficult task. In fact, their job is to elevate the team's performance. Honoring the hierarchy, the power of their superiors, and the chain of command is a natural tendency. It also makes for a convenient excuse if things don't work. Blame can be shifted to the established systems. In fact, supervisors have an obligation to surface new ideas and challenge entrenched methods if they are detrimental to performance. No one is suggesting that after ninety days in the position, a supervisor should suggest changing everything. What is suggested is that as supervisors grow, they advocate for change in a manner that will be effective.

NEW SUPERVISORS

The first insight, if one is to succeed as a supervisor, is to change your perspective from "I" to "we." It is not about just doing the technical aspect of your job. It is about helping others do their job. You will be evaluated on your collective success. New supervisors may have formal authority; that is, they have been designated as supervisor and formally imbued with the requisite power and authority. Or they may by default be a supervisor if they are the lone professional responsible for guaranteeing work output for a shift. The single most critical issue for new supervisors is establishing their credibility.

As a new supervisor, your staff members may be willing to overlook your inexperience as you grow into the job. The one thing not likely to be ignored is if they believe you are unfair in your treatment of staff. It is ingrained in most of us that fairness implies equal treatment, that everyone be treated the same. Certainly, there should be equal pay for equal work, and people need to be respected for their basic human dignity. In terms of the "goodies" associated with work, there should be equity. But how you and I communicate may be affected by age, gender, circumstance, and nationality. Some will want personal attention, others to be left alone; some will require external motivators, while others are self-motivated. The tension for the supervisor is to be seen as fair and equitable while still meeting individual and idiosyncratic needs.

Credibility is a function of your willingness to do, and insist upon, the right thing regarding the actual job. It is a prejudice, but I believe all people want to be part of something outside themselves, something bigger than themselves, something that makes them feel good at the end of the day. It is yours to give, if you have the character and the courage to do the right thing, the hard thing. Most work is repetitive and mundane; the task is to convince the staff members not that they are laying bricks, but that they are building a cathedral that will last a thousand years.

How to actually begin? A therapy technique for countering depression is to "fake it until you make it." This approach sets up a positive feedback loop. It is good advice for a new supervisor. It is not likely on the first day of a job as a supervisor that you will feel confident or assured. The best idea is to project an air of confidence, despite your internal feelings. Caution is warranted in that projecting an air of arrogance signals insecurity covered by overcompensation. An aid in projecting confidence is to think of a time and circumstance when you were confident. Alternatively, think of someone you know who is confident and emulate that person's behavior. Or think of a character in the movies who is confident and emulate his or her behavior. In times of transition, Ibarra (2015b) argues that thinking and introspection should follow action. In other words, don't worry too much about how you will do; just act like you know what you are doing, and the rest will catch up with you.

THE SAME OR NOT

Much of what happens at work is outside of supervisory control. Much of the time is spent in reacting to the day's issues and problems. It is important to remember what is in your control. What you control is your thoughts, emotions, and behaviors in dealing with employees. In this case how you treat people is in your control.

Whether all employees should be treated the same is an ongoing issue for any supervisor. Consistency in dealing with staff, not exactness, is the standard. Chapter 2 established a professional value of respect for others. All staff members should be consistently respected for their dignity as a human and their contributions to the organization. But in dealing with individual issues on a day-to-day, one-on-one basis, flexibility is the winning approach. The art of supervision is to read people and respond in a manner most likely to further organizational goals. This dynamic is captured in the ideas and techniques of emotional intelligence—reading people and crafting a behavior appropriate to the context. People are different; act accordingly. Supervision is an art, not a protocol.

TOUCHPOINTS

As a supervisor/manager your role is to develop and utilize relationships to accomplish organizational objectives. There is always a tension between the individual's needs and the organization's goals. Between individuals there are always issues, some of which are theirs alone, some of which are yours alone, and some of which are mutual. Supervision requires balancing individual needs, organization goals, and issues. Each one-on-one interaction with a colleague is an opportunity to either strengthen or erode the relationship. One-on-one is the critical touchpoint (Conant and Norgaard 2011) where you as a supervisor are measured and where deposits are made into your relationship bank.

Like word-of-mouth advertising, if handled well, these touchpoints mushroom into a network of goodwill and motivation to perform. If handled poorly, supervisory nightmares ensue. People are not distractions. The engine of effective supervision is the relationship—in this chapter the one-on-one relationship.

RELATIONSHIPS

Relationships at work can be categorized as one of the following:

- **Collegial:** equal power, trust, and respect
- **Collaborative:** mutual power, trust, and respect
- **Student-teacher:** either party can be the student or teacher, both parties willing to listen, teach, and learn
- **Friendly stranger:** little trust and acknowledgement, may be courteous but formal
- **Hostile, adversarial, and abusive:** negativity in tone and action (adapted from Schmalenberg et al. 2005)

Collegial relationships have all the features of a collaborative relationship with the added dimension of equality and should be viewed as the ideal between and among professionals of the same rank. Collaborative relationships are the ideal for supervisor and staff, though student-teacher relationships are also important. Collaborative relationships reflect working together and sharing responsibilities for solving problems. These relationships are based on trust, respect, teamwork, and open communication. Trust derives from meeting other's expectations and knowing that the other professional has integrity. Even if a colleague is not likable, he or she is deserving of respect. Open communication is the ability to say what needs to be said without involving egos. It is the ability to question and be questioned without defensiveness. Teamwork is the movement of collaboration from individual relationships to all involved.

All work and professional relationships are subject to power differentials. Effectiveness as a supervisor rests in part on one of the five bases of power described below. One person may combine all of the bases of social power, though it is not likely. In dealing with other professionals and staff, it is critical to understand the bases of their power and yours.

- **Coercive power:** The ability to force someone to do something they don't want to do; the goal is compliance. This type of power relies on threats and punishment.

- **Reward power:** The ability to provide someone with something they want or remove something they don't want. Raises, promotions, and compliments typify this type of power. In an academic context, grades are used to reward behavior.
- **Legitimate power:** This stems from the position one occupies. A director of a pharmacy has legitimate power.
- **Referent power:** This is power derived from respect for another person, someone who is exceptionally good at his or her job.
- **Expert power:** This is power derived from the information, knowledge, or expertise that an individual has (French and Raven 1959).

CONVERSATIONS

In many ways the world is overconnected and overcommunicated. The quest for open dialogue often leads to much noise with little insight or true understanding. The technology of supervision is talk, conversations. In interacting with the world, each of us makes our own observations, which we then interpret and from which we draw our unique conclusions. We may each observe the same situation, but we will each notice different things, attend to different cues, generally influenced by our past experiences, and apply our own unique rules to the situation. These rules have been developed and tested over time. One of us has learned that taking excessive risks is never warranted, while another believes only he who dares, wins. Finally, the conclusions and recommendations based on our unique observations and interpretation of events reflects our self-interest, what is best, easiest, or most familiar to us. In dealing with colleagues, to say that their position is based on their perceptions (and, thus devalue) is to acknowledge the truth; just as our position is based on our perceptions. Also, we often have beliefs about colleagues that are counterproductive. For example, they are selfish, naive, controlling, irrational, or inexperienced.

Many of the conversations between staff and professionals are difficult and contentious. In any difficult conversation, it helps to understand that there are actually three conversations occurring. First, there is the "what happened" conversation. This is about attempting to get the facts right, coming to an agreement on the substance of the issue. There is also a "feelings" conversation, understanding if my feelings about the situation are valid, appropriate, and functional; as well as the feelings of the other person. Finally, these conversations have aspects that touch our identity, our sense of competence, worthiness, goodness, love, self-esteem, and self-image. Conversations that impinge on our worth as a person often escalate as we seek to defend our ego. Working through a difficult conversation requires that we suspend the assumption that we are right and the other is wrong, that we know the intentions of the other, and that the other is to blame. In any difficult conversation, it is important to remember that the only person we control is ourselves. The standard for conduct is that of a professional who acknowledges the three levels of conversation and fosters a learning conversation in pursuit of the best outcomes for the patient.

Certain techniques are helpful in facilitating a difficult conversation with a colleague. One is to develop a series of catchphrases for dealing with difficult people, situations, and conversations. For example, if someone is upset, rather than engaging with them, say, "You seem to be upset right now, let's talk later when you feel better." Or if someone is distant and unfriendly, say, "Is there something I have done that we should talk about?" Over time, develop these fallback phrases to short-circuit a conversation that is about to go wrong and either delay it or redirect it in a more appropriate direction.

If time allows, prepare for the conversation by scripting out the various ways the conversation could flow and preparing responses for each one. For example, in dealing with a staffer who is late, the preferred answer to receive would be along the lines of "I apologize, I have had day care issues but I will take care of it." What is likely are responses that are defensive, angry, excuses. The idea is to prepare for each possible scenario so as not to be surprised by a particular response.

COACHING AND FEEDBACK

As a supervisor/manager, the job is to get people to perform. Sometimes people are deficient in their ability and skills to perform. If that deficiency is due to personal issues (health, behavioral, circumstances), then counseling is warranted. If situational depression is causing a staff member to be less than customer focused, then counseling is the strategy. If the deficiency is in the area of the person's skills and abilities related to the job, then coaching is the approach.

Coaching is a form of training or teaching aimed at helping someone improve. It is generally one-on-one. Coaching at work begins with a belief that an individual can improve, that growth and improvement are possible. Coaching is about finding solutions that let people contribute more effectively and increase their productivity. Effective coaching is not about telling people how to be better but helping them find their own path to improvement. It involves developing a partnership and a commitment to results. It requires an appreciation of the uniqueness of each individual, empathy, and compassion. Coaching requires the willingness of both parties to do the work to get better.

The mechanics of a coaching session are as follows:

1. Declare and define specifically and collaboratively what it is that is to be improved.
2. Determine if it is a long-term development plan, a debrief of a project or event and how it could be handled differently, or a short-term problem-solving session and how it is to be handled.

3. Seek to understand the source of the deficiency in performance, lack of preparation, deficient skills, outdated thinking, and so on by using open-ended questions.
4. Ask for suggestions on how to eliminate the declared deficiency.
5. Close with a declaration and mutually agreed-upon action plan with a declared timetable.
6. It is important for both parties to keep their agreements.
7. As a supervisor, any improvements require your acknowledgement, both formally and informally.
8. The best coaching is not a formal, stand-alone event. It happens day-to-day in the interaction between supervisor and staff. At the supervisory level it is best to coach in the moment.

Implicit in a coaching session is the idea of deficiency. For most people this evokes feelings of fear, anxiety, defensiveness, and anger. Coaching and feedback are at the heart of supervision. To be effective, all the skills of this chapter are required: civility, trust, empathy, and emotional intelligence. It matters how you say it. Coaching and feedback without civility and empathy is like surgery without anesthesia—effective but unnecessarily painful. Above all, effective coaches are honest. They convey information people don't want to hear. They are willing to have you be upset with them, if it will help you.

RECIPROCITY

If relationships are the engine of supervision and conversation is the technology, then reciprocity, civility, empathy, and trust are the lubricants for that engine. Relationships are at the core of the definition of management, using people to accomplish objectives. The essence of sustaining any relationship is the idea of reciprocity. No relationship will persist over the long term unless it is mutually beneficial to both parties. Mutual benefit is captured in the idea of reciprocity. Reciprocity implies a state of indebtedness between parties. If I do this for you, you will do this for me. Seldom is this expectation explicit. It tends to be implied. Reciprocity involves a rough and ongoing calculation of cost to me relative to benefits gained. There is a dark side to this equity—the idea of revenge, that evil on your part will be met with retaliation on my part. Relationships, at a very simplistic level, can be reduced to a calculation of an I want/they want ratio. Relationships are maintained and may prosper if equity in this ratio is maintained. As a supervisor, the objective is to use the relationship as a mechanism to influence others to accomplish organizational goals. Along with respect, openness, and trust, the key to influencing others is mutual benefit (Cohen and Bradford, 1991).

This idea of relationships and reciprocity rests on the notion of matching personal inputs with expected payback. As well as matching, an attitude of giving can be adopted as a reciprocity style. In his book *Give and Take,* Adam Grant (2013a) makes the case for the effectiveness of a giving approach to reciprocity and relationships. Grant found that givers are likely to end up at the bottom of the success ladder; he also found they were likely to end up at the top. Givers at the top were not lucky or altruistic; they just pursued success with a different strategy. The benefit of a giving approach to relationships for supervisors is this—it spreads and cascades. The benefits of giving as a reciprocity style on customer service and work environment are obvious.

CIVILITY

It is impossible to adhere to the professional values espoused in this book, specifically respect for others, and not be civil to one another. Civility is linked to manners, courtesy, and politeness, though it is not quite the same. Civility is best thought of as being civilized, a good citizen, and a good neighbor. To be civil is to "lessen the burden of living for those around us" (Forni 2002, 4). To be civil, to be civilized, is to adhere to rules and standards that can't be enforced; for example, giving up a seat on a subway to a pregnant woman or withholding a sarcastic remark.

Incivility in the workplace is not without consequences. Targets of incivility react, and there are tangible costs, as Porath and Pearson (2013) found:

- Forty-eight percent intentionally decreased their work effort.
- Forty-seven percent intentionally decreased the time spent at work.
- Thirty-eight percent intentionally decreased the quality of their work.
- Eighty percent lost work time worrying about the incident.
- Sixty-three percent lost work time avoiding the offender.
- Sixty-six percent said their performance declined.
- Seventy-eight percent said that the commitment to the organization declined.
- Twelve percent said that they left their job because of the uncivil treatment.
- Twenty-five percent admitted to taking their frustration out on customers.

Incivility may be prompted by actual malice, though it is more likely to be the result of thoughtlessness, stress, pressure, or insensitivity. Whereas bullying tends to be obvious, incivility is more insidious. Spreading overt lies about colleagues or demeaning them in public is one thing and leaves a tangible wake, but quietly dismissing another's ideas does not. For the supervisor the path to a civil workplace and civil relationships is to model it, teach it, hire for it, and reward it.

EMPATHY

Communicating negative information is, unfortunately, an unattractive aspect of the job of a supervisor. People are told they are being let go, not getting a promotion, acting inappropriately, not getting a raise, and so on. An essential aspect of effectively communicating this type of information is the ability to be empathic. Empathy is the ability to understand and share the feelings of another. While unattractive communications are unavoidable, insensitive communications are not. Before communicating such information, consider how it is going to impact someone and what their likely response will be; give them the time to react, a chance to maintain their dignity, and the respect due them as a human being. Think how you would want to be treated. It is a professional obligation to act empathically.

TRUST

Trust is the belief that you can count on another person. To get it, you must give it. To trust others is to be vulnerable to their actions. To trust is to believe that others will keep their word. At work, trust is a function of individual character, that a person will keep his or her word. It is also a function of competence; that I can trust others to do their job and be good at it. As a belief, trust is an element that can be developed, destroyed, or rebuilt.

Building trust is difficult. It is done in small increments on a daily basis. Numerous supervisory and managerial behaviors can erode trust, including the following:

- **Inconsistent messages:** announcing that meeting are important, then canceling three out of the first six; or announcing a new quality-improvement program then not following through
- **Inconsistent standards:** a belief by employees that supervisors and managers play favorites, that on the core values and objectives certain people are above reproach
- **Misplaced benevolence:** out of a false sense of benevolence, carrying an incompetent employee, indulging an excessively negative staffer, or tolerating incivility
- **False feedback:** not being appropriately and professionally honest in dealing with employee deficiencies
- **Failing to trust:** delegating responsibility to others, then utilizing micromanaged oversight
- **Elephants in the room:** failing to deal with obvious but painful and political situations
- **Lack of transparency:** allowing rumors to replace reliable information about key organizational initiatives
- **Consistent corporate underperformance:** lack of realism in establishing performance goals and measures (adapted from Galford and Drapeau 2003)

When trust is broken, it can be repaired by first acknowledging what happened, and then allowing feelings about the incident to surface. If the betrayal is significant, support from outside may be required. Next, beliefs about the situation can be reframed by putting the event in a different context and seeing it not as a personal slight but as an experience for growth and a rite of passage to higher insights. It is also helpful to consider your contribution to the betrayal, what you missed, and so on. Finally, it is necessary to forgive yourself and others following these circumstances. Mark Twain captured the potential dysfunctional response to a betrayal with the following quote: "We should be careful to get out of an experience only the wisdom that is in it and stop there lest we be like the cat that sits down on a hot stove lid. She will never sit down on a hot stove lid again and that is well but also she will never sit down on a cold one anymore" (http://www.goodreads.com/quotes/52127-we-should-be-careful-to-get-out-of-an-experience).

That one person betrayed your trust does not mean that all people will betray you. A good piece of advice for work is to trust the dealer but cut the cards anyway.

TRANSFERENCE

All current relationships are colored by past relationships. Some people we immediately like; others we find immediately difficult. This is explained by the idea of transference. All human relationships have an element of transference; it is a universal phenomenon. Transference is a confusion of time and place in that we read and respond to someone as if they were, for example, our father or mother, a coach from the past, a former supervisor, and so on. In responding in such a distorted fashion, we miss the "truth" of what is happening in the current situation. The idea is to be aware of this phenomenon and to check yourself for the extent of its intrusion into the current situation.

PSYCHOLOGICAL CONTRACT

In taking a new job and being socialized into the organization, many of the expectations for performance are explicitly conveyed through employment contracts and policy formulations. In addition, certain aspects of the job are implicit. Those aspects, the implicit expectations, are embodied in the idea of a psychological contract that is unspoken and unwritten. As with all contracts, the expectations are beliefs of mutual obligation to one another. These beliefs embody the expected exchange between the individual and the organization and are anticipated to be beneficial for both parties. When aspects of the psychological contract are breached, negative employee behaviors is the result, such as absenteeism, leaving, and so on. The supervisor's role in this is to maintain his or her side of the "bargain" as a method of influencing performance.

It is important to understand that all relationships have two aspects: the observable social aspect and the psychological aspect. The point is that relationships always have a subtext that may or may not conform to what is actually said and observed. This subtext is often a powerful influence on the quality of the relationship.

INNER WORK LIFE

Imagine that about an hour before you are to leave for work, there is a call from your son or daughter's pediatrician. This subject of the call is that your child's blood work has come back with several abnormal values, and more tests are required. As you work through your day, how focused will you be on your tasks? Will you be distracted? Might you miss some key signals or information? In a meeting, will your mind wander? Of course, the answer is yes to all of the above. This scenario points out that everyone at work, you included, has an inner work life that has the potential to diminish productivity. Performance at work is affected by the interplay of perceptions, emotions, and motivations triggered by workday events and events in one's personal life. The most important workday event is the supervisor's or manager's behavior. When work was manual—shoveling, digging, lifting, and so on—this may not have been such a problem. But for knowledge workers, for professionals, distractions in perceptions, emotions, and motivations are critical. The supervisory response to negate an employee's negative work life involves enabling the employee to achieve a goal, solve a problem, and be successful at work, which will lead to positive feelings. The worst days at work are when goals are not met and there is a feeling of inadequacy and frustration. The other factor that negates a negative work life is being treated decently as a human being by a supervisor. Here is the secret to making people feel good about themselves at work: Help them accomplish their assigned goals and tasks, and then genuinely acknowledge their work and convey your appreciation for their efforts.

SET THE MOOD

Your first task as supervisor is to set the mood for the department. What has been found is that productivity is impacted by the supervisor's mood. This requires you to manage your inner work life. This is best handled if one is emotionally intelligent. Emotional intelligence is understanding your emotions and using them in a way that is appropriate to the context. It is not about indulging your emotions or suppressing them. It is about being aware of how your emotions impact your behavior and thus the mood of the department. The people who work for you will read you like the weather. They want to know if you are predictable or if there will be fronts moving through. Can they count on you? Their careers and their lives depend on you. It is not dissimilar from a small child's relationship with his or her mother. All the good things come from you: affirmation, recommendations, promotions, a pleasant work environment, accomplishment. The aspiration is a mood that is "optimistic, authentic, high energy" (Goleman, Boyatzis, and McKee 2001, 4).

APPRECIATIVE INQUIRY

People get told they are deficient all the time. Many come through school intensely aware of their deficiencies. Rather than pointing out where people are deficient, look for what they are good at—and then ask them for more of that. Everyone has talents. If you were an admissions director, would you focus on reasons to exclude people from a program, or would you look for reasons to admit them? Look for reasons why people will be good at their job, and then let them know you appreciate what they do. Tell them you trust them, that they are competent—and they will work for you. Recognize their goodness, and there is no limit to what you can ask of them, because they won't want to disappoint you. If you don't believe this, I suspect that a substantial part of your life has been an attempt to honor your mother or father's expectations for you, or if they had none, to prove them wrong.

CONNECT

The age-old supervisory conundrum is this: Is it better to be loved or feared? Expressed another way: Is warmth or strength and competence the winning hand? Being judged competent but lacking warmth provokes envy, a complicated emotion involving both respect and resentment. Being judged warm but incompetent elicits pity, which invokes compassion and lack of respect, and thus neglect. Projecting strength and competence, prior to establishing trust, generates fear, which undermines cognitive potential, creativity, and problem solving. Having to choose, the way to influence is to begin with warmth (Cuddy, Kohut, and Neffinger 2013). Being a new supervisor, you will be judged on your warmth before your competence is assessed. Warmth induces trust. And trust at work begets openness, sharing, and honest communication, and it enhances the potential for a supervisor to change attitudes and beliefs and the "sweet spot" of influence (Cuddy, Kohut, and Neffinger 2013). How to project warmth?

- Be genuine. There is a natural tendency to overdo it when trying to project warmth. Behavior that is exaggerated is read as inauthentic. Better to project warmth by behaving in a way that lets people know that you are leveling with them, speaking as if you were talking to a friend, even sharing an appropriate personal story that feels like you are confiding in them.

- To get people to agree with you, first agree with them. Validating their ideas demonstrates empathy and that you have common sense. If a meeting is tense, acknowledge that fact. People appreciate your honesty.
- According to the French diplomat and dramatist Jean Giraudoux, "The secret of success is sincerity. Once you can fake that you've got it made" (https://en.wikiquote.org/wiki/Jean_Giraudoux).
- Not true. Warmth cannot be faked. The final recommendation to project warmth is to smile—and smile sincerely. If you don't feel happy and a smile is a struggle, use the actor's trick of recalling a time and circumstance when you were.

SPECIAL RELATIONSHIPS: YOUR BOSS

It's obvious that one does not supervise a boss. It is important, however, to manage that relationship. It is an important relationship with many implications for personal and departmental achievement. Certain key assumptions are useful in the process of managing your boss: (1) You own 50 percent of your relationship with your boss, (2) you are 100 percent in control of your own behavior, (3) the way you behave toward your boss teaches him or her how to treat you, (4) the relationship with your boss is one of mutual dependence, and (5) you are both fallible human beings

Some people see themselves as extremely dependent on their boss. As such, they adopt an infantile posture toward their boss. They see their boss as omnipotent and infallible. In fact, the boss is, as are all humans, insecure and uncertain. One needs to recognize just how dependent the boss is on his or her subordinates. Through your actions you can do your boss considerable harm. Bosses are imperfect. They are fallible. They don't have all the answers. Nor are they the enemy.

Understanding your boss's strengths and weaknesses, as well as your own, is the foundation for crafting a positive relationship with your boss. First, if your boss's preferred work style is one of formal communication via memos and reports, then you should adjust your behavior to that style—whether you like it or not. Second, mutual expectations for one another should be explicitly declared. Typically, your boss won't do this, and it is your job to solicit this information. Third, keep a flow of information moving upward toward your boss. You may need to find a way to frame information that your boss doesn't want; failures and problems, for example. Fourth, be dependable and honest in dealing with your boss. It is the only way he or she will learn to trust you and confide in you. Fifth, be judicious in your demands on your boss's time.

While you can't change your boss's behavior, you can shape it. Remember that bosses are human. They want affirmation, strokes, and compliments like everyone else. So in shaping your boss's behavior, keep the following in mind: (1) Remember that bosses like praise for their good points, like everyone else; (2) voice public and private support for your boss's goals; (3) simplify your boss's job by taking on tasks that speak to your strengths and compensate for his or her weaknesses; (4) offer to be a sounding board for your boss's ideas and problems. No matter what, you will have some type of relationship with your boss. As with all relationships, a successful relationship with your boss is based on mutual understanding, respect, and benefit.

OTHER PROFESSIONALS

There are two problems in supervising professionals. The first is that the dictates of the profession have a powerful influence on their behavior. Individuals are socialized into their profession in school, typically when they are relatively young. Also, mentors at work continuously reinforce professional standards. Your colleagues may have been acclaimed for their adherence to professional ideals. They likely believe that professional obligations supersede organizational mandates. They may believe there is an iron floor separating the practice site from the corporate suite. In short, there is a countervailing influence to your influence as a supervisor.

The second problem in supervising other professionals is that they are likely to be very smart, very driven, extremely independent, in short supply, disdainful of the role of management as not being real work, and indifferent to formal positioning on corporate charts. They may think of themselves as "the talent" and managers and supervisors as "the suits." The suits' job is to make their lives easier by dealing with the minutiae of administration while the talent focuses on the important issues. They may generate significant corporate revenues and profits. The actual supervisory problem is likely to be this—they know what to do, they just don't want to do it. Think of managing a nineteen-year-old, world-class athlete with a guaranteed contract to get the flavor of this.

For the reasons above, the normal command and control approach to management and supervision with professionals is not likely to work. Inspiration rather than supervision is preferred. Professionals want to know why they are asked to do something, not how. They already know how and have demonstrated by their accomplishments that they are self-motivated. They want to collaborate on projects that they deem important and worthy of their talents and that will have an impact on their career. They do not need to be micromanaged. "Engineers hate being micromanaged on the technical side" (Garvin 2013, 78).

While professionals hate to be micromanaged on the technical side, "they love being closely managed on the career side" (Garvin 2013, 78). The best at managing professionals support them in their careers and their development. Professionals want to know they are winning and doing a good job as they advance. Feedback to professionals must be smart and steady, delivered with a light touch, and judicious in its occurrence. Professionals expect to be provided with new and exciting projects to engage them. "It's the care and feeding of our professionals that make the whole organization work" (Broderick 2011, 41).

The best supervisors and organizations do the following regarding their professional staff: They adopt a stewardship mindset moving from the idea that we own them or they work for us to how can professionals be nurtured to success in their careers. Professionals need to know and feel that you care about them.

Google used its expertise in data management and analytics to determine if managers mattered and to determine what the best managers and supervisors did. Remember this is a company composed of ultra-high-achieving engineers and programmers. Their efforts identified eight key behaviors for the most effective managers. They concluded that a good manager of professionals

1. Is a good coach
2. Empowers the team and does not micromanage
3. Expresses interest in and concern for team members' success and personal well-being
4. Is productive and results oriented
5. Is a good communicator
6. Helps with career development
7. Has a clear vision and strategy for the team
8. Has the technical skills to advise the team (adapted from Garvin 2013)

One method of considering professional relationships is to examine the nature and types of transactions between professionals. First, consider the perspectives individuals might adopt when interacting with one another.

Consummate professional: A consummate professional's sole focus is on the job. To act as a consummate professional is to consider the situation and the available information in an objective, unbiased manner, to arrive at unprejudiced conclusions. Personal issues and agendas, ego, insecurities, politics, and emotional distortions are absent when acting as consummate professionals. Consummate professionals are in control of themselves and recognize they are *only* in control of themselves, and not any other professional.

The boss: To act as the boss is to act based on the idea of should and ought; that there are standards that need not be examined for validity and appropriateness and are invoked in an unthinking manner. The boss thinks: This is the way it is done, why don't you know this? The professor/boss may say one thing and do something else. In other words, bosses are willing to impose standards on you but cut corners for themselves. Much of what the professor/boss believes is appropriate. These well-structured and strongly held beliefs expedite outcomes. The boss is never in doubt. The boss believes he or she is in control of everything. Any problems that arise in a professional relationship are your fault.

The employee: There are two aspects to the employee perspective. The first is inappropriate and may be dysfunctional. Employees believe they are not responsible for anything, not even themselves. Their fallback attitude is: I was just following the rules, the protocols, what you told me. Employees tend to blame others for outcomes and take no responsibility for the consequences of their actions. The second perspective is positive. In this case employees are engaged in understanding how they might improve. They willingly defer to expertise in any form to facilitate improved performance. The forty-year practitioner committed to excellence will, at times, adopt this perspective.

All professionals exhibit aspects of each perspective over the course of their professional lives. In fact, they may exhibit each perspective in a single transaction. The key is to understand when each is appropriate. The ideal professional transaction obviously involves two consummate professionals acting with equal power and trust in a collegial relationship to positively impact performance based on objective criteria. Problems arise when both professionals want to act as the boss, or when each wants to avoid responsibility and act as the employee.

The above framework borrows from the work of Berne (1964), *Games People Play*, and Harris (1969), *I'm OK—You're OK*. In their work, transactions are analyzed from the perspective of the parent (professor/boss), the adult (consummate professional), and the child (student/employee). In any professional transaction, think of who is acting like the critical, controlling parent; the functioning, objective adult; and the passive, weak child.

DIVERSITY

Any casual observer walking down a city street will notice the diverse types of people. Supervisors no longer can expect to manage people like themselves. Staff will vary as to age, ethnicity, culture, sexual orientation, and physical challenges. Astute supervisors accept this challenge and seek to accommodate that diversity within the framework of professional obligation and organizational objectives. More than accommodate, effective supervisors in this area value the diversity. In accepting this challenge it is important for supervisors and managers to recognize that (1) a diverse workforce is the reality of the age, that there will be different approaches to work and productivity, and to value this variety; (2) diversity presents challenges but also contains the opportunity to learn and grow; (3) despite this diversity, the organization has the right to expect the same standards for performance from everyone; (4) the organization must support openness and the free exchange of ideas; (5) personal growth and development must be encouraged; and (6) workers must feel valued. As to the mechanics of managing diversity, Thompson and Gregory (2012, 244) write:

- "Invest the time and effort in cultivating genuine and meaningful relationships with their employee."
- "Engage in behavior that builds mutual trust with their employees."
- "Adopt a coaching approach. . . ."
- "Assume an individual consideration approach to working with their employee."

SUMMARY

The focus of this chapter was supervision at the one-on-one level. What follows are several additional observations and strategies that are helpful in managing relationships.

- Be open about yourself and curious about others.
- Don't give mixed signals. Does your body language align with your words?
- Be mannerly, be civil, and care.
- Have a sense of humor about yourself.
- Take feedback well.
- Trust and be trusted.
- Be angry only when appropriate.
- Acknowledge the other person's feelings and point of view.
- Explain your decisions when warranted.
- Give feedback sparingly that is objective and constructive. Avoid ad hominems.
- Like yourself (adapted from Bradberry and Greaves, 2009).

EXERCISES

Summarizing
Write a one-page executive summary of the chapter.
Discuss with your classmates how you would teach this material.
Write a two-page case from your experience on this topic that would be instructional for other students.
Develop a mental model for this chapter based on the mind mapping technique.

What's Important to You in the Chapter?
With several of your classmates, discuss the most important ideas from the chapter. Which ideas do you think will be most useful to you in your career? Which ideas do you think you will remember in six months?

What Do the Practitioners/Others Say?
Discuss with your colleagues or someone at work any of the ideas in the chapter. Alternatively, read an article from any source on supervision and be prepared to summarize its message.

Questions

1. Read the following quote. Do you agree with this observation? Is it something you would do?

   "New leaders who are perceived as having low status—because of their age, education, experience, or other factors—face different rules. They get better ratings and results from teams when they take charge, set the course, and tell subordinates what to do. For those bosses, it pays to be bossy" (Sauer 2013).

2. What ten things should every supervisor know?

3. Consider whether the following comments regarding reciprocity apply to you.
   a. In your dealings with colleagues and others, do you provide each other with equal benefits?
   b. Do you balance your dealings with others?
   c. Are you fair in your dealings with others?
   d. Do the benefits you provide and receive even out over time?
   e. If there are problems with another, do you discuss those problems, redress them, and make the other aware?

4. Much of the advice on supervision revolves around the ideas of reciprocity, of trading with others to influence them. An alternative finding suggests that it might be better just to give things to people with little expectation of payback. Adam Grant (2013b), in his article "In the Company of Givers and Takers," concluded generosity is an effective work strategy. What Grant is saying is that the most effective way to get things done at work is not based on exchange and reciprocity but on helping others without expecting anything in return. What is your perspective on this idea?

5. Will you be more comfortable with the scientific, craft, or artistic aspect of supervision?

6. Take some of the ideas and themes of this chapter and condense them into a poster. In other words, can you visually represent the ideas in the chapter in an appealing way?

Beliefs about People

From your mind map at the beginning of the chapter, compile your specific beliefs about people in general and people in their role as employees and staff. Discuss with several of your colleagues what the implications of these beliefs are for your likely effectiveness as a supervisor.

What would you conclude about an individual who was rude to wait staff in a restaurant? Would you want to work with such a person?

For the following situations, discuss with several of your classmates the "perfect" phrase to deal with the situation.

- Unfriendly colleague
- Argumentative colleague
- Negative colleague
- Bully
- Complainer

- Angry colleague
- Micromanaging colleague

Develop a script for the conversation to deal with each of the following situations; compare with several of your classmates.

- Telling a staff member they need to improve their personal hygiene
- Telling your boss that you find some of the jokes he or she tells offensive
- Telling a staff member you won't recommend him or her for a promotion

With several classmates, discuss one work relationship and one personal relationship that is problematic. From these discussions, offer three suggestions to improve both work and personal relationships.

REFERENCES AND WORKS CONSULTED

Amabile, T.M., and S.J. Kramer. 2007. "Inner Work Life." *Harvard Business Review* (May): 2–12.

Benjamin, S.F. 2008. *Perfect Phrases*. New York: McGraw-Hill.

Bennett, F.L. 1996. *The Management of Engineering*. New York: Wiley.

Berk, M.S., and S.M. Anderson. 2000. "The Impact of Past Relationships on Interpersonal Behavior: Behavioral Confirmation in the Social-Cognitive Process of Transference." *Journal of Personality and Social Psychology* 79 (4): 546–62.

Berne, E. 1964. *Games People Play*. New York: Ballantine.

Bradberry, T., and J. Greaves. 2009. *Emotional Intelligence 2.0*. San Diego: Talent Smart.

Broderick, M. 2011. *The Art of Managing Professional Services*. Upper Saddle River, NJ: Prentice Hall.

Cialdini, R.B. 2007. *Influence*. New York: Collins Business.

Cohen, A.R., and D.L. Bradford. 1991. *Influence without Authority*. New York: Wiley.

Conant, D.R., and M. Norgaard. 2011. *Touch Points*. San Francisco: Jossey-Bass.

Cuddy, A.J.C., M. Kohut, and J. Neffinger. 2013. "Connect, Then Lead." *Harvard Business Review* (July–August): 53–61.

Dietz, J., and E.P. Kleinlogel. 2014. "Wage Cuts and Manager's Empathy: How a Positive Emotion Can Contribute to Positive Organizational Ethics in Difficult Times." *Journal of Business Ethics* 119: 461–72.

Dimitrius, J., and W.P. Mazzarella. 2008. *Reading People*. New York: Ballantine Books.

Earley, P.C., and E. Mosakowski. 2004. "Cultural Intelligence." *Harvard Business Review* (October): 139–46.

Espinoza, C., M. Ukleja, and C. Rusch. 2010. *Managing the Millennials*. Hoboken, NJ: Wiley.

Feinberg, R.A., and J.T. Greene. 1995. "Transference and Countertransference Issues in Professional Relationships." *Family Law Quarterly* 29 (1): 111–20.

Forni, P.M. 2002. *Choosing Civility*. New York: St. Martin's Griffin.

Forni, P.M. 2008. *The Civility Solution*. New York: St. Martin's.

French, J.R.P., and B. Raven. 1959. "The Bases of Social Power." In *Group Dynamics,* edited by D. Cartwright and A. Zander. New York: Harper & Row.

Gabarro, J.J., and J.J. Kotter. 2005. "Managing Your Boss." *Harvard Business Review* (January): 92–99.

Galford, R., and A.S. Drapeau. 2003. "The Enemies of Trust." *Harvard Business Review* (February): 1–7.

Garvin, D.A. 2013. "How Google Sold Its Engineers on Management." *Harvard Business Review* (December): 75–82.

Goffee, R., and G. Jones. 2005. "Managing Authenticity." *Harvard Business Review* (December): 1–8.

Goffee, R., and G. Jones. 2007. "Leading Clever People." *Harvard Business Review* (March): 72–79.

Goffee, R., and G. Jones. 2009. *Clever.* Boston: Harvard Business Press.

Goleman, D. 1995. *Emotional Intelligence.* New York: Bantam Dell.

Goleman, D. 1998. *Working with Emotional Intelligence.* New York: Bantam Dell.

Goleman, D., R. Boyatzie, and A. McKee. 2001. "Primal Leadership: The Hidden Driver of Great Performance." *Harvard Business Review* (December): 3–11.

Grant, A. (2013a). *Give and Take.* New York: Viking.

Grant, A. (2013b). "In the Company of Givers and Takers." *Harvard Business Review* (April): 90–97.

Groysberg, B., and M. Slind. 2012. "Leadership Is a Conversation." *Harvard Business Review,* 2–10.

HBR Guide to Coaching Employees. 2015. Boston: Harvard Business Review Press.

HBR Guide to Managing Up and Across. 2013. Boston: Harvard Business Review Press.

Harden-Fritz, J.M. 2013. *Professional Civility.* New York: Land.

Harris, T.A. 1969. *I'm OK—You're OK.* New York: Harper.

Hill, L.A. 2007. "Becoming the Boss." *Harvard Business Review* (January): 2–9.

https://en.wikiquote.org/wiki/Jean_Giraudoux

http://www.starwars.com/news/the-starwars-com-10-best-yoda-quotes

http://www.goodreads.com/quotes/52127-we-should-be-careful-to-get-out-of-an-experience

Hurley, R.F. 2006. "The Decision to Trust." *Harvard Business Review* (September): 55–62.

Huy, W.N. 2001. "In Praise of Middle Managers." *Harvard Business Review* (September): 72–79.

Ibarra, H. 2015a. *Act like a Leader, Think like a Leader.* Boston: Harvard Business Review Press.

Ibarra, H. 2015b. "The Authenticity Paradox." *Harvard Business Review* (January–February): 53–59.

Jackman, J.M., and M.H. Strober. 2003. "Fear of Feedback." *Harvard Business Review* (April): 3–8b

Kets de Vries, M.F.R. 1988. "Prisoners of Leadership." *Human Relations* 41 (3): 261–80.

Kets de Vries, M.F.R. 2005. "The Dangers of Feeling like a Fake." *Harvard Business Review* (September): 1–8.

Kim, W.C., and R. Mauborgne. 2002. "Fair Process: Managing in the Knowledge Economy." *Harvard Business Review,* 3–11.

Kramer, R.M. 2009. "Rethinking Trust." *Harvard Business Review* (June): 2–9.

LeBoeuf, M. 1985. *Getting Results.* New York: Berkley.

Mayer, R.C., J.H. Davis, and F.D. Schoorman 1995. "An Integrative Model of Organizational Trust." *Academy of Management Review* 20 (3): 709–34.

McKenna, P.J., and D.H. Maister. 2002. *First among Equals.* New York: Free Press.

Mintzberg, H. 1998. "Covert Leadership: Notes on Managing Professionals." *Harvard Business Review* 76 (6), 140–48.

Mintzberg, H. 2013. *Simply Managing*. San Francisco: Berrett-Koehler.

Patterson, K., J. Grenny, R. McMillan, and A. Switzler. 2002. *Crucial Conversations*. New York: McGraw-Hill.

Pervan, S. J., L.L. Bove, and L.W. Johnson. 2009. "Reciprocity as a Key Stabilizing Norm of Interpersonal Marketing Relationships: Scale Development and Validation." *Industrial Marketing Management* 38: 60–70.

Pollan, S.M., and M. Levine. 1996. *Lifescripts*. Indianapolis, IN: Wiley.

Porath, C., and C. Pearson. 2013. "The Price of Incivility." *Harvard Business Review* (January–February): 115–21.

Reina, D.S., and M.L. Reina. 2006. *Trust and Betrayal in the Workplace*. San Francisco: Berrett-Kohler.

Robbins, S.P. 2013. *The Truth about Managing People*. Upper Saddle River, NJ: FT Press.

Runion, M. 2010. *Perfect Phrases for Managers and Supervisors*. New York: McGraw-Hill.

Sasser, W.E., Jr., and F.S. Leonard. 1980. "Let First-Level Supervisors Do Their Job." *Harvard Business Review* 58 (2): 113–21.

Sauer, S.J. 2013. "Why Bossy Is Better for Rookie Managers." *Harvard Business Review* (May): 30.

Schmalenberg, C., M. Kramer, C.R. King, M. Krugman, C. Lund, D. Poduska, and D. Rapp. 2005. "Excellence through Evidence: Securing Collegial/Collaborative Nurse-Physician Relationships, Part 2." *Journal of Nursing Administration* 35 (11) 507–14.

Schoorman, F. D., R.C. Mayer, and J.H. Davis. 2007. "An Integrative Model of Organizational Trust: Past, Present, and Future." *Academy of Management Review* 32 (2): 344–54.

Stone, D., B. Patton, and S. Heen. 1999. *Difficult Conversations*. New York: Penguin.

Sutton, R.I. 2010. *Good Boss, Bad Boss*. New York: Business Plus.

Tamm, J.W., and R.J. Luyet. 2004. *Radical Collaboration*. New York: Collins Business.

Thomas, D.A., and R.J. Ely. 1996. "Making Differences Matter: A New Paradigm for Managing Diversity." *Harvard Business Review* (September–October): 79–90.

Thompson, C., and J.B. Gregory. 2012. "Managing Millennials: A Framework for Improving Attraction, Motivation, and Retention." *Psychologist-Manager Journal* 15: 237–46.

Tuchman, B. 1981. *Practicing History*. Ballantine: New York.

Uhl-Bien, M., and J.M. Maslyn. 2003. "Reciprocity in Manager-Subordinate Relationships: Components, Configurations, and Outcomes." *Journal of Management* 29 (4): 511–32.

5 SUPERVISING YOURSELF

ALEX

There it was right in front of him. The letter began, "Congratulations, you have been accepted as a fellow. ..." It was everything Alex had ever wanted. All through school Alex knew he was destined for advanced training. It was a long tradition in the family. But what was that feeling; why wasn't he happy? Setting off for a late afternoon jog, Alex was aware that his running shorts seemed tighter than usual. Alex set the app on his phone to record the distance, adjusted the earphones, set the sound right, queued up his favorite play list, and set off. It was unseasonably mild today, almost sixty degrees when the thirties were the norm. He settled in and let her mind wander.

Wow! Those fellowships are hard to get, my family will be proud.

I really don't want to move.

I couldn't be gaining weight, could I?

I don't really want to give up my spare time for two years to study.

I seem to be winning the staff over, finally. It only took six months.

I don't think the prior supervisor will ever come back.

If I get the supervisor job permanently, I wonder how much the raise will be.

I like being in control at work.

What's with the senior staff? They don't seem to be warming up to me.

If I had more income, I could take a winter vacation, or maybe get a new car.

I really like having money.

What do I tell them if they offer me the supervisor job permanently?

Why are these shorts so tight?

Only two more miles to go.

MENTAL MODELS

In the center of the space below, write the word *me*. Next, write the words that come to mind when you think of this topic. Do not edit your thoughts or collaborate with anyone. There is no right or wrong answer.

If things are related, connect them with an arrow. If the relationship is reciprocal (they both affect each other), put arrows at both ends of the line. If one relationship is stronger than another, make the arrow darker and thicker.

The goal is to capture your mental model of what you believe about yourself. This is the starting point for the discussion on marketing, marketing services, and customer service.

LEARNING OBJECTIVES

- Discuss the advantages to a supervisor of having self-awareness.
- Clarify your commitment to the professional values described in the book.
- Describe the Big Five of personality.
- Discuss the concept of emotional intelligence.
- Discuss the idea of personal schemas.

SELF-AWARENESS

Supervision, for the most part, is about managing professional relationships. It is about managing relationships with your boss, your subordinates, and your professional colleagues. Often neglected in the writing and thinking on managing these relationships is the single most critical relationship to be managed as a supervisor. It is the relationship with yourself.

Almost all advice on being successful at anything begins with some variation of the idea of "know thyself." Knowing yourself requires introspection, work, clarifying your values, understanding the impact of your family and past circumstances on your behavior and attitudes, reflection, being uncomfortable as sensitive lines about yourself are broached, changing how you think about the world and your place in it, maturity, and accepting feedback about yourself, both formal feedback and the informal kind of feedback we get every day from the world. It also requires you to stop making excuses and to accept limitations. The prospect of being an effective supervisor is enhanced by accepting who you are. A professional will set about to change the things about themselves that can be changed and accept the things about themselves that can't be changed. Having done this, you can have an authentic relationship with yourself, unfettered by deceit and denial. From this foundation of personal honesty about yourself you can begin to build authentic relationships with those you are tasked with supervising and your professional associates above and lateral to you.

Effective supervisors and managers know themselves. They are aware of their behavioral tendencies, their emotions, how they think, what their values are, what their dreams and aspirations are, what their personal schemas are, the impact of their personal family history, the way their body responds to stress, their beliefs and assumptions about the world, the contour of their inner terrain, how they impact other people, and the composition of their self-talk (the mental tapes playing in their head), and on and on. They have an objective database of how they interact in the world, what their personal modus operandi is in any situation. A long tradition of advice on knowing yourself extends from the ancient Greeks, flows from Shakespeare's pen, and is ubiquitous in today's world. Supervisors and managers possessing this type of personal insight are argued to be more effective; they are recognized as being authentic, as being themselves. The daily human tensions and frictions of supervision and management are smoothed by a supervisor or manager who has done the work of understanding themselves and thus understands the mirror tensions and frictions of those being supervised, acts accordingly, and builds enduring relationships—relationships being the human technology that drives organizational effectiveness. Authentic and self-aware people are "real."

Self-awareness is an intrapersonal phenomenon. It requires individuals themselves to become the focus and object of attention. Self-awareness begins with a simple, conscious understanding of one's inner life in relation to the world; requires a period of self-reflection, where one makes sense of it all; ultimately yielding something called self-awareness. Self-awareness, in addition to its internal focus also entails a comparison to external standards. By linking self-awareness to an external standard the idea that one is sometimes not "ideal" is introduced. Understanding that one is not always ideal, not always perfect is to require the individual to accept their "dark" side. Ultimately, self-aware people become self-accepting of themselves and of their strengths and their deficiencies.

The idea of a self is not singular. Each of us contains multiple selves. There is the authentic or real self—what is true; the repressed self—the part kept in check to conform to society; the autonomous self—the self that through rationality and reflection recognizes they have power and a choice in how to act; the storied self—the self of the stories we tell ourselves about who we are; and the entangled self—that part of us enmeshed in and a function of our relationships. In other words, the self we are seeking to understand varies with context, situation, and relationship.

There are at least two barriers to an accurate self-assessment. First, in seeking to understand themselves, individuals acquire information that may be painful or is inconsistent with their view of themselves. When this information challenges deeply held beliefs about themselves, a sensitive line is broached, and individuals tend to defend themselves psychologically by offering explanations and rationales for this discrepancy. However, information that is confirmed by others ameliorates the potential discomfort associated with the sensitive line. The implication of the sensitive line is that when approached, it is defended and limits the chance for learning and development. The second barrier to self-knowledge is time and energy. One must take an active role as an observer. Students and working professionals may not have the time or the psychic energy to indulge in the "luxury" of self-observation and self-awareness. Both self-observation and self-awareness require conscious mental activity. If none is available due to sheer exhaustion, then no insight will occur. What is gained is only what is put into it.

In seeking self-awareness it is important to remember the following. You are not on trial. It is a journey not a personal tribunal. You may not find what you are looking for so keep looking. Sometimes personal truths emerge from the give and take of dialogue with others. You may not like what you find. Respect your courage to seek this information and honor the quest to improve. It is important to remember to live the life in front of you. An obsessive and compulsive inward self-focus is not useful.

There is an almost infinite number of things people could learn about themselves. Increasing self-awareness is a lifelong activity. For this chapter, the following topics are discussed as grounding for that process: schemas, personality, values, and emotional intelligence.

SCHEMAS

A schema is a map, a theory, a blueprint, a mental model of something. It is the aggregated beliefs about something, some aspect of the world. Formally, schemas are defined as "a pattern imposed on reality or experience to help individuals explain it, to mediate perception, and to guide their responses" (Young, Klosko, and Weishaar 2003). Schemas are important in that they help us interpret reality and solve problems. They help us make sense of our experiences. Schemas comprise our memories, emotions, cognitions, and bodily sensations and are formed in early childhood and adolescence, though they may form later in life as well. Schemas provide us with cognitive consistency in dealing with the world. There is a potential issue if the need to maintain cognitive consistency (maintain our blueprint) overrides the reality of current experience. Thus, schemas may be adaptive or maladaptive. Summarizing:

- Schemas lend structure to experience. Schemas are activated from long-term memory in response to a new circumstance.
- Schemas determine the information that will be encoded and retrieved from memory.
- Schemas affect processing time, speed of information flow, and speed of problem solving.
- Schemas permit the observer to fill in missing data when data are missing or ambiguous.
- Schemas provide a basis for problem solving.
- Schemas provide a basis for evaluating experience.
- Schemas provide a basis for making plans, establishing goals, and developing behavioral routines to accomplish objectives (adapted from Narvaez and Mitchell 2000).

Just as individuals hold schemas about the world, they have personal schema that encapsulate what individuals believe about themselves. Page 27 of the exercises describes many of the schemas that individuals hold about themselves. The ones described are negative and may be maladaptive. Note that not all schemas that individuals hold about themselves are negative. One of a supervisor's tasks is to first identify if any of these maladaptive schemas are ones that they hold and then to understand how the particular schema influences their behavior. For example, there is a schema described as failure to achieve that may inordinately influence the attainment of objectives, personal and organizational. In the exercise section, you will be asked to review these schemas for their applicability to you and their potential impact on you as a supervisor.

PERSONALITY

To ask who I am is to ask what my personality is. Personality is a relatively enduring pattern of thoughts, feelings, and behaviors that distinguish individuals from one another. It has been shown that as much as 50 percent of the variation in personality may be attributed to genetics. However, the environment can moderate that tendency. Children raised by a depressive parent may not become depressed. Life's experiences may reinforce certain genetic tendencies or ameliorate them. There are as many personalities as there are people on the planet. In thinking about personality it is helpful to remember that each person is:

> Like all other people,
> Like some other people, and
> Like no other people (Kluckhohn and Murray 1953, 53)

The Big Five
Although there are as many personalities as there are people on the planet, we are all alike at some level. In fact, we are more alike than different. That similarity is captured in the dominant view of personality today—the "Big Five" description of personality. This theory suggests that all personality variables and traits can be collapsed into the following five factors: conscientiousness, agreeableness, neuroticism, openness to experience, and extraversion (CANOE).

Conscientiousness
People who score high in this trait are disciplined, organized, goal driven, and self-controlled compared to low scorers, who are impulsive and spontaneous. Those high in conscientiousness are described as perfectionists and workaholics, and often people who score high in this trait find it difficult to be flexible when adjusting to a change of routine. People who score high in this trait are often perceived as being intelligent, dependable, always prepared, liking order, following a schedule, paying attention to details, and getting work done right away. Occupational success is more closely related to the trait of conscientiousness than to other traits. Six useful subscales are associated with conscientiousness:

- Self-efficacy: taking pride in your work, performing in a competent fashion
- Orderliness: neat, tidy, scheduled
- Dutifulness: related to job delinquency, substance abuse
- Achievement striving: the desire to move up

- Self-discipline: the ability to keep working
- Cautiousness: related to impulsive behavior

Agreeableness

Individuals who score high in this trait are often described as being cooperative, trusting, and empathic, in contrast to low scorers, who can be described as cold, hostile, and nonco-operative. Paying attention to the mental states of others, helping others, and having good interpersonal relationships is a description of someone who scores high in agreeableness. Those who score high in agreeableness are also described as being interested in people, aware of other's emotions, having a soft heart, taking time for others, and being sympa-thetic to other's feelings. Research in personality has discovered that women score higher in agreeableness than men. Subscales related to agreeableness include:

- Trust: believing the best about people
- Morality: a strong sense of right and wrong
- Altruism: the desire to help others
- Cooperation: wanting to get along
- Modesty: not thinking of oneself as special
- Sympathy: concern for others

Neuroticism

Individuals who score high in neuroticism tend to be anxious, insecure, and prone to stress and worry and are more affected by the daily hassles of life than low scorers. Neuroticism has been described as the response to the negative emotions of fear, anxiety, shame, guilt, disgust, and sadness. Neuroticism has been related to depression, anxiety disorders, phobia, eating disorders, post-traumatic stress disorder, and obsessive-compulsive disorder. People who score on the high end of neuroticism often have low self-esteem and are constantly wondering if they have taken the right path in life. Self-doubt is a common theme. People on the low end of neuroticism tend to be calm and display emotional stability. The subscales related to neuroticism are:

- Anxiety: nervousness, unease
- Anger: annoyance, displeasure, hostility
- Depression: despondency, hopelessness, inadequacy
- Self-consciousness: social anxiety, unassertiveness
- Immoderation: poor impulse control
- Vulnerability: easily flustered, difficulty in performing under stress

Openness to Experience

The trait of openness to experience refers to those individuals who are creative and imaginative and prefer variety over routine. High scorers are open to experience, are intellectually curious, have an appreciation for art, and are aware of their feelings. They like uniqueness. A high scorer in openness to experience would be full of ideas, quick to understand things, have a vivid imagination, spend time reflecting on things, and have a rich vocabulary. The subscales related to openness to experience include:

- Imagination: creative, can get lost in their thoughts
- Artistic interests: interest in music, art, and so on
- Emotionality: experience and express emotions
- Adventurousness: love of the new and different
- Intellect: high value on intellectual pursuits
- Liberalism: support for the liberal perspective

Extraversion

Carl Jung introduced the terms *extroversion* and *introversion*. His idea of extroversion was someone who was focused outward, liked action more than reflection, and enjoyed other people's company. In contrast, the introvert was described as someone who is in tune with his or her own thoughts and feelings and seeks solitude to reflect. The core of extroversion is sociability. Extroverts tend to be ambitious, enjoy gaining status, receiving social attention, and have lots of positive emotion in their daily lives. Someone high in extraversion would be described as being comfortable around people, being the life of the party, starting conversations, and being the center of attention. The subscales linked to extraversion include:

- Friendliness: kind and pleasant
- Gregariousness: sociable, fond of company
- Assertiveness: socially appropriate expression of thoughts and feelings
- Activity level: doers
- Excitement seeking: trying new things, taking a calculated risk
- Cheerfulness: happy, optimistic

Does Personality Change?

The question is whether personality is stable or whether it changes. It would be convenient if there were an absolute answer to this question. Unfortunately, this is not possible. It is possible to make some statements about personality change, though not unequivocally. People and personalities change as people mature. For example, conscientiousness and agreeableness may increase with age, while openness to experience may increase through early adulthood but decline with age. Meaningful life events, first job, marriage, birth of a child, unemployment, and so on may cause personality to change. The point is that personality does change. At the genetic, biochemical, neuroscience-level personal genetics argues for personality stability, while the findings on brain plasticity support personality change. To reiterate, the answer to "Is personality fixed or does it change?" is—YES.

Personal Intelligence

Personal intelligence is the "capacity to reason about personality and to use personality and personal information to enhance one's thoughts, plans, and life experience" (Mayer 2007–2008, 210). "Personal intelligence involves the abilities: (a) to recognize personally relevant information from introspection and from observing oneself and others, (b) to form that information into accurate models of personality, (c) to guide one's choices by using personality information where relevant, and (d) to systemize one's goals, plans, and life stories for good outcome" (Mayer 2007–2008, 215). Individuals learn about themselves and their personality from introspection—eavesdropping on one's feelings and thoughts, paying attention to one's inner world; self-observation—paying attention to our external acts and drawing conclusions from them as to who we are; information from informants—information gleaned from others about ourselves; and paying attention to others and their general personality traits and the link between personality trait and their expression in the world. This process lets the individual understand that certain personality traits, those they possess and that others possess, are predictive of certain things, such as getting along, being liked, being accepted, and being respected.

Personality and Supervision

People vary along continuums regarding their personality-anchored behavior. For example, someone might be extremely conscientious regarding work but willing to be more flexible regarding certain family obligations. Personality measurements capture tendencies, not specificities. Certain personality traits are associated with a greater likelihood of success in certain jobs. In a job high in social contact, extraversion is an asset. It does not mean that the more introverted cannot learn to be effective in this role. Those high in an openness to experience would likely prosper in a high-tech, research environment, whereas those less inclined to experience the new would be happier in a more regimented work environment. Someone high in the traits linked to the agreeableness traits of trust, cooperation, and sympathy might find supervision a more natural fit. The point is intuitive; certain personality traits make supervision easier. Since no one is completely lacking in any specific personality trait, everyone has the potential for professional level supervision, it just may be more difficult. Similarly, all the staff in a department are expressions of their personalities, and understanding their individual variances and collective similarities is a requirement of effective supervision.

WHAT ARE VALUES?

Values are enduring and stable elements of personality. They are the constellation of beliefs that sets the course of a life, influences decision and choices, and defines who we are. Values are not arrived at rationally but emerge from the emotional world. Values are anchored in the country of origin, the specific culture within that country to which we belong, and our families. It is important to note that individuals differ in their level of value development. In other words, value priorities change over a lifetime as people move through different stages of maturity. As individuals mature, they tend to move from values related to the self, through a stage that focuses on conformity to external standards, and finally to a stage that focuses on universal principles.

The subtitle of this book indicates that it is a text for professionals. Therefore, the professional values of accountability, altruism, duty, honor, integrity, excellence, and respect for others are at the core of this effort. For students, the exercise in self-awareness and values is to assay whether they hold to these values emotionally and intellectually, conform to the dictates inherent in these values, strive to use them in their work, and aspire to improve their adherence to these requirements. In other words, are they important? Are they an integral part of the personality? Are they honored both in word and in deed?

EMOTIONAL INTELLIGENCE

The core belief and assumption of this chapter is that the most important relationship individuals ever have is with themselves. Emotional intelligence is the ability to understand my emotions and your emotions and to craft a functional behavior that is suitable to the context. Emotional intelligence does not require that emotions be suppressed or denied; rather, emotions are used to achieve objectives. Some people are better at understanding themselves, understanding the needs of others, and building successful and productive relationships. These people are emotionally intelligent. Emotional intelligence is more accurately thought of as a skill. If the ability to understand yourself and other people is an intelligence in the strictest sense of the word, then it would not be possible to get better at it. It is possible with reflection and insight to recognize, name, and appropriately respond to our inner emotional world and do the same in dealing with other people. In other words, you can elevate your emotional intelligence and get better at this aspect of supervision.

Emotions

Emotions affect everything we do. We can be mindful of them, we can suppress them, but we can't ignore them. Even presumably highly rational decision processes are influenced by our emotional state. Positive and negative moods impact how we decide. Many situations demand that we control or suppress our emotions. Emotions contain information for us about what is going on in the world around us. They are tangible. They can be measured in the body. Daniel Goleman, author of the book *Emotional Intelligence*, which brought the idea of emotional intelligence to a larger readership, defines an emotion as "a feeling and its distinctive thoughts, psychological and biological states, and range of propensities to act" (1995, 289). Emotions have a cognitive component, a physiological component, and a behavioral component. The sequence regarding emotions is this: Something happens in the environment that is attended to. This stimulation causes the centers of the mid brain to engage and prompts one to act. The same stimuli, slightly delayed, also progress to the higher cortex regions of the brain. In certain life-threatening situations where milliseconds count, individuals react without thinking. In most situations, there is time to think about the stimuli and choose a more appropriate response. It is the distinction between an unthinking reaction and a measured response that defines emotional intelligence. Because of the cognitive aspect of emotions it is not accurate to say that something makes you uncontrollably mad. Except for the life-threatening situation, the emotional reaction to any situation is always a choice. *In other words, you are in control of your emotions.*

There are four primary emotions (fear, anger, sadness, and enjoyment) recognized around the world, even by preliterate cultures. These four emotions, and their variants, can be blended to create innumerable and subtle emotional shadings. Just as artists see shades and hues of color, emotionally astute individuals can understand and describe the shades and hues of their emotional lives. People who are emotionally literate, emotionally intelligent, can identify the various shadings of their emotional environment and act with finer grained precision. The sadness generated from a poor test result requires a different response from the sadness evoked about a dying child.

Emotions are both functional and dysfunctional. For example, anger may motivate you to act or alienate you from other people; fear will alert you to a threat or interfere with thinking; sadness may motivate you to reevaluate what you want from life or inhibit you from taking any action at all; while happiness promotes positive relationships or leads you to unrealistically favorable expectations.

Each of us is addicted to certain emotions. Every morning, we get up and put on our own familiar and comfortable emotional coat. Even though the emotion may be negative and not self-serving, it is the one we choose on a daily basis. This emotional addiction is based on the fact that neurons that fire together create neural networks. These networks reflect the experienced patterns of our emotions, thoughts, and behaviors. This explains why, on a daily basis, we tend to feel like a victim, or slightly sad, or optimistic and why similar situations and people always evoke the same emotional response. It is only your neural network responding as it always does to this circumstance. Paradoxically, negative emotions like anger and sadness can be strangely comforting due to their familiarity.

Though we might be addicted to a specific emotional pattern, we can, with conscious effort, change these patterns.

Emotions that are muted but persist for an extended period (a day or two) are moods, while the tendency toward a specific mood over a very long time is temperament. Emotions arise from identifiable stimuli, while moods are feelings that often occur for unknown reasons. Moods may be the "aftershock" of emotional events. Think of an emotion as a wave lapping the shore, while a mood is the tide changing every twelve hours.

Emotional Regulation and Self-Management

Emotional regulation is the process by which individuals modulate their emotions. The goal is to control the intensity, duration, occurrence, or expression of emotions. Self-management does not mean that one never feels emotion or never lets them show. It would be a cold heart that rounded on a pediatric floor with children suffering from leukemia and felt nothing. Denial of emotions is not the ideal. Nor is the universal suppression of emotions the ideal. A child who violates a mutually agreed-upon course of action should see and experience a measure of a parent's displeasure. This is a difficult admonition. These situations are subtle, fluid, and multilayered. An expectation that one can be perfect at this is unreasonable.

In managing your emotions and managing yourself, the following options are available.

- Don't put yourself in situations that you know have the potential to cause you to lose control or focus.
- If you can, alter situations that have the potential of causing you to lose control. If a specific individual gets under your skin, try never to meet with him or her alone.
- Focus on those aspects of people and circumstances that do not arouse you rather than the elements that do.
- Reappraise the circumstances that cause emotional turmoil. A critical test is just a series of questions on a piece of paper, rather than a measure of your self-worth.
- Control and modulate your response to the arousing circumstances. In other words, take a deep breath or walk away for a moment, alter your thought process, and respond rather than react unthinkingly. At the extreme, the emotion is suppressed. If a superior is berating you, this may be your only option in the short term.

Emotional highjackings, or flashpoints, are circumstances, people, or objects that provoke uncontrolled emotional reactions. Road rage following being cut off in traffic exemplifies an emotional highjacking. Lashing out at someone if you feel belittled is another example. Emotional highjackings, or reacting without thinking, can be considered a form of emotional *unintelligence*. A significant aspect of emotional intelligence is understanding and managing emotional highjackings.

The Domains of Emotional Intelligence

Emotional intelligence has four domains or core skills: self-awareness, self-management, social awareness, and relationship management. The first two skills, self-awareness and self-management, are primarily about the individual; they are internal. The second two skills, social awareness and relationship management, are about the individual's relationship to the world; they are external.

Self-Awareness

Self-awareness was discussed above in the context of its importance to the relationship you have with yourself and your ability to act authentically. Self-awareness is the ability to understand who you are. The level of self-awareness that is appropriate does not require plumbing the inner depths of your soul and subconscious. Instead, ask yourself in an objective way, do you understand how you operate in the world? The key aspect of self-awareness is objectivity. It is an exercise in self-reality, not wish fulfillment. Self-awareness is complicated by the tendency to defend our ego when the sensitive line on certain issues is approached. Also, for some people self-awareness about what they are good at is difficult, as people tend to diminish themselves in the guise of false modesty or self-devaluation, illustrating Groucho Marx's observation about not wishing to join any club that would have him as a member. Further, being aware of one's tendencies is a beginning, but it is the understanding of self that is the goal. This takes work and time. For a professional student, time for this pursuit is not likely to be a priority, as it is crowded out by other, more immediate and compelling tasks.

Self-Management

Self-management is what you do, or not do, that is appropriate to the context. Context is key. Self-management requires monitoring your behaviors in specific, discrete circumstances, as well as your entrenched tendencies. Self-management requires sublimating your immediate emotional needs for your longer term success.

The key to self-management is to recognize that you are in control of everything you feel and think and how you behave. You always have a choice. People or circumstances may anger, but only you decide whether to express that anger and in what format. If you see an injustice, you can't stop the feelings you have, but you do control your reaction to it. Feeling emotion is fine, showing emotion is fine, and suppressing emotion is fine. A self-managed individual knows which response is appropriate for any circumstance and can execute the appropriate response. As Aristotle wrote, "Anybody can become angry—that is easy, but to be angry with the right person and to the right degree and at the right time and for the right purpose, and in the right way—that is not within everybody's power and is not easy."

Social Awareness

Social awareness requires paying attention to the people and the world around you. You have to look and listen—effectively. This requires that you stop talking and stop listening to the internal dialogue in your head. Social intelligence requires seeing people as they are, not as you would like them to be.

In the social context we read vast amounts of information. We explicitly attended to or unconsciously absorb this information. We run mental checklists or intuitively draw conclusions. We are analyze the "shows" that people want us to understand about them and their unconscious "tells" that give them away. We process our first and subsequent impressions of people. We will never be completely right in reading someone. What we can do is to gather enough information to establish a consistent pattern. If pieces of information about people present an incongruent picture, then we should be cautious. If we have an assessment of someone or a situation that seems to hang together or make sense, then this is probably the best we can do.

Relationship Management

Relationships are the key to everything in both personal and professional contexts. Relationship management is a delicate balance between doing things to preserve the relationship and doing things to preserve personal integrity. A familiar refrain in dealing with another person is something like, "Things would be OK if you would just. ..." Implicit in this comment is the notion that the relationship would improve if the other person would change. And if they won't change, my task is to change them to suit my needs. This misses the key point regarding change in humans; *you can never change another person*. Whatever you think about supervision and what your power is, this statement still holds true. As a supervisor, you can coerce people to behave in certain ways, but they have not changed; they have merely complied with external pressure. The aspect of the relationship that you control completely is yourself. If you want someone to be more considerate of your feelings, then be considerate of theirs. If you want someone to be more open about their issues, then be open about yours. It is the reciprocity phenomenon discussed above.

Relationships are work. Successful relationships don't just happen. Everyone has a myriad of needs, wants, and aspirations. Some, they are not even aware of. Inevitably, frictions result as two people pursue these needs, wants, and aspirations. A good counsel to keep in mind is that other people are not out to take advantage of you; but they are out for themselves. The key point is that just because a relationship takes work does not mean that it is defective.

To maintain and strengthen relationships, we must assert ourselves in an appropriate manner. Passive acceptance and disregard is not the path to a functioning relationship. In assessing how to handle a difficult issue in a relationship it is helpful to assess what is more important, the issue or the relationship. Typically, maintenance of the relationship is more important.

Long-term, successful relationships are characterized by the following.

- **Collaborative intent:** Partners to a relationship make a mutual commitment to the relationship.
- **Truthfulness:** Partners commit to both telling and listening to the truth. This is accomplished by creating an atmosphere of openness and trust where the difficult issues can be considered.
- **Self-accountability:** Partners accept responsibility for their lives, the choices they make, and the consequences of their choices. Accountability trumps blaming.
- **Awareness of self and others:** Partners to the relationship commit to enhancing self-awareness, understanding the context of their circumstances, and issues that motivate others.
- **Problem solving:** Partners to the relationship commit to engaging in effective problem solving rather than subtle competition (adapted from Tamm and Luyet 2004).

Successful relationships are collaborations between people in pursuit of mutually beneficial goals.

YOUR THINKING IS A CHOICE

Things happen to people; they are reprimanded for being late or they turn in a substandard assignment. A natural response might be to blame the other person to alleviate the feelings of shame or embarrassment. The option to blame the other is a choice, just as it is a choice to accept responsibility for your behaviors. The variance in the cascade of behaviors that follow from this choice is significant. One path likely leads to hostility and conflict, the other to maturity and effective behaviors. In fact, it is this belief—that I am in control of how and what I think that is the first, and most critical step, on the path to self-awareness and supervising yourself.

If something negative happens to us, that experience can be termed an activating event. Because of that event, we respond in a certain way; for example, we lash back or take a tone. That is the consequence of the event. What is missing from this scenario—and what determines our response, both emotionally and behaviorally—is our belief about the event. If we believe we are aggrieved, then we might feel justified in our lashing out. If we believe it was a misunderstanding, then we seek to calmly discuss and clarify the misunderstanding. This sequence can be reduced to the famous and easily understood formula developed by Albert Ellis (2001):

$\underline{A}$ (activating event) + $\underline{B}$ (belief) = $\underline{C}$ (consequence)

Effective thinking means that we examine the beliefs we apply to any circumstance to see if they meet an empirical test (where is the proof that this belief is true); a functional test (does my belief help me or make things worse); and a logical test (does it meet a test for commonsense). Self-management requires that we engage in an internal debate with ourselves, that we dispute with ourselves the validity of our beliefs. If our beliefs are found wanting, then our task is to alter them so that our beliefs, and hence our behaviors, are functional.

Anyone who has ever come through a significant life event or trauma often recognizes after the fact that while in the midst of the circumstance, they were thinking "crazy." Self-supervision requires an ability to recognize whether we are thinking appropriately or whether our thinking is "crazy." David Burns, in his book *Feeling Good*, has detailed the ways that people's thinking can be flawed. They are worth reviewing.

All-or-nothing thinking: You see things in black-and-white categories. If your performance falls short of perfect, you see yourself as a total failure.

Overgeneralization: You see a single negative event as a never-ending pattern of defeat.

Mental filter: You pick out a single negative defeat and dwell on it exclusively so that your vision of reality becomes darkened, like the drop of ink that colors the entire beaker of water.

Disqualifying the positive: You dismiss positive experiences by insisting they don't count for some reason or other. In this way you can maintain a negative belief that is contradicted by your everyday experiences.

Jumping to conclusions: You make a negative interpretation even though there are no definite facts that convincingly support your conclusion.

Mind reading: You arbitrarily conclude that someone is reacting negatively to you, and you don't bother to check this out.

The fortune-teller error: You anticipate that things will turn out badly, and you feel convinced that your prediction is an already established fact.

Magnification (catastrophizing) or minimization: You exaggerate the importance of things (such as your goof-up or someone else's achievement), or you inappropriately shrink things until they appear tiny (your own desirable qualities or the other fellow's imperfections). This is also called the "binocular trick."

Emotional reasoning: You assume that your negative emotions necessarily reflect the way things really are: "I feel it, therefore it must be true."

Should statements: You try to motivate yourself with should's and shouldn'ts, as if you had to be whipped and punished before you could be expected to do anything. "Must's" and "ought's" are also offenders. The emotional consequence is guilt. When you direct should statements toward others, you feel anger, frustration, and resentment.

Labeling and mislabeling: This is an extreme form of overgeneralization. Instead of describing your error, you attach a negative label to yourself: "I'm a loser." When someone else's behavior rubs you the wrong way, you attach a negative label to him: "He's a louse." Mislabeling involves describing an event with language that is highly colored and emotionally loaded.

Personalization: You see yourself as the cause of some negative external event, which in fact you were not primarily responsible for.

TECHNIQUES AND STRATEGIES TO ENHANCE SELF-AWARENESS AND SELF-SUPERVISION

Bradberry and Greaves (2009), in their book *Emotional Intelligence 2.0*, provide a checklist of strategies for enhancing self-awareness and self-management. A summary of those strategies follows.

Strategies to Enhance Self-Awareness

Do not attached labels of good and bad to your feelings. They are just your feelings. They simply convey information about the world around you.

Observe the impact of your emotions. Going off on someone may cause you to lose a friend; at a minimum, it will strain a relationship. Emotions are contagious.

To change and become self-aware, you have to lean into the discomfort of confronting the emotions that may be hurtful or scare you.

Seek to understand the link between your emotions and their impact on your body. When stressed, which muscles tense?

Understand what your hot buttons are, those people and circumstances that have the potential to cause you to lose your composure.

Take a bird's-eye view of yourself. Imagine if a drone were recording your behaviors, what this would reveal about you.

Record your emotional life in a journal. Try to understand what caused them, how you responded, and their effectiveness.

Become aware of your moods, the good and bad ones that may cloud your judgment.

Periodically review your core values and your commitment to them.

Stop and look in the mirror periodically; does your face, posture, and appearance express what is going on inside?

Notice which characters in books, movies, and videos you identify with and how they express their emotions.

Ask others to confirm your beliefs about your emotional world and behaviors. Do they agree you are happy-go-lucky?

Reflect on how you deal with stress, how you behave, what it does to your body, and what goes on in your brain.

Self-Management Strategies

Take a few deep, slow focused breaths before you act when stressed.

Count to ten.

Before deciding or acting, create a logic versus emotion list. Determine where emotions are clouding your judgment and where logic is causing you to ignore important emotional cues.

Sleep on it. Big decisions deserve at least twenty-four hours before you decide and act.

If you don't think you can do it, think of a different time or circumstance when you did, or emulate someone who knows how to do it.

Smile more, it's contagious; laugh more. Most things aren't that serious.

Disconnect from the world and take some time to think.

Monitor your self-talk.

Visualize the outcomes you want.

Get more and better sleep.

Focus on possibilities versus limitations.

If you have a problem, get an outsider's opinion, someone not invested in the outcome.

You can't work all the time or take care of everyone else all the time; indulge yourself some each day.

Whatever the circumstance, it will probably change sooner or later. Change is the constant (adapted from Bradberry and Greaves 2009).

We can't control what we feel. The world bombards us daily with information. Some of that information evokes our emotions, those we cannot control. Our response to those emotions, our thoughts about those emotions and circumstances, are with practice and insight controllable. Channeling those emotions into functional responses is emotional intelligence. It is a skill, and it can be learned. Emotionally intelligent supervisor/managers are self-aware and self-managing; they are also effective.

SUMMARY

This chapter was on self-awareness and self-supervision. It began by discussing the idea of self-awareness and then introduced the idea of personal schemas and their relationship to supervision and management. Personality, personal values, and emotional intelligence were then discussed. The key idea from the chapter is that self-aware and self-managing people understand that they are in control of their emotions, their beliefs about those emotions, and their behavioral response to those emotions—and that this is the beginnings of effective supervision and management.

EXERCISES

Summarizing
Write a one-page executive summary of the chapter.

Discuss with your classmates how you would teach this material.

Write a two-page case from your experience on this topic that would be instructional for other students.

Develop a mental model for this chapter based on the mind mapping technique.

What's Important to You in the Chapter?
With several of your classmates, discuss the most important ideas from the chapter. Which ideas do you think will be most useful to you in your career? Which ideas do you think you will remember in six months?

What Do the Practitioners/Others Say?
Discuss with your colleagues or someone at work any of the ideas in the chapter. Alternatively, read an article from any source on self-awareness and self-supervision and be prepared to summarize its message.

Self-Talk
Self-talk is the voice in our head. If, after an argument with someone, you go over what each of you said and come up with something like "I should have said this," you are engaging in self-talk. For the next five minutes, listen to the voice in your head. What are you saying to yourself? This self-talk is you "thinking out loud" to yourself and captures an element of your thinking.

Mindfulness
Mindfulness is open and active engagement in aspects of our thinking and feeling in a nonjudgmental way. For some it is a practice in meditation. For the next several days, try to be mindful of your thinking about what is going to happen with your job or school. Record in a journal to capture your thought process.

What Are My Values?
Most students are vaguely aware of what their values are. As should be expected, one's values will become clearer with experience. What follows is a brief exercise aimed at clarifying one's values.

Answer the following questions.

1. As a student, what is the most important thing to me? (list 3)
2. In my personal life, my highest aspirations are. (list 3)
3. My career will be a success if I accomplish the following. (list 3)
4. For each of the values listed above, consider how much time is spent on a weekly basis in pursuit of these values.

What Is Your Life Story?

A valuable technique to aid in enhancing self-awareness is to take a few moments to write the story of your life. In writing this story, use the left side of the page to record the narrative. In the expanded right margins, note critical events and your reactions. Look for patterns and tendencies. Conclude the story with a brief summary explaining these patterns and tendencies.

Schemas

Many of the schemas that people hold about themselves are negative and termed maladaptive.

People cope with schemas in three ways, described as follows:

Schema surrender is everything the person does to keep the schema going, by remaining in the situation and doing things to keep the schema going; for example, if someone has a defectiveness schema and they stay in a relationship with someone who has criticized them, they are surrendering to the schema, they are staying in the situation but allowing themselves to be criticized, thus enhancing the schema.

Schema avoidance is avoiding the schema either by avoiding situations that trigger the schema or by psychologically removing yourself from the situation so you don't have to feel the schema. An example of avoidance might be the person with a mistrust schema who avoids making friendships because of the fear of being hurt or taken advantage of. This action only tends to reinforce the belief when others pick up the coolness and distance themselves.

Schema overcompensation is an excessive attempt to fight the schema by trying to do the opposite of what the schema would tell you to do. So if someone has a subjugation schema, they might rebel against the people who are subjugating them. If the overcompensation is too extreme it ultimately backfires and reinforces the schema. A form of overcompensation is externalizing the schema by blaming others and becoming aggressive. Another way can be achieving at a very high level, whereby a person who feels defective works eighty hours a week to overcompensate.

The list below, adapted from Bricker, Young, and Flanagan (1993), includes many of the common maladaptive schemas. Read through them quickly and see which seem to match your internal beliefs about yourself.

Extrapolate from the chosen schema as to how this belief about yourself might influence your behavior at work both as an employee and as a supervisor. Determine if your approach to your schema is to surrender, avoid, or overcompensate.

Abandonment/Instability

Definition: The essence of this schema is the perceived instability or unreliability of those available for support and connection.

Characteristics: Because of their exaggerated fear of being left alone and abandoned, these individuals are usually very clinging in relationships, sometimes to the point of unwarranted jealousy.

Abuse/Mistrust

Definition: The essence of this schema involves the expectation that other people will hurt, abuse, humiliate, cheat, lie, manipulate, or take advantage of one. A fear of angry or violent outburst from others is often also included in the schema. People holding this schema experience other people's negative behaviors as intentional or as resulting from extreme and unjustifiable negligence.

Characteristics: Abused individuals are hypervigilant to harm, manipulation, or being cheated by others. They frequently distort events, read hidden meanings into statements, or attribute negative intentions to others' behavior. They can be accusatory, be openly suspicious, and test others' motives. If they think they are being cheated, they can behave in an unfeeling, cruel, or vengeful way.

Emotional Deprivation

Definition: Emotional deprivation involves the expectation that one's desire for a normal degree of emotional support will not be met by others. The person may feel deprived of nurturance, protection, or empathy. Deprivation of nurturance involves an absence of attention, and warmth from others.

Characteristics: Depending on the specific nature of the deprivation (nurturance, protection, or empathy), these individuals advertise their deprivation in both obvious and subtle ways. They can come across as demanding and controlling or can be cold, uncaring, insensitive, and withholding. Emotionally deprived people often report high levels of loneliness. Frequently, they avoid intimacy and closeness or pull away from nurturance because its unfamiliarity generates discomfort.

Functional Dependence/Incompetence

Definition: This schema relates to the feeling of not being able to handle one's everyday responsibilities competently or without considerable help from others.

Characteristics: These individuals constantly avoid new tasks or even minor decisions; consequently, they exhibit a pervasive passivity. However, these people attribute even real experiences of success or mastery to luck or a fluke.

Vulnerability to Harm and Illness

Definition: This schema involves an exaggerated fear that disaster—financial, medical, criminal, or natural—will strike at any time and that one is unable to protect oneself from disaster.

Characteristics: These individuals usually show a whole range of unrealistic fears—of having a heart attack, of getting AIDS, of going crazy or broke, of being mugged, and so on. They frequently suffer from anxiety disorders (panic disorder, generalized anxiety disorder, phobias, or hypochondriasis). The inherent unpredictability and uncertainty of everyday living is extremely anxiety provoking to them.

Enmeshment/Undeveloped Self

Definition: The essence of this schema is excessive emotional closeness and involvement with one or more significant others at the expense of full individuation and normal social development.

Characteristics: Depending on their degree of enmeshment, these individuals find it extremely difficult to function separately from the family unit or enmeshing other. They spend a lot of time at home and usually remain living there will beyond the normal age for leaving the nest.

Defectiveness/Shame

Definition: This schema involves the feeling that one is inwardly defective, flawed, or invalid and that one is therefore fundamentally unlovable or unacceptable. Consequently, people who hold this schema have a deep sense of shame concerning their perceived internal inadequacies and a constant fear of exposure and further rejection by significant others.

Characteristics: Individuals holding this schema expect rejection and blame from others. They are therefore hypersensitive to even minor slights or criticisms. They are usually also very self-critical and exaggerate their own defects. By and large, they avoid intimacy and self-disclosure and therefore the risk of being exposed to rejection.

Social Undesirability/Alienation

Definition: This schema involves the belief that one is *outwardly* undesirable to or different from others. Individuals may feel that they are ugly, sexually undesirable, poor in social skills, dull, boring, or low in status. Therefore, they feel self-conscious and insecure in social situations and have a sense of alienation or isolation from the rest of the world. These individuals frequently feel that they do not fit in, that they are not part of any group or community.

Characteristics: These individuals feel more comfortable when alone, since social situations trigger self-consciousness and perceived pressure to perform or to pretend that they are enjoying themselves. They usually minimize their social contacts or stay on the periphery of groups. Privately, they remain feeling totally detached and alienated.

Failure to Achieve

Definition: This schema involves the belief that one will inevitably fail or is fundamentally inadequate relative to one's peers in areas of achievement. It often involves the related belief that one is stupid, inept, untalented, or ignorant.

Characteristics: These individuals usually have a sense that they have failed in comparison to their peers, either at their job or at school. Often they actually are underachieving, but even individuals whose performance is adequate or excellent still have considerable anxiety concerning the possibility of failure.

Subjugation

Definition: This schema involves an excessive surrendering of control over one's own decisions and preferences—usually to avoid anger, retaliation, or abandonment.

Characteristics: Subjugated people frequently present a very compliant and unassertive picture. They exaggerate the likelihood of retribution if they express their needs rather than deferring to others. They are therefore excessively eager to please. Because they catastrophize the devastating impact of others' anger, they avoid conflict and confrontation at all cost. They frequently harbor anger at those they perceive as subjugating them, but their inability to manage and express this anger sometimes translates into passive-aggressive behavior.

Self-Sacrifice/Overresponsibility

Definition: This schema involves a voluntary but excessive focus on meeting the needs of others at the expense of one's own gratification. The most common reasons for this self-sacrifice are to prevent causing pain to others, maintain the connection with others who are perceived as more needy, avoid guilt, or gain in self-esteem. Self-sacrifice often results from an acutely tuned sensitivity to the pain of others. However, it leads to a feeling that one's own needs are not being met and sometimes to resentment of those for whom one sacrifices.

Characteristics: By and large, these people put the needs of others first, and in doing so, they tend to overextend and overcommit themselves. If they feel resentful that their needs are not being met by others, they may then feel guilty at their own selfishness. Guilt predominates—guilt that they caused the other person pain, guilt that they were not there when needed, guilt that they did not do the right thing, guilt that they let the other person down. Guilt is the primary force in maintaining the schema.

Emotional Inhibition

Definition: This schema involves excessive inhibition of emotions and impulses—most frequently, anger. The person expects the expression of emotions and impulses to result in loss of self-esteem, embarrassment, retaliation, abandonment, or harm to oneself or others.
Characteristics: Emotionally inhibited individuals can seem cold and controlled or logical and pragmatic to the point of lacking spontaneity and sensitively. This is because they are very uncomfortable around displays of even positive emotions. They find it extremely difficult to handle their own emotions and frequently harbor fears of losing control. Socially, they are often construed as killjoys because their seriousness can make other people feel self-conscious and immature.

Unrelenting/Unbalanced Standards

Definition: This schema involves the relentless striving to meet high expectations of oneself at the expense of happiness, pleasure, relaxation, spontaneity, playfulness, health, and satisfying relationships.
Characteristics: Predictably, these individuals are often very successful and accomplished, but they are also depressed and anxious or suffer from various psychosomatic complaints. They tend to exaggerate any deficits or flaws in themselves and to see things in rigid black-and-white categories. They work too hard, at the expense of feelings of well-being, good health, and relationships. In relationships, they look for perfection and can be very controlling and critical. In either case these individuals tend not to invest the necessary time in their relationships; career pursuits and achievements take priority.

Entitlement/Self-Centeredness

Definition: Central to this schema is the feeling that one is entitled to whatever one wants, regardless of the cost to others or of what others or society might regard as reasonable.
Characteristics: People who hold this schema are egocentric and narcissistic. They have an exaggerated view of their own rights and worth in relation to others and the world and also an underdeveloped sense of their moral and social obligations. These people can therefore come across as arrogant, selfish, demanding, and controlling. They lack empathy for others' needs and tend to treat people carelessly. They often have an employment history of being fired because they could not get along with bosses or coworkers or of walking out when they did not get what they wanted.

Insufficient Self-Control/Self-Discipline

Definition: This schema involves pervasive difficulty exercising sufficient self-control or tolerating frustration long enough to achieve personal goals or to refrain from emotional outbursts or impulsive behaviors.

Characteristics: These individuals may exhibit problems of emotional and impulse control, overeating, alcohol and substance abuse, promiscuity, aggressive outbursts, and criminal behaviors.

(adapted from Bricker, Young, Flanagan, 1993)

Who Are My Emotional Role Models?

Our attitudes toward our emotions are derived from our earliest caregivers, typically family. Those we meet during childhood and adolescence shape our emotional world. Take a few moments to identify your emotional role models by answering the following questions.

What positive emotional traits did you pick up from your mother and father? What negative emotional trait did you pick up from your mother and father?

What Are My Emotional Triggers?

All of us have people and situations that provoke strong emotional reactions. Take a moment to consider what your emotional triggers are.

Describe a time when you lost control of your emotions.

What was the precipitating event?

Is there a pattern to when I lose control of my emotions?

What things cause you to lose your composure?

Emotional Catalogue

For the next week, keep a record of your emotions, the events that caused them, their length, and their impact on the day.

Date	Emotion	Circumstances (what happened, what was going on that day)
Monday		
Tuesday		
Wednesday		
Thursday		
Friday		
Saturday		
Sunday		

Based on this log, do you see any patterns? Are these patterns helpful or not helpful?

What's the Emotionally Intelligent Thing to Do?

With several of your classmates, discuss the emotionally intelligent response in the following scenarios. Also, consider how not to handle these situations.

The Dinner

You and your fiancée planned a romantic weekend together to celebrate the end of the semester. The only thing left to do before moving and taking the job you want is graduation. The night before leaving, you want to go out for dinner. There is considerable disagreement over the restaurant choice. Following a lengthy discussion, you agree to the restaurant your fiancée prefers. Unfortunately, the food, service, and ambience are terrible. As you pay the rather expensive bill, you are fuming at the waste of money. What do you advise?

The Grade

You always felt that your professor didn't really like you. You are not sure why, but others noticed that the professor seemed aloof with you; whereas with other students, the professor was warm and giving. You just received your first evaluation from the professor. You were graded as deficient on everything. Even though you had some difficulties and came to one presentation ill prepared, it was not likely you would be inadequate on all dimensions. You know for a fact that the other clinical staff enjoyed working with you. This evaluation was personally hurtful, the first time something like this happened to you. It was a stress you did not need. You just found out your mother was going in for tests following a course of treatment for breast cancer. What do you advise?

REFERENCES AND WORKS CONSULTED

Beitman, B., G. Viamontes, A. Soth, and J. Nittler. 2006. "Toward a Neural Circuitry of Engagement, Self-Awareness, and Pattern Search." *Psychiatric Annals* 36 (4): 272–80.

Bradberry, T., and J. Greaves. 2009. *Emotional Intelligence 2.0*. San Diego: Talent Smart.

Bricker, D., J.E. Young, and C.M. Flanagan. 1993. "Schema-Focused Cognitive Therapy: A Comprehensive Framework for Characterological Problems." In *Cognitive Therapies in Action*, edited by K.T. Kuehlwein and H. Rosen. San Francisco: Jossey-Bass.

Brinthaupt, T.M., M.B. Hein, and T.E. Kramer. 2009. "The Self-Talk Scale: Development, Factor Analysis, and Validation." *Journal of Personality Assessment* 9 (1): 82–92.

Burns, D. 1980. *Feeling Good: The New Mood Therapy*. New York: HarperCollins.

Caruso, D.R., and P. Salovey. 2004. *The Emotionally Intelligent Manager*. San Francisco: Jossey-Bass.

DePape, A.R., J. Hakim-Larson, S. Voelker, S. Page, and D.L. Jackson. 2006. "Self-Talk and Emotional Intelligence in University Students." *Canadian Journal of Behavioral Science* 38 (3): 250–60

Eckroth-Bucher, M. 2010. "Self-Awareness: A Review and Analysis of a Basic Nursing Concept." *Advances in Nursing Science* 33 (4): 297–309.

Ellis, A. 2001. *Overcoming Destructive Beliefs, Feelings, and Behaviors: New Directions for Rational Emotive Behavior Therapy*. New York: Prometheus Books.

Epstein, S. 1998. *Constructive Thinking: The Key to Emotional Intelligence*. Westport, CT: Praeger.

Ferrari, M., and R.J. Sternerg. 1998. *Self-Awareness: Its Nature and Development*. New York: Guilford.

Forni, P.M. 2011. *The Thinking Life*. New York: St. Martin's.

George, B. 2015. *Discover Your True North*. Hoboken, NJ: Wiley.

Goffee, R., and G. Jones. 2005. "Managing Authenticity." *Harvard Business Review* (December): 1–8.

Goleman, D. 1995. *Emotional Intelligence*. New York: Bantam.

Gonzalez, M. 2012. *Mindful Leadership*. Mississauga, ON: Wiley.

Gross, J.J., and R.A. Thompson. 2007. "Emotion Regulation." In *Handbook of Emotion Regulation*, edited by James J. Gross. New York: Guilford.

Holland, J.L. 1997. *Making Vocational Choices: A Theory of Vocational Personalities and Work Environments*. 3rd ed. Odessa, FL: Psychological Assessment Resources.

Howard, P.J., and J.M. Howard. 2010. *The Owner's Manual for Personality at Work*. Charlotte, NC: Center for Applied Cognitive Studies.

Jung, C.G. 1923. *Psychological Types: or The Psychology of Individuation*. Oxford, England: Harcourt, Brace.

Kluckhohn, C.M.K., and H.A. Murray. 1953. "Personality Formation: The Determinants." In *Personality in Nature, Culture and Society*, edited by C.M.K. Kluckhorn, H.A. Murray, and D. Schneider, 53–67. New York: Knopf.

Mayer, J.D. 2007–2008. "Personal Intelligence." *Imagination, Cognition and Personality* 27 (3): 209–32.

Mayer, J.D., A.T. Panter, and D.R. Caruso. 2012. "Does Personal Intelligence Exist? Evidence from a New Ability Based Measure." *Journal of Personality Assessment* 94 (2): 124–40.

Mayer, J.D., P. Salovey, and D.R. Caruso. 2004. "A Further Consideration of the Issues of Emotional Intelligence." *Psychological Inquiry* 15 (3): 249–55.

Mayer, J.D., R. Wilson, and M. Hazelwood. 2010–2011. "Personal Intelligence Expressed: A Multiple Case Study of Business Leaders." *Imagination, Cognition and Personality* 30 (2): 201–24.

Narvaez, D. and Mitchel, C. 2000. "Schemas, Culture and Moral Text." In *Moral Education and Pluralism*, edited by M. Leicester, C. Modgil, and S. Modgel, London: Falmer Press. 000-000.

Nave, C.S., R.A. Sherman, D.C. Funder, S.E. Hampson, and L.R. Goldberg. 2010. "On the Contextual Independence of Personality: Teachers' Assessments Predict Directly Observed Behavior after Four Decades." *Social Psychology and Personality Science* 1 (4): 1–9.

Orloff, J. *Emotional Freedom*. 2009. New York: Harmony.

Schutte, N.S., R.R. Manes, and J.M. Malouff. 2009. "Antecedent-Focused Emotion Regulation, Response Modulation and Well-Being." *Current Psychology* 28: 21–31.

Segal, J. 1997. *Raising Your Emotional Intelligence: A Practical Guide.* New York: Owl.

Seibert, S.E. and M.L. Kraimer. 2001. "The Five-Factor Model of Personality and Career Success." *Journal of Vocational Behavior* 58: 1–21.

Silvia, P., and T.S. Duval. 2001. "Objective Self-Awareness Theory: Recent Progress and Enduring Problems." *Personality and Social Psychology Review* 5 (3): 230–41.

Specht, J., B. Egloff, and S.C. Schmukle. 2011. "Stability and Change of Personality across the Life Course: The Impact of Age and Major Life Events on Mean-Level and Rank-Order Stability of the Big Five." *Journal of Personality and Social Psychology* 101 (4): 862–82.

Spradlin, S.E. 2003. *Don't Let Your Emotions Run Your Life.* Oakland, CA: New Harbinger.

Sull, D.N., and D. Houlder. 2005. "Do Your Commitments Match Your Convictions?" *Harvard Business Review* (January): 82–91.

Szasz, P.L., A. Szentagotai, and S.G. Hofmann. 2001. "The Effect of Emotion Regulation Strategies on Anger." *Behavior Research and Therapy* 49: 114–19.

Tennant, M. 2005. "Transforming Selves." *Journal of Transformative Education* 3 (2): 102–15.

Young, J. E., Klosko, J. S. and Weishaar, M. E. 2003. *Schema Therapy.* New York: Guilford Press.

6 SUPERVISING TEAMS

ALEX

Alex couldn't believe it. Within three months, half the people in the department retired, two took other jobs, one was let go, and one was promoted to a new position. Also, two staffers were on maternity leave and wouldn't be back for six months. In the past three months, six new people had been added, one position was still open, and two temporaries had been brought in to cover the maternity leaves. There were clear splits in the department. The old hands were sticking to themselves. Among the new employees, they were separating themselves by age and gender, and the temps did not seem too interested in mixing with anybody. Everyone was just interested in doing their job and getting their hours in. Not surprisingly productivity in the department was down. The latest figures for the quarter were not good, both output and service levels were off 15 percent. While Alex's superiors had expressed sympathy for the dilemma, it was also clear that Alex's bonus for the year was in jeopardy. Alex daydreamed on the way home.

It feels just like the schoolyard again.

I've already booked the vacation; I really need the bonus.

Why can't they just get along?

What's with that one temp? They "creep" me out.

Maybe I should have a Super Bowl party and invite everyone?

All most of them care about is getting their hours.

I wish it would stop snowing; winter here is so depressing.

The monthly supervisor's meeting will not be good; it looks like the department has dropped to the bottom of the performance rankings.

How embarrassing.

I wonder if the other temp is single?

Who else is going to retire or get pregnant?

Alex walked in the door, threw his briefcase on the sofa, clicked on the TV, poured a glass of wine, and immediately went "brain dead."

MENTAL MODELS

In the center of the space below, write the word *team*. Next, write the words that come to mind when you think of this topic. Do not edit your thoughts or collaborate with anyone. There is no right or wrong answer.

If things are related, connect them with an arrow. If the relationship is reciprocal (they both affect each other), put arrows at both ends of the line. If one relationship is stronger than another, make the arrow darker and thicker.

The goal is to capture your mental model of what you believe about teams and team development. This is the starting point for the discussion on this process.

LEARNING OBJECTIVES

- Discuss the stages of team development.
- Discuss the various team roles.
- Describe and discuss emotional intelligence in teams.
- Discuss how to handle conflict and conduct a negotiation.
- Discuss the leader's role in team development.
- Describe the various team norms.
- Discuss how to deal with multicultural and diverse teams.

Teams are characterized as a group of people committed to a common purpose with a specific set of objectives that will hold them mutually accountable for results. A supervisor's task is to turn a department of disparate members into a team. Teams with high performance standards and that act cohesively are the engines of increased productivity. The supervisor's task is to change people's thinking from "me" to "we." Red Auerbach, the longtime coach and general manager of the dynastic Boston Celtics, commented that a player's salary was not based on his individual statistics but the overall performance of the team and that the dominant motivating force in the player's success was the pride associated with the team winning (Webber, 1987). The standard for a supervisor is this: "to assess managerial effectiveness, you also have assess the effectiveness of the unit. And not only that: you have to assess the contribution the manager made to that effectiveness" (Mintzberg 2013, 164).

Effective teams have the technical expertise to accomplish their assigned task; they have individuals with good problem-solving and decision-making abilities; and they have members with good interpersonal skills, people who listen, give feedback, and are good at dealing with conflict. Also, individual personalities influence team effectiveness. People higher in "average levels of extraversion, agreeableness, conscientiousness, and emotional stability" (Robbins 2013, 156) contribute to higher performing teams.

STAGES IN TEAM DEVELOPMENT

People don't just coalesce into a highly functioning team overnight. They typically go through the following five stages.

Forming is the stage where people get to know one another. People begin to learn what the objectives of the team are and what their role in that process is. The supervisor and senior members are important in that they establish and model how the team will function. This stage is often somewhat stressful and confusing.

Storming is a stage for working out how the team will function, what roles will be, who will dominate and lead, who will facilitate, whose ideas will prevail, how decisions will be made, and so on. In this stage groups, relationships, and factions emerge. Some perceive themselves as winning or losing. Members need to learn to tolerate differences among themselves. This stage may be contentious and unpleasant, especially for those who shy away from conflict.

Norming is the stage of agreement and accommodation. People understand what their role is, what the objectives are, and how work will get done. People feel they are part of something worthwhile, something bigger than themselves. Trust and respect develop.

The **performing** stage is where the group, now a team, accomplishes its assigned tasks and meets its objectives. The team functions as a unit.

Adjourning is a stage that not all teams go through; it is dependent on their purpose. Disbanding a highly functioning and productive team may leave team members with a sense of loss.

TEAM ROLES

Any functional athletic team has defined roles for its members: offense, defense, scorer, passer, captain, and so on. Similarly, functioning work teams have defined roles for their members. With the exception of the team leader (think formal supervisor), those roles are informal and emerge through the stages of group formation. Those roles fall into three broad categories; roles focused on accomplishing the task, roles focused on maintaining group harmony, and roles that emerge from individuals attempting to gratify their personal needs, which is generally disruptive. Specific roles are as follows (adapted from Mudrack and Farrell, 1995):

Task Focused
Coordinator: coordinates activities
Elaborator: expands on suggestions
Energizer: prods the group to act
Evaluator-critic: questions and critiques
Information giver: offers facts and opinions
Information seeker: seeks information
Initiator-contributor: proposes and suggests
Opinion giver: states beliefs and opinions
Opinion seeker: asks for opinions and clarification
Orienter-clarifier: summarizes
Procedural technician: performs routine tasks
Recorder: keeps records

Maintenance

Compromiser: offers compromise

Encourager: offers praise

Follower: passively goes along

Gatekeeper and expediter: keeps communication open and facilitates participation

Harmonizer: reconciles disagreements

Observer and commentator: comments and interprets on process

Standard setter: expresses standards

Individual

Aggressor: attacks others

Blocker: is negative and resistant

Dominator: asserts and manipulates

Evader: strays off the subject

Help seeker: expresses insecurity for sympathy

Playboy/playgirl: displays lack of involvement

Recognition seeker: calls attention to him- or herself

Special-interest pleader: speaks for special groups

Teams do not necessarily have all of these roles. Teams function better if there is only one person in each of these roles. For example, teams function better if there is only a single member acting as the coordinator. When multiple people contest for a role within the team, the potential for conflict and confusion is increased.

EMOTIONAL INTELLIGENCE OF TEAMS

Team effectiveness is a function of trust among the members, a sense of group identity, and a sense of group efficacy. Like individuals, teams are unique, with each having its own identity. Emotionally intelligent individuals do not necessarily guarantee an emotionally intelligent team. Team emotional intelligence is complicated by the interplay of multiple individuals. What is required is a team norm that supports regulation and awareness of emotions, both inside the group and outside the team. People take their emotional cues from each other. Individuals' emotions are regulated through norms of both confrontation and caring. When individuals violate agreed-upon norms, they need to be confronted on their deviation. Such confrontations are best leavened with humor and a caring attitude. While people may violate agreed-upon standards, they still need to feel that they are valuable contributors to overall group performance. Team members also need to develop a group self-awareness, specifically the emotional state of the group, the group's strengths and weaknesses, its modes of interaction, and how the group members process their tasks. Emotionally competent teams are aware of how they operate, both emotionally and in solving problems. Effective teams attempt to develop a collective enthusiasm while also working out methods for venting frustrations. An affirming environment, a sense of optimism, and a proactive approach to solving problems facilitates the overall group emotional state. Group emotional intelligence is also about the small things, the thank-you, the respect for others, the open sharing of what is real within the group, no matter whether it is pleasant or not. Emotionally intelligent teams also develop the capacity to understand the broader organizational context and how they are influenced by it and how they, as a group, influence that context. Emotionally intelligent teams are aware and understand the implications of individual emotions and group emotions, both internally and externally (adapted from Druskat and Wolff, 2001)

CONFLICT

Conflict is an inevitable part of organizational life. It is impossible to avoid. Conflict in groups is usually over the task, relationships, or the process of how work is done, with relationship conflicts most often leading to dysfunctional groups. In dealing with conflict, a supervisor/manager has at least five options. The first is to avoid it. Generally, there is always a low level of "rumblings" between people at work. The prudent supervisor recognizes this fact and attempts to stay out of it, letting individuals work out their differences. However, when the conflict negatively impacts performance, then it becomes an issue for consideration. The second approach is to accommodate; that is, to give in. This is beneficial if an issue is not important or if the relationship is more important than the issue in contention. Third, a resolution can be forced. Forcing is used when one has formal authority; in other words, the power to impose a resolution; if time is critical; or if a decision is correct but unpopular. Compromise is the fourth option and is particularly effective in dealing with interpersonal conflicts. With compromise, both parties to the conflict give up something. Finally, conflicts can be resolved via collaboration; the option characterized as win-win, where people work together to mutually resolve their issues.

If people always agree, then some members of the team or group are redundant. A group or team where everyone agrees can be accused of groupthink; the process where people try to minimize conflict at the expense of effective decisions. One of the strengths of a group is that multiple perspectives are brought to bear on a problem. Multiple perspectives and multiple personalities will inevitably generate disagreement and conflict. *Conflict* is not a "dirty word." Nonproductive conflict, where issues are not resolved and relationships are strained, is wasted time and energy. Constructive conflict leads to better decisions, fosters more creativity and innovation, begets engagement and buy-in, helps clear the air, and leads to change and improvement.

Management teams and departments have to learn how to have a good fight. The tactics and strategy of a good fight are these. First, the tactic is to base the discussion on current, factual information and then develop multiple alternatives for discussion. Next, keep the overall goals of the effort in mind. Use humor to soften the discussion. Though there may be differences in formal power within the group, recognize that certain individuals have power within their areas of expertise. In other words, a too-dominant leader or a weak leader will beget ineffective conflict. And it is best to resolve issues without forcing a consensus. These tactics can be arrayed under three broad strategic recommendations. First, focus on issues and not personalities. Second, believe that all involved have the best interest of the department or company in mind and that their heart is in the right place. Finally, all must believe that the discussion and the process were guided by a rubric of fairness and equity.

NEGOTIATION

People negotiate because another person has something they want and there is a difference of opinion, or conflict, as to what constitutes a fair exchange. Negotiation is a fact of life for any supervisor and for any member of a department. It is a skill that can be learned and practiced. There are two broad approaches to a negotiation. The first is integrative, in which both parties seek a balance in their priorities. This approach is collaborative, seeks a win for both parties, and recognizes the value of preserving the relationship. A distributive approach to a negotiation is an attempt to divide a fixed number of resources. In this approach, one party is a winner and the other loses. These negotiations tend to be adversarial and competitive, with little concern for preserving the relationship.

Effective negotiators first prepare and plan for the negotiation. They gather information, analyze what the other party wants, decide strategy and tactics, and determine how to present their argument. They consider what their ideal result is, decide what their bottom line is, and determine a zone of acceptability for a resolution. Next, the ground rules for the negotiation are declared. Where it will be held, who will be there, what the issues on the agenda are, and what behavior is acceptable for both parties are established. As the negotiations begin, goals are clarified and justification for seeking this outcome is revealed. Having declared objectives, both parties begin to bargain and seek solutions to problems, and options are discussed and analyzed. Effective negotiations begin to narrow choices to ones that are acceptable. Terms and conditions are introduced and haggled over until a resolution is attained. In the last stage the terms, conditions, and agreement are reviewed and finalized into a formal statement that codifies the result.

Effective negotiators separate issues from personality. They manage themselves; they control their emotions; they read the other person; they establish rapport with their opposite number. In other words, they are emotionally intelligent. One technique for negotiations is to script ahead of time several different scenarios of how the negotiation might proceed.

What happens if the negotiations are friendly, constructive, or obstructionist, if they play "hard ball"? If a proposal is made, what are the likely responses, and how should each be responded to? Crafting scenarios eliminates the possibility of surprise, of being taken off guard and not having a considered response available. Effective negotiators practice their craft and understand it is "just business."

LEADER

Teams just don't happen. They require work, they are built, they are nurtured, and they are shaped. The responsibility for this development resides with the head of the department, the supervisor; it means acting as a leader.

Mood

Supervisors need to understand the power of their emotional state on the mood of the team or department. There is a biological basis for the social and emotional intelligence necessary to forge a team and establish a mood. That biological basis is the mirror neuron. When an individual senses someone else's mood, mirror neurons in the brain reproduce those emotions. Thus, a leader's moods and emotions provoke followers to mimic those feelings. The leader's task is to be conscious of his or her emotions and moods as they are projected on and reflected by the staff. Emotions and moods resonate back and forth between leader and staff. It is crucial then that the leader create a positive mood on the assumption that if people feel better, they will perform better. A sour, disgruntled supervisor will create an atmosphere that is unpleasant and that poisons the work experience. People in a positive mood are more likely to be engaged, be creative, and want to come to work.

Related to the idea of mood is an atmosphere of fun and the use of humor at work. Work is serious business; it just doesn't need to be taken seriously. A key aspect of the idea of emotional intelligence is that emotions be appropriate to the context. On a normal day, routine activity at work can be enlivened with fun and stress reduced with humor. However, at peak demand or during a crisis, fun and humor are not warranted. Focus on the task is the priority, as it should be.

Purpose

People come to the team or department from various backgrounds, different experiences at work, and different aspirations for their career and the future. Each could be argued to possess a different mindset regarding these issues. The supervisor's role is to develop and reinforce a sense of shared purpose and a communal mindset. Purpose is what gives meaning to an activity. It is larger, grander, and hopefully more inspiring than a simple statement of mission or detailing of goals and objectives. As an instructor, my goal is to cover the material in a palatable and engaging manner. My purpose is to influence student's lives, to instruct and perhaps inspire. Parents' mission is to see their children advance as far as possible in their education; their purpose is to nurture and care. Soon all work, no matter how exciting or important, takes on the aspects of laying bricks—another day, another case, another client, and so on. The supervisor's task is to convince staff that they are not laying bricks; rather, they are part of building a cathedral that will last a thousand years as a testament to their passion, as a sign of shared purpose. The most effective technique available to supervisors regarding shared purpose and their department is to live it every day. Living a shared purpose is contagious and gives meaning to work and life. Tony Hsieh, the creator of Zappos, observed that the longest type of happiness is derived from purpose, from being part of something bigger than yourself.

Appreciative Inquiry

The supervisor/leader is tasked with molding a group of individuals into a functioning team that is more productive collectively than the members would be individually. The discussions above regarding mood, morale, and purpose are descriptive, and thus limited regarding application. What is required is an approach, philosophy, or technique for influencing the mood, morale, and purpose of the team. Appreciative inquiry is all three.

Most business issues are approached as a problem to be solved; in this case how to build a functioning team. The familiar problem approach requires first identifying the issue to be fixed, analyzing the causes and deficiencies, evaluating alternative solutions, selecting a preferred course, and then developing an action plan for resolving the issue. Focusing on problems casts a negative shadow over the group. Deficiencies are highlighted and negative aspersions cast regarding individuals. A problem focus highlights limitations and weaknesses. What gets discussed, what is focused on creates the group "reality." It is difficult to pivot a group of people from a belief that they are deficient to a belief that they are efficacious, that they have the potential and the will to accomplish stated objectives.

Rather than focus on problems and the negative, appreciative inquiry asks people to focus on what is best about the team and the individuals in it. From this platform, the group is then asked to consider how what is best about the team can be expanded and brought to bear on other issues and in other contexts. The process of appreciative inquiry moves from appreciating and valuing the best of what is, envisioning what might be, discussing and deciding what should be, and then innovating and developing the steps to what will be.

Appreciative inquiry begins with asking the members of the team to recall the best team experience they have ever had. Each member of the new team is asked to describe the experience. Those discussing the peak team experience are asked to consider what it was about themselves, the situation, the task, and the others that contributed to making the peak experience. From these shared discussions a consensus and list of the attributes of a highly effective team are described and compiled. This shared, appreciative discussion is the beginning of relationships that lets people get to know one another in a nonconfrontational way. Also, after this list is compiled, group members can be asked how they or any other member contributed in this session to meeting those ideals. In other words, early on people are recognized for their contribution to the process and to meeting the standard. This inquiry shapes individual and interpersonal behaviors. The mechanism for this is that what gets discussed creates the future reality of the group. Appreciative inquiry focuses on best practices and positive experiences, creating a self-fulfilling prophecy of optimism and accomplishment.

TEAM NORMS

In developing a team, specific norms for behavior need to be established. The more explicitly they are declared, honored, and reinforced, the better the team. Norms of use in developing any team include collaboration, citizenship, commitment, and altruism.

Collaboration

Collaboration is mutually caring about other team member goals and willingly and freely working to achieve each other's goals. People at work can be characterized as collaborators as defined above; those who cooperate as a method of minimizing conflict and ill will within the group; competitors who seek to win at another's expense; enslavers who seek to control others for their personal gain; and predators who focus only on their needs and goals with complete disregard for others.

Collaboration is driven by the following:

- Communication about important, sensitive, and ignored issues; the open and honest consideration of personal, team, and organization realities
- Understanding the issues, aspirations, and goals of others and where they overlap and where they diverge as people get to know one another and build bridges
- Competence; are potential collaborators an asset or a liability, either technically or to work with
- Respect; is there mutual tolerance and respect for what each brings to the table
- Trust, which facilitates communication, understanding, and respect
- Safety; the degree to which people will let themselves be vulnerable in the group

Citizenship

Citizenship in an organization is voluntary and not necessarily recognized by the formal reward system. It contributes to the effective functioning of the group. Team and organizational citizenship include the following elements:

- Helping behaviors are aimed at helping others or preventing work-related problems and are exemplified by peacemaking activities, cheerleading dimensions, interpersonal facilitation, and courtesy in dealing with others.
- Sportsmanship is the ability to tolerate the negative aspects of work without complaining, maintain a positive attitude, not be easily offended, and not take rejection personally.
- Loyalty to the organization involves remaining committed and protecting and defending the organization from external threats.
- Organizational compliance is the acceptance and honoring of the established norms.
- Individual initiative is the willingness to go above and beyond the requirements of the job.
- Civic virtue is a willingness to participate in the governance of the organization.
- Self-development is the willingness to voluntarily engage in activities to improve personal knowledge, skills, and abilities that will benefit the organization.

Commitment

People commit themselves to their profession, the job, a group, or an individual. Commitment is a measure of the strength of an attachment or identification with something outside oneself; in this case the team. People commit attitudinally; that is, they have a mindset in which their values and goals reflect those of the team and the organization. They commit behaviorally to the agreed-upon norms of the team and the organization. In other words, they commit to "walking the walk." The reasons for this commitment vary and reside in the psychology of the individual, the nature of the task, and the organizational dynamics. People who commit link their identity with the team. They voluntarily suppress their ego and sublimate some of their desires for the betterment of the group. Why would someone do this? Because at its fruition, when a team is fully functioning and productive, it simply feels better when the collective, rather than individual, goals are met. Commitment is facilitated by a supervisor who understands how to align as much as possible individual and team goals; who understands how to convince people of the importance of the team and its purpose; who understands how to give trust; and who models the individual sacrifices for the betterment of the group.

Team Altruism

Team altruism is voluntarily engaging in behavior to benefit other team members or the team as a whole that involves self-sacrifice and is not mandated or coerced. This is in contrast to behaviors that maximize self-interest. People are motivated to act altruistically because it makes them feel good; an evolutionary perspective suggests that such behaviors have survival value for the individual and the group. Motivation for team behaviors range from those that are driven by egoism to those enforced by the organization and are undertaken to maximize self-interest, avoid punishment, or seek individual rewards. Pure altruistic team behaviors are also motivated by a desire to get along or adherence to a moral principle. Altruism can be argued to be the central dynamic for team collaboration, citizenship, and collaboration.

MULTICULTURAL TEAMS

Multicultural and diverse teams add an additional element to the development and supervision of teams and departments. Potential difficulties arise from communication patterns. Some team members will use explicit and direct communication, while others will be more indirect. Various team members will see these differences as impediments to effective relationships. Language may be a hindrance, preventing the access of member expertise or a perception by some of incompetence. Different cultures take a different approach to hierarchy. For some members, status in the hierarchy is important, while those from egalitarian cultures will not be concerned with this issue. Finally, some cultures favor a more expeditious approach to decision making, while others will demand more deliberation and analysis. Team members may approach these issues in various ways, such as (1) some members may adapt to the differences; (2) a structural intervention utilizes a change in the relationships within the team or a member's position in the team to negate problems; (3) a managerial intervention might require the team leader to reinforce the team norms or change the norms to enhance compliance and performance; and (4) some problems may be insurmountable, requiring that a team member be voluntarily or involuntarily removed.

DELEGATION AND EMPOWERMENT

It is impossible to build a team that is committed to a shared purpose without people feeling a sense of ownership regarding the team. In other words, people need to feel empowered. To empower someone is to share information, rewards, responsibility, and power. Empowered employees are more loyal, more engaged, and more creative. With empowerment comes delegation. Individuals are delegated to perform a specific task. Effective delegation requires an assignment of responsibility for a specific task. Transferring responsibility also requires transferring authority, including the resources to accomplish the task. With delegation and empowerment, people must also be held accountable for their performance. As a supervisor, even though you have delegated a task to someone, you are still ultimately responsible for team and departmental performance. If the delegated performance is substandard, then coaching for improvement is appropriate. To reiterate, as a supervisor, you are still ultimately responsible, since you selected those to delegate to and trained them. Their performance is your handiwork.

MEETINGS

Teams spend a significant amount of their time in meetings. It makes sense that those meetings should be as productive as possible. Meetings can be called for various purposes, such as to include the sharing and dissemination of information, to solve a problem, to make a decision, or for social reasons. There are some basic recommendations that, if utilized, will increase the effectiveness of team meetings. First, decide if a meeting is really necessary. Determine if face-to-face interaction is the best way. If so, determine who is required to be there, establish the location and time, and develop and disseminate the agenda. Announce the length of the meeting so people can schedule accordingly and understand how much time will be devoted to the issue. Stick to this time constraint. See to it that the meeting venue is conducive to a productive meeting. At the beginning of the meeting, announce the objective, the agenda, and the rules for the meeting. Manage the process. Encourage the recalcitrant to speak, and limit the excessively verbose. Gently chide those who don't follow the accepted ground rules for the meeting. Recognize when the discussion wanders or becomes redundant, and call for a resolution. Having worked through the agenda, summarize the results of the meeting. Ask for comments regarding the conduct of the meeting and people's satisfaction with the process. Send a follow-up communication in writing that summarizes the outcomes of the meeting, and thank participants for their efforts and adherence to the meeting protocols.

SUMMARY

Building an effective team or department is elusive. It is hard. It is a fundamentally human activity with all the subtleties and complications of weaving multiple personalities, agendas, and aspirations into a functioning unit. The steps to the process are well known and simple to understand; their application, however, is not easy. This is where the "art," the "touch," and the "feel" of the leader emerges. To summarize the process, it is convenient to review the ideas in the book *Five Dysfunctions of a Team* and their impact.

First, there is an **absence of trust** because team members are not open about themselves, their weaknesses, and their mistakes. There is an unwillingness to let themselves be vulnerable within the group. The absence of trust leads to a **fear of conflict**, limiting the free flow and discussion of ideas. The lack of open and productive conflict results in a **lack of commitment**. People don't commit, because their ideas and opinions did not get a fair hearing; therefore, no one commits to team decisions. Because no one is actually committed,

accountability for results is negligible. No one accepts or holds others responsible for their performance. Finally, there is a **lack of attention to results**. People put their personal agendas ahead of team performance.

The role of the supervisor, the leader of the team, in negating these dysfunctions is as follows. To build trust, supervisors must first create an environment that does not punish genuine vulnerability. The method for this is for supervisors to express their own vulnerability first. They must admit some of their fears and weaknesses in front of the group. Once it is seen that this is acceptable, others in the group will follow. Now feeling secure within the group, members can engage in productive conflict. The supervisor must let members resolve their own issues themselves. Restraint is in order. Focus on issues and not people is the rule. As with vulnerability, the supervisor models for the group what is acceptable regarding conflict. Through conflict, ideas and resolutions are discussed and vetted. It then is up to the supervisor to decide and clarify the team's goals in such a manner that members can rally around and commit to the objective. Having committed to the goals, highly functioning teams hold one another accountable. In other words, the team disciplines itself. The supervisor only steps in when necessary, but it must be understood that he or she will intervene if commitments are not honored. Team leaders must convey that team results are the only standard and the only focus. Personal agendas have no place in a highly functional team.

There is a great deal of common sense to the prescription for building a team. It is the uncommon application of these commonsense ideas that separates highly functioning teams from ineffective groups.

EXERCISES

Summarizing
Write a one-page executive summary of the chapter.
Discuss with your classmates how you would teach this material.
Write a two-page case from your experience on this topic that would be instructional for other students.

What's Important to You in the Chapter?
With several of your classmates, discuss the most important ideas from the chapter. Which ideas do you think will be most useful to you in your career? Which ideas do you think you will remember in six months?

What Do the Practitioners/Others Say?

Discuss with your colleagues or someone at work any of the ideas in the chapter. Alternatively, read an article from any source on teams and be prepared to summarize its message.

Exercises

Develop a mental model for this chapter based on the mind mapping technique.

With several of your classmates, develop a ten-question assessment to determine if a team is effective.

Research an athletic team, professional or amateur, and present the "secret" of the team's success.

For your particular professional or career circumstance, what would be a worthy shared purpose that would inspire a team to greater performance?

With several classmates, develop several approaches to deal with a fellow team member who is:

- Not carrying his or her weight in the team
- Won't accept responsibility for his or her performance
- Doesn't contribute at team meetings
- Dominates the conversation in meetings
- Engages in personal attacks on other team members

What role are you most comfortable in fulfilling on a team? Leader, someone who focuses on the task, or someone who focuses on human relationships?

REFERENCES AND WORKS CONSULTED

Blanchard, A. L., O.J. Stewart, A. Cann, and L. Follman. 2014. "Making Sense of Humor at Work." *Psychologists-Manager Journal* 17 (1): 49–70.

Brett, J., K. Behrar, and M.C. Kern. 2006. "Managing Multicultural Teams." *Harvard Business Review* (November): 89–96.

Bushe, G.R. 1998. "Appreciative Inquiry with Teams." *Organization Development Journal* 16 (3): 41–49.

Bushe, G.R. 2001. "Meaning Making in Teams: Appreciative Inquiry with Pre-identity and Post-identity Groups." In *Appreciative Inquiry and Organizational Transformation: Reports from the Field*, edited by R. Fry, F. Barrett, J. Seilling, and D. Whitney, 39–63. Westport, CT: Quorum.

Druskat, V. U. and Wolff. S. B. 2001. "Building the Emotional Intelligence of Groups." *Harvard Business Review* 79.3: 80–91.

Freund, A., and A. Carmeli. 2003. "An Empirical Assessment: Reconstructed Model for Five Universal Forms of Work Commitment." *Journal of Managerial Psychology* 18 (7/8): 708–25.

Harvard Business Essentials. 2003. *Negotiation*. Boston: Harvard School Press.

Harvard Business Review. 2013. *On Collaboration*. Boston: Harvard Business Review Press.

Haskins, M.E., J. Liedtka, and J. Rosenblum. 1998. "Toward an Ethic of Collaboration." *Organizational Dynamics* (Spring): 34–50.

Lencioni, P. 2002. *The Five Dysfunctions of a Team: A Leadership Fable*. San Francisco: Jossey Bass.

Lewis, S. 2011. *Positive Psychology at Work*. West Sussex, UK: Wiley-Blackwell.

Li, N., B.L. Kirkman, and C.O.L.H. Porter. 2014. "Toward a Model of Work Team Altruism." *Academy of Management Review* 39 (4): 541–65.

Manley, K., H. O'Keefe, C. Jackson, C., J. Pearce, and S. Smith. 2014. "A Shared Purpose Framework to Deliver Person-Centered, Safe and Effective Care: Organizational Transformation Using Practice Development Methodology." *International Practice Journal* 4 (1). http://www.fons.org. library/journal.aspx.

Markova, D., and A. McArthur. 2015. *Collaborative Intelligence*. New York: Spiegel and Grau.

Meyer, J.P., and N.J. Allen. 1991. "A Three-Component Conceptualization of Organizational Commitment." *Human Resources Management Review* 1 (1): 61–89.

Mintzberg, H. 2013. *Simply Managing*. San Francisco: Berrett-Koehler.

Mudrack, P.E., and G.M. Farrell. 1995. "An Examination of Functional Role Behavior and Its Consequences for Individuals in Group Settings." *Small Group Research* 26 (4): 542–71.

Owler, K., R. Morrison, and B. Plester. 2010. "Does Fun Work? The Complexity of Promoting Fun at Work." *Journal of Management and Organization* 16: 338–52.

Peelle, H.E., III. 2006. "Appreciative Inquiry and Creative Problem Solving in Cross-Functional Teams." *Journal of Applied Behavioral Science* 42 (4): 447–67.

Podsakoff, P. M., S.B. Mackenzie, J.B. Paie, and D.G. Bachrach. 2000. "Organizational Citizenship Behaviors: A Critical Review of the Theoretical and Empirical Literature and Suggestions for Future Research." *Journal of Management* 26 (3): 513–63.

Robbins, S.P. 2013. *The Truth about Managing People*. Upper Saddle River, NJ: Pearson.

Sharma, S., K. Joneson, and S. Hosler. 2015. *Purpose Drives Performance*. Seattle, WA: Knotted Road.

Webber, A.M. 1987. "Red Auerbach on Management." *Harvard Business Review* (March): 84–91.

Willis, S. 2012. *Power through Collaboration*. San Rafael, CA: Author.

SECTION II
| PEOPLE |

Best ideas are defined as those ideas from the chapters in this section that you believe will be the most influential in your practice and that you will retain over time. Take a few moments to compile your ten best ideas. Consider these as the residue of the effort and time put into these readings and discussion. In other words, what did you learn?

IDEA ONE

IDEA TWO

IDEA THREE

IDEA FOUR

IDEA FIVE

IDEA SIX

IDEA SEVEN

IDEA EIGHT

IDEA NINE

IDEA TEN

ORGANIZATIONAL ISSUES

The first section laid the intellectual framework for the book. The second section discussed supervising people. This section focuses on organizational issues. The issues discussed are leadership, culture, politics, and change.

Chapter 7: Leadership

Chapter 7 is about leadership and provides several perspectives on the topic to include a definition of leadership, the distinction between leaders and managers, whether leaders are born or made, the idea of authenticity, Level 5 leadership, emotional intelligence and leadership, followers, and toxic leaders.

Chapter 8: Culture and Politics

Chapter 8 presents the ideas of organizational culture and organizational politics. Culture is the shared beliefs that bind an organization together. Politics is how power is used to accomplish organizational goals. The key idea is that both culture and politics are not readily accessible; they are the hidden aspects of organizations. To be effective, a supervisor must develop tacit knowledge or practical intelligence—the understanding of how to get things done.

Chapter 9: Change, Innovation, and Entrepreneurship

This chapter begins by discussing the idea of the organizational life cycle and the rarity of organizations that survive intact for a hundred years. The mechanism for ensuring corporate survival is change, innovation, creativity, and entrepreneurship. The chapter discusses the value of failure in facilitating change.

7 LEADERSHIP

ALEX

The financials for the year were bad and not likely to improve in the next three to five years. Consequently, the executive group decided that two positions in the department would be eliminated and no overtime hours would be approved for the next six months. Alex was saddened by the impact on the two that would be let go and the reduced paychecks for several staffers who counted on the overtime to make ends meet. Alex considered how to handle the dismissals and the overtime announcement. Troubling Alex was the fact that it looked like the best date for the bad news was right before he was scheduled to leave for a conference in Florida for a week. Alex had looked forward to the conference all year and was gradually working his way into the rotation to become a national officer. How would it look if the day after Alex dismissed the two staffers and made the overtime announcement, he left on the trip?

I really like Florida.

They will all be mad.

Morale will drop through the floor.

I'm planning to stop and see my family on the way back. ... Dad is almost 90 now. Hard to believe.

I really liked the bicycle outing yesterday.

I think I will go to the movies tonight.

I really like eating out.

How should I phrase it?

How do I make it palatable?

At least they get some severance.

My stomach is starting to hurt.

I'm thinking too much.

I need to compartmentalize.

MENTAL MODELS

In the center of the space below, write the word *leadership*. Next, write the words that come to mind when you think of this topic. Do not edit your thoughts or collaborate with anyone. There is no right or wrong answer.

If things are related, connect them with an arrow. If the relationship is reciprocal (they both affect each other), put arrows at both ends of the line. If one relationship is stronger than another, make the arrow darker and thicker.

The goal is to capture your mental model of what you believe about corporate culture. This is the starting point for the discussion on these topics.

LEARNING OBJECTIVES

- Define what leadership is.
- Discuss the difference between leadership and management.
- Discuss whether leaders are born or made.
- Discuss the impact of authenticity on leadership.
- Discuss the relationship between leaders and followers.
- Discuss Level 5 leadership.
- Describe what transformational leadership is.
- Discuss the power and appeal of toxic leaders.
- Discuss emotional intelligence and leadership.

LEADERSHIP DEFINED

Leadership is a topic much researched and written about, yet a precise definition is elusive. However, most people have an intuitive sense of what leaders do, who they are, and what they are like. Leadership is a complex phenomenon involving the leader, the followers, and a situation. Thus, in thinking of leadership, the personality, traits, and behaviors of the leader are a focus, as well as the type and quality of the relationship between the leader and the followers. Finally, the aspects of the situation are also of interest. A sampling of the perspectives on leadership include the following:

- Leadership as a focus or pivotal point for various group processes
- Leadership as a personality type and its impact on others
- Leadership as a behavior; what leaders do
- Leadership as a force for goal achievement
- Leadership as integrating the efforts of others to accomplish something
- Leadership as initiating and providing structure
- Leadership as inducing compliance
- Leadership as influencing others
- Leadership as persuasion
- Leadership as power

Leadership can also be viewed from a psychological, sociological, economic, or historical perspective. Taken together, a workable definition of leadership is that it is a process whereby the intentional activity of one person influences others toward the attainment of a goal.

LEADERSHIP VERSUS MANAGEMENT

The classic distinction between leadership and management is that managers do things right, while leaders do the right thing. Effective managers are associated with efficiency, procedures, control, and consistency; whereas effective leaders are associated with vision, change, and dynamic environments. Further distinctions between leaders and managers include the following:
- Managers administer; leaders innovate.
- Managers maintain; leaders develop.
- Managers control; leaders inspire.
- Managers have a short-term view; leaders have a long-term view.
- Managers ask how and when; leaders ask what and why.
- Managers imitate; leaders originate.
- Managers accept the status quo; leaders challenge it (Bennis, 1989).

BORN VERSUS MADE

Whether leaders are born or made is an age-old question and is a variant of the familiar nature-versus-nurture debate. As with any nature-versus-nurture debate, the answer is yes. Clearly, possessing certain traits or behaviors is helpful to a leader. For example, taller candidates for the US presidency received more popular votes, were more likely to be reelected, and were much taller than men in general (Stulp et al. 2012). Certain psychological and cognitive traits may be an advantage to a leader. But neither physical or psychological gifts guarantee that an individual will become a leader or, more important, an effective leader. Leaders emerge from a coincidence of personal gifts, situational opportunity, and personal development. The answer to the question of whether leaders are born or made is yes.

FOLLOWERS

There can be no leaders without followers. The most desirable followers have two attributes. First, they have a bias for action; they want to accomplish something. Second, they can distinguish between and support only effective and ethical leaders. Desirable followers are not sheep. Followers can be categorized as to their level of engagement. Followers can be isolates, those barely aware of what is going on; bystanders who observe but do not participate; participants who are engaged in some manner; activists who have strong feelings about the organization and act accordingly; and diehards willing to go down with the ship. Leaders don't "do things" to followers; it is a symbiotic dance. Leaders may have formal authority, but followers are not without power; nor are they all the same. Astute leaders understand this (adapted from Kellerman 2007).

AUTHENTICITY

Authentic leaders are self-aware, reveal their true selves to their followers, are aware of their strengths and weaknesses, and don't hide their mistakes or weaknesses. In the book *Discover Your True North*, Bill George (2015) introduced the idea of an onion, with the authentic self at the core surrounded by less-revealing layers. At the core is our authentic self, surrounded by an understanding of our life story, blind spots, vulnerabilities, and shadow sides. In the next layers are values, motivations, strengths, weaknesses, needs, and desires. At the outmost layer are the things about ourselves that can be observed by anyone, including attire, body language, appearance, and leadership style. Authenticity is argued to be a prerequisite for effectiveness as a leader. It is also a prerequisite for finding the "sweet spot" in life and career—the place where personal motivations and talents can best be expressed. Authentic leaders are grounded and true to themselves. They integrate their personal and professional lives and are the same person in all environments. They are the same whether talking with the custodial staff or another CEO, and they share personal information about themselves appropriate to the situation. Authentic leaders are also guided by internal moral standards that are utilized to self-regulate.

Life is argued to be a very effective therapist in that it will teach you what you need to know about yourself if you take time to search for and integrate the lessons it is giving you. The search for authenticity is a conscious choice and it takes work; it is a choice to let our true selves be seen. The search for authenticity will always be a work in progress. Suggestions for developing authenticity include the following:

- List the attributes of effective leaders and assess yourself relative to this list.
- Ask the people you work with what your strengths are, when you are at your best, and what circumstances evoke your best.
- Develop transparency. What information about yourself are you comfortable sharing with others. Why?
- Given a moral choice, what values determine your behavior?

Effective leaders can't be and shouldn't be genuinely authentic in all circumstances. Contingency theory in the next section confirms this view. Effective leaders manage their authenticity and reveal different aspects of themselves to different audiences at different times. At some level leadership is acting; you have to give the audience what they want. Remember, one of our most authentic presidents, Ronald Reagan, was a professional actor.

CONTINGENCY

The target audience for this book, professionals, or about-to-be professionals, likely are educated and practice in disciplines with relatively rigid and standardized protocols, expectations, and standards of practice. Therefore, they are likely to be accustomed to seeking the "right" answer and may intellectually be uncomfortable with ambiguity and contingency. Leadership would be simple if there was one best way, one set of behaviors for all circumstances that once mastered were applied over and over. Unfortunately, like all human interactions, one size does not fit all. It makes no sense to think that a team of seasoned professionals could be influenced by the same messages, behaviors, and techniques as a team of novices. Leadership is a contingent activity, varying with the leader, the type of followers, and the situation.

Researchers have developed various contingency theories of leadership. The various theories consider different situational variables as influencing leader behavior. Variables that have been considered include time urgency; amount of physical danger; external stress; degree of autonomy; degree of job scope; meaningfulness of the work, how boring, ambiguous, or unstructured the task; the degree to which situations are favorable to the leader; the level of maturity of the followers; the followers' job readiness; and the psychological commitment of the followers to the task. A recognized contingency approach to leadership suggests that leaders should focus on the task and consideration for the individual at an appropriate level. Consider any coach in preseason. To build teamwork, it would be appropriate to take time to enrich relationships by asking players for their input regarding plays for the upcoming season. The time to focus on player input and personal relationships is not when there is one play to call to win a championship; the coach needs to focus on the task and make the call. Leadership styles that are useful for different situations are supportive (concern for the individual), directive (telling what to do), participative (seeking input), and achievement oriented (focus on the task). Leaders who are more behaviorally complex, in that they have a greater repertoire of behaviors and thus have more options for dealing with situations, may have an advantage relative to leaders who are behaviorally restricted. Contingency is not an overly complicated idea; it simply counsels leaders to adapt to circumstances.

LEVEL 5 LEADERSHIP

When thinking of leaders, many people envision an individual who has charm, or the ability to communicate something intangible about their personality that influences people to follow them. Examples of charismatic leaders include Martin Luther King Jr., John F. Kennedy, Pope John Paul II, Bill Clinton, Lee Iacocca, and Jack Welch. Charismatic leaders are the heroes of myth. In fact, charisma is not what makes for exceptional leadership. It is something Jim Collins (2001) labels Level 5 leadership.

Collins and his research group looked at Fortune 500 companies from 1965 to 1995 to identify firms that produced financial returns three times the Fortune 500 average. Of 1,435 Fortune 500 companies, only 11 met this criteria. In seeking to understand what separated these 11 companies, the researchers found that a significant contributor was a Level 5 leader.

In reaching Level 5 leadership, executives need to possess the capabilities of the lower levels plus the unique attributes of Level 5 leadership. The levels of capabilities are as follows:

- **Level 1:** Highly capable individual who make productive contributions through talent, knowledge, skills, and good work habits
- **Level 2:** Contributing team member who works effectively with others in a group setting in contributing to group objectives
- **Level 3:** Competent manager who efficiently and effectively organizes to accomplish objectives
- **Level 4:** Effective leader who offers a compelling vision, stimulates the group to high standards, and catalyzes commitment to the vision
- **Level 5:** Builds greatness through a paradoxical combination of personal humility and professional will

Collins elaborates on the personal humility of Level 5 leaders, describing them as having a compelling modesty that avoids public adulation and is not boastful. They act with a quiet, calm determination and rely on inspiring standards rather that personal charisma to motivate. Personal ambition is channeled into the company and positions successors for ever greater success. It is not about the self. Level 5 leaders believe that poor results cannot be attributed to circumstance, luck, or other people. They are willing to accept responsibility for company performance.

Regarding personal will, Collins (2001) writes that Level 5 leaders set the standards for enduring success and operate with unwavering resolve, will do whatever it takes to accomplish that success, and will settle for nothing less. Level 5 leaders apportion success to other people, deflecting their impact. The former Alabama football coach Bear Bryant captured this idea by declaring, "If anything goes bad, I did it. If anything goes semi-good, we did it. If anything goes really good, then you did it. That's all it takes to get people to win football games for you" (https://www.saturdaydownsouth.com/2012/bear-bryant-50-quotes/).

In addition to humility and personal will, the following contribute to greatness as a leader:

- Rather than focusing on strategy, first focus on getting the right people involved; in Collins's words, getting the right people on the bus, moving the wrong people off, and the right people in the right seats.
- James Stockdale survived more than seven years in a Vietnamese POW camp relying on two distinct and contradictory beliefs. The first is a willingness to confront the brutal facts of the current situation, coupled with a belief that ultimately the individual will

prevail in the end. This way of thinking is termed the Stockdale paradox—focusing on the facts while having faith in the future.

- Success at the beginning is not an overnight process. Rather, it a relentless push until a critical point is reached where momentum accelerates.
- Focus on simplicity, characterized by what are we the best at, what are the economics of the situation, and how best to excite the passions of people. This is termed the "hedgehog concept."
- Instill a culture of discipline, specifically disciplined people, disciplined thought, and disciplined action.

Taken together, Level 5 leadership provides a picture of and a blueprint for greatness as a leader that is at odds with what is commonly believed about leadership.

TRANSFORMATIONAL LEADERSHIP

Transformational leaders do big things. Abraham Lincoln and Franklin D. Roosevelt were clearly transformative. Transformational leaders are contrasted with transactional leaders, who use contingent rewards to motivate. Transformational leaders motivate by elevating and transforming followers' attitudes, beliefs, and values. Transformative leaders inspire followers to transcend their self-interest. Transformative leaders arouse passions and energize others. Transformative leaders may be charismatic in that they inspire change through the strength and appeal of their personalities.

Transformative leaders inspire by articulating a vision of an ideal world that is communicated in an inspirational way arousing both the emotions and the intellect. Transformative leaders are supportive; they are concerned for their followers and take account of their needs. They also engage followers intellectually and arouse interest in problems and thinking about problems in different ways. Finally, transformative leaders are adept at recognizing the contributions of followers, value follower accomplishments, and provide reward and recognition for follower contributions.

EMOTIONAL INTELLIGENCE AND LEADERSHIP

Goleman, Boyatzis, and McKee (2001) argue that the primal task of all leaders is to set the emotional tone. The leaders' task is to drive follower emotions in a positive direction and negate the impact of toxic emotions. Leaders are emotional guides for the organization. It is how leaders handle their relationships with followers that sets the emotional direction and is a function of a leader's emotional intelligence. Effective leaders also are attuned to the emotions of a group; they resonate or are in sync with those emotions. They then begin to move follower's emotions, if necessary, in a positive direction. The explanation for a leader's ability to move emotions is that emotions are contagious; this has to do with the physiology of the human brain. Leaders who don't resonate with the group are termed discordant, out of sync, and out of touch. Discordant leadership may be calculated in that the leader believes an abusive style is appropriate; it may be subtle in that the leader believes a manipulative style is effective and most likely the result of a leader who is just clueless, insensitive, or lacking in empathy. Leaders and followers who resonate are analogous to finely tuned instrument; the emerging sounds are harmonious and pleasing.

TOXIC LEADERS

Leaders have and give power. They can use that power to benefit others, or they can use it destructively. It doesn't take long to develop a list of toxic leaders—Hitler, Stalin, Saddam Hussein, Kim Jong-un. Toxic leaders by their behaviors and personal characteristics harm followers, organizations, and nonfollowers. Between 1933 and 1945, Hitler and Stalin killed an estimated 14 million people through famine, shootings, incarceration in prison camps, and general terror (Snyder 2010). Some leaders are intentionally toxic and are deliberate in their efforts, while others are unintentionally toxic, the harm derived from their carelessness, recklessness, or incompetence. Toxic leader behaviors include the following:

- Deliberating demeaning, imprisoning, torturing, intimidating, seducing, marginalizing, disenfranchising, killing, and so on
- Violating basic human rights
- Engaging in corrupt, criminal, and unethical behaviors
- Depicting themselves as the only one who can save the followers
- Playing to base fears
- Stifling the truth
- Subverting structures designed to ensure honesty, justice, and fairness
- Behaving incompetently

These toxic behaviors emerge from a personality characterized by a lack of integrity, insatiable ambition, outsized ego, arrogance, amorality, avarice, and cowardice.

Toxic leaders only exist if followers are willing to tolerate and accept their behaviors. Follower acceptance of toxic leaders emerges from the psychology of followers. That psychology includes the need for an authority figure to replace our parents, the need for a sense of self as significant, and our fear of confronting a powerful leader. Followers are also attracted to toxic leaders for pragmatic reasons, political access, and additional tangible benefits. Toxic leaders also speak to existential needs to live a life of meaning as one of the chosen, as a member of something outside the self. Toxic leaders also can offer order in a messy world or allow us vicariously to bask in the accomplishments of the toxic leader.

Adolph Hitler satisfied many of these wants for the German people when he put them back to work during the Depression, brought order to the chaos of hyperinflation, and told the Germans that they were the most cultured people in the world and were helping to build a thousand-year Reich.

SUMMARY

This chapter offered a definition of leadership and discussed the following topics: whether leaders are born or made, toxic leadership, contingency theories of leadership, authenticity and leadership, emotional intelligence and leadership, Level 5 leadership, and transformational leadership. Despite the considerable intellectual power devoted to this topic and the innumerable studies and writings on the topic, the conclusion is that like all the important things in life, leadership is a topic best considered from an aesthetic rather than a scientific perspective.

EXERCISES

Summarizing
Write a one-page executive summary of the chapter.
Discuss with your classmates how you would teach this material.
Write a two-page case from your experience on this topic that would be instructional for other students.

What's Important to You in the Chapter?
With several of your classmates, discuss the most important ideas from the chapter. Which ideas do you think will be most useful to you in your career? Which ideas do you think you will remember in six months?

What Do the Practitioners/Others Say?
Discuss with your colleagues or someone at work any of the ideas in the chapter. Alternatively, read an article from any source on leadership and be prepared to summarize its message

What leader, alive or dead, would you like to have lunch with? That is, what leader do you admire? What do you admire about this individual? Compare with several of your classmates and determine if there is any commonality across the leaders, such as looks, behavior, personality, and so on.

Prepare a one-page summary of the latest president, assessing his effectiveness as a leader. What strengths and weaknesses contributed to his performance?

Identify the characteristics of an effective leader. How do you rate yourself on these dimensions?

John Gagliardi, over a fifty-eight-year coaching career at St. John's University, won 377 games. In doing so, he compiled a list of 108 no's that guided the program. Examples of those no statements include the following:

14. No creating busy work. Eliminate the unnecessary.
18. No goals needed. We just expect great things to happen.
20. No mission statement. Just win.
25. No rules except the Golden Rule.
29. No player meetings.
35. No playbooks.
36. No statistics posted.
38. No excuses.
40. No blaming anyone else for your or their mistakes.
75. No big deal when we score. We expect to score.
77. No trying to "kill" the opponent.
91. No dwelling on bad things.
107. No promises. Just results.

(Collison, 2001).

Comment on this list as a style of leadership. In what circumstances would this style be suitable and with what type of players.

The chapter suggested that effective leaders are both emotionally intelligent and humble. In contrast, Roderick Kramer (2006), in his article "The Great Intimidators," suggested that sometimes leaders need to be scary and that sometimes fear works. Comment on this idea and consider what types of industries and in what circumstances fear might be required.

The search for authenticity begins by answering the question: Who are you? Reflect on your life by sketching the highlights of your life story. Think of your life as a path, and on the timeline below, record the highlights of your life, including the memorable events, accomplishments, and setbacks that have shaped who you are.

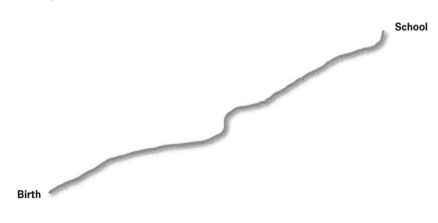

Fig. 7.1. Life timeline

How do you tell the story of your life: as a hero, a victim, a bystander, an achiever, as happy, as fulfilled? Remember you can tell the story of your life from multiple perspectives. What is the central lesson of your life?

It has been suggest that women and men use different leadership styles (Rosener 1990). From your experience, do you believe this to be true? Do you have a preference for a male or female superior? Do you believe the "glass ceiling" for women was broken when Hillary Clinton was chosen as the first female candidate for the presidency?

REFERENCES AND WORKS CONSULTED

Avolio, B.J., F.O. Walulmbwa, and T.J. Weber. 2009. "Leadership: Current Theories, Research, and Future Directions." *Annual Review of Psychology* 60: 421–49.

Avolio, B.J., and T.S. Wernsing. 2008. "Practicing Authentic Leadership." *Positive Psychology: Exploring the Best in People* 4: 147–65.

Bennis, W.G. 1989. *On Becoming a Leader*. Reading, MA: Addison-Wesley.

Burns, J.M. 1978. *Leadership*. New York: Harper & Row.

Collins, J. 2001. "Level 5 Leadership: The Triumph of Humility and Fierce Resolve." *Harvard Business Review* 79 (1): 66–76.

Collison, J. 2001. *No-How Coaching*. Herndon, VA: Capital.

Craig, N., B. George, and S. Snook. 2015. *The Discover Your True North Fieldbook*. Hoboken, NJ: Wiley.

George, B. 2003. *Authentic Leadership*. San Francisco: Jossey-Bass.

George, B. 2015. *Discover Your True North*. Hoboken, NJ: Wiley.

Goffee, R., and G. Jones. 2005. "Managing Authenticity." *Harvard Business Review* (December): 1–8.

Goleman, D., R. Boyatzis, and A. McKee. 2001. "Primal Leadership: The Hidden Driver of Great Performance." *Harvard Business Review* (December): 42–51.

Goleman, D., R. Boyatzis, and A. McKee. 2002. *Primal Leadership*. Boston: Harvard Business School Press.

Graef, C.L. 1997. "Evolution of Situational Leadership Theory: A Critical Review." *Leadership Quarterly* 8: 153–70.

House, R.J. 1971. "A Path-Goal Theory of Leader Effectiveness." *Administrative Science Quarterly* 16: 321–38. https://www.saturdaydownsouth.com/2012/bear-bryant-50-quotes/

Ibarra, H. 2015. "The Authenticity Paradox." *Harvard Business Review* (January–February): 1–9.

Johnson, A.M., P.A. Vernon, J.M. McCarthy, M. Molson, J.A. Harris, and K.L. Jang. 1998. "Nature vs. Nurture: Are Leaders Born or Made? A Behavior Genetic Investigation of Leadership Style." *Twin Research* 1: 216–23.

Kellerman, B. 2007. "What Every Leader Needs to Know about Followers." *Harvard Business Review* 85 (12): 84–91.

Kramer, R.M. 2006. "The Great Intimidators." *Harvard Business Review* (February): 1–9.

Lipman-Blumen, J. 2005. *The Allure of Toxic Leaders*. New York: Oxford University Press.

Lorsch, J. 2010. "A Contingency Theory of Leadership." In *Handbook of Leadership Theory and Practice*, edited by N. Nohriaand R. Khurana, 411–29. Boston: Harvard Business Press.

Nohria, N., and R. Khurana. 2010. *Handbook of Leadership Theory and Practice*. Boston: Harvard Business Press.

Rosener, J.B. 1990. "Ways Women Lead." *Harvard Business Review* 68 (6): 119–25.

Snyder, T. 2010. *Bloodlands: Europe between Hitler and Stalin*. New York: Basic.

Stulp, G., A.P. Buunk, S. Verhulst, and T.V. Pollet. 2012. "Tall Claims? Sense and Nonsense about the Importance of Height of US Presidents." *Leadership Quarterly*. http://dx.doi.org/10.1016/j.leaqua.2012.09.002

Vroom, V.H., and P.H. Yetton. 1973. *Leadership and Decision Making*. Pittsburgh: University of Pittsburgh Press.

8 CULTURE AND POLITICS

ALEX

Alex thought the presentation had gone well. His arguments were well reasoned, and the data that supported it were comprehensive and well researched. His presentation was flawless. The joke he told had everyone laughing. On the way out the door, everyone congratulated him on the effort. Alex thought that within a week he would be called in to the COO's office and they would discuss the next step needed to implement his proposal. Now it was a month later, and he hadn't heard anything. He asked around and found out that two of the senior executives had sabotaged his proposal in private meetings with the COO. As Alex thought about it, the monthly meeting rarely resulted in the adoption of any proposal as presented. There was always a delay, a modification, or a rejection. Alex also remembered the two senior executives walking down the hall with the COO following the meeting. Alex wondered what had happened as he walked to the car.

I put a lot of time in on that presentation; it was really good.

I always see the same two executives with the COO at lunch.

I think all three went to the same school.

How do I do my budget for next year?

I wish I hadn't told the staff that I thought it was a done deal.

I can't believe the cafeteria raised their prices again.

I'm glad we could get the student intern into counseling; they seemed very depressed.

I need to schmooze more. I'm not very good at schmoozing.

Poor Jack, I heard he had a heart attack right outside the copy room.

I'm so sore. I should know better than to run that far on the first day out.

Meetings seem like such a waste of time here; everything is already decided.

The only proposal that was ever accepted went through the COO's administrative assistant.

I wonder who will win the best picture of the year. I really like the Oscar presentation.

I can't wait to get home

MENTAL MODELS

In the center of the space below, write the words *corporate politics*. Next, write the words that come to mind when you think of this topic. Do not edit your thoughts or collaborate with anyone. There is no right or wrong answer.

If things are related, connect them with an arrow. If the relationship is reciprocal (they both affect each other), put arrows at both ends. If one relationship is stronger than another, make the arrow darker and thicker.

The goal is to capture your mental model of what you believe about corporate culture. This is the starting point for the discussion on these topics.

LEARNING OBJECTIVES

- Discuss the definition of organizational culture and why it is important.
- Discuss the idea of prudent paranoia.
- Discuss the idea of political skill.
- Discuss the ideas of tacit knowledge and practical intelligence and how they relate to culture and politics.

As a student, consider the atmosphere in various classes. How was discipline handled, was the relationship with the instructor formal or informal, was discussion encouraged, was disagreement tolerated, was the instructor a knowing sage or a facilitator. Was the class fun or a drudge? While the syllabus may have officially declared the rules for the class stories on campus would have conveyed the "truth" about the class. The syllabus might say questions encouraged but in reality they were met with a peevish and condescending response from the instructor. Each class was different. That difference could be attributed to the culture of the class.

ORGANIZATIONAL CULTURE

"Organizational culture is the pattern of basic assumptions that a given group has invented, discovered, or developed in learning to cope with its problems of external adaptation and internal integration, and that have worked well enough to be considered valid, and, therefore, to be taught to new members as the correct way to perceive, think and feel in relation to those problems" (Schein 1984, 3). Culture explains how work is done in a specific organization and emerges from the founder and founding group. It is their beliefs and assumptions about the nascent organization, its role, and how its objectives are to be accomplished that ground the culture. Organizational culture is a system of shared meaning. Organizational culture is expressed in the tangible artifacts of the organization, which includes elements such as architecture, office layout, accepted dress, visible behavior patterns, and public documents. The espoused values of the organization explain behavior at work. Espoused values are what people say about work, the rationalization for their behavior. One aspect of culture that is difficult to access is the underlying unconscious assumptions that members hold. It is these unconscious assumptions that drive how people think, feel, and perceive at work. These assumptions have been tested over time and been found to work, thus continually confirming their validity. These assumptions are taken for granted; for example, that the purpose of a business is to generate profit, or the purpose of health care is to cure disease.

Culture is embedded and transmitted through the following mechanisms:
- Formal statements of philosophy, charter, or creed
- Design of physical space
- Deliberate role modeling, teaching, coaching
- Explicit reward and promotion criteria
- Stories, legends, parables about key people and events
- What is measured
- Leader reaction to critical events
- Design and structure of the organization
- Organizational systems and procedures
- Criteria used for hiring, promotion, retirement (adapted from Schein, 1995)

Table 8.1. Levels of organizational culture

Symbolic artifacts; behaviors	Surface level	**SEEN**
What people say; how decisions are made	Expressed values and beliefs	**HEARD**
Beliefs and assumptions; rarely discussed	Unconsciously held assumptions and beliefs	**BELIEVED**

For some organizations there is congruence across all the dimensions shown in table 8.1. For other organizations there is a dissonance between what is said and expressed explicitly and what is actually enacted. For example, a corporate statement may declare that the company values its employees above all else, but if downsizing is required, the process is ruthless and demeaning. Or a company says it values innovation but doesn't give employees release time to work on it.

A specific department has its own culture or subculture within the larger organizational culture. In other words, there is a hospital culture and a pharmacy or nursing subculture. The subculture is about how work is done within that department. As with the larger culture, the departmental culture emerges from the history of the department and all those who have passed through. There are also subcultures within an organization based on criteria other than departments. For example, there may be an "old timer" subculture, those who have worked there for a long time. Or there may be subcultures based on ethnicity, gender, or some other attribute.

The tasks of a supervisor are first to understand the larger organizational culture and how their department is impacted, and second to both understand and shape their department's culture. It is also important to understand the strength of both the departmental and the organizational culture. A cult, for example, that entices members to excessive and self-destructive behaviors epitomizes a strong culture. Culture is important to a supervisor in that it establishes constraints on what is or is not acceptable and on what a supervisor can do.

POLITICS

Facts of Life

There are certain facts of organizational life that must be accepted. Of themselves, they are neither good nor bad. Those facts are that (1) organizations are not democracies, (2) some people have more power, (3) all decisions are subjective, (4) your boss has a great deal of control over your life, and (5) fairness is an impossible goal (McIntyre 2005). Another fact that must be accepted is that all organizations are political. Politics are inevitable and unavoidable. Politics is organizational gamesmanship, it is organizational astuteness, it lubricates and eases the friction between people and departments. Politics fills in the gap between the idealized workings of the organization and the reality of human behavior. Politics is about power, its acquisition and use to accomplish personal and professional objectives. The ultimate political reality is that the person with the most power wins. One can choose to play the political game or not. One can choose to be a winner and a skilled adversary who accomplishes both personal and professional objectives. Or one can accept being taken advantage of due to a lack of political skill or of acting the martyr. Never forget that the ultimate organizational fact of life is that the person with the most power wins.

Politics and Paranoia

A theme that pervades many of the chapters in this book is the importance and value of trust at work. In thinking politically at work, it is important to recognize that being too trusting can be detrimental. Some people will play the political game ruthlessly. It is important to recognize that there is always something happening at work that may impact you both personally and professionally. It is important to view the work situation with a healthy level of paranoia; paranoia not in the clinical sense of a debilitating pathology, but rather as a healthy suspicion regarding the intentions of others at work. A healthy suspicion requires a keen and penetrating observation of what is going on at work. Who is in favor, who is out, who is allied with whom, what projects are being advanced or tabled, what are the idiosyncrasies of decision makers that can be leveraged for advantage, what is being gossiped about, what is in the rumor mill, and so on. Reading the political, behavioral, and emotional landscape is an element of emotional intelligence. Prudently paranoid and suspicious people gather data from as many sources as possible; they question their interpretation of this information searching for the reality contained, unpleasant though it may be. This perspective on organizational life does not lessen the power and utility of trust at work; it confirms the idea that trusting the dealer is OK, but it's still wise to cut the cards anyway.

Politics is a competitive game. There are, however, limits to what is fair in playing that game. It is not a ruthless winner-take-all, zero-sum game. Certain political strategies are appropriate, while others are excessive and unwarranted. Appropriate political strategies include the following:

- Assertiveness: speaking up for your rights
- Bargaining: trading, give and take
- Reciprocation: offering something to someone and assuming they will respond in kind
- Coalition building: building groups to accomplish objectives
- Ingratiation: getting people to like you, building rapport
- Inspirational appeals: appeal based on emotions and values
- Consultation: seeking input before making decisions
- Rational persuasion: using logical arguments
- Pressure: using demands
- Networking: staying connected to sources of information and power

Political behaviors that are not appropriate include intimidation, innuendo, manipulation, obstructionism, controlling information, blaming, attacking, controlling promotions, or merging with a group to silence them. Yet, other political behaviors are even less appropriate, including sabotage, duplicity, and open rebellion. It is good to remember that in playing politics at work, "never advance your own interests by harming the business or hurting other people" (MacIntyre 2005, 17). In other words, there is an ethical constraint to playing politics at work.

Organizational politics is about using leverage in pursuit of objectives. Leverage results from a higher position, status, having something the other wants, being the only one who can do something, having influence with people in power, having a good reputation, and having a good relationship with others (adapted from McIntyre 2005). If you have ever asked to speak to a manager following bad service, you have used and understand the concept of leverage.

Certain organizations suffer from a toxic political environment in which (1) power plays and power struggles predominate, (2) management egos require constant stroking, (3) entire departments are at war, (4) time is spent covering yourself rather than accomplishing the objective, (5) gossip and backbiting predominate, and (6) disagreements are personal (adapted from MacIntyre 2005). The recommendation in this case is to simply leave, as you will not, as a supervisor, be able to change the organizational environment.

Effective political players are skilled in that they are socially astute. They observe others and their interactions. They identify with others. They are unassuming and have a personal style that impacts others. They understand the situation and will use an influence tactic that is appropriate, such as one of the following:

- Rational persuasion: using logical facts and arguments to persuade someone
- Consultation: seeking others' help as a method of getting them to buy in

- Inspirational appeal: arousing enthusiasm by appealing to values, ideals, and aspirations
- Ingratiation: trying to get someone in a good mood
- Personal appeal: appealing to someone's loyalty or friendship
- Exchange: trading favors
- Coalition: seeking the help of other people
- Legitimizing: establishing the legitimacy by appealing to authority
- Pressure: using demands or threats (adapted from Yukl, Falbe, and Youn 1993)

The politically skilled develop individual networks, particularly with groups and individuals that hold valued assets. They are subtle in building friendships and alliances and are adept at negotiation and making deals. Finally, politically skilled individuals appear to be sincere and to have high levels of integrity. They are thought of as genuine and honest. They are seen as having no ulterior motives. Politically skilled people know how to get things done and have the contacts and ability to get them done, all the while appearing as if acting in the best interest of others. In other words, they are political without appearing to be so.

LIKABILITY AND IMPRESSION MANAGEMENT

The classic question in management and supervision is whether it is better to be liked or respected, with the collective wisdom indicating that respect is the desired commodity. In the political game at work, it is shortsighted to discount the impact of being liked. When people need to get things done at work, research indicates that people choose congeniality and likability over competence (Casciaro and Lobo 2005). It is not hard to understand that people like other people who are like them; who are similar in their beliefs, attitudes, and behaviors; and with whom they resonate. There is a biologic underpinning to this truth (Goleman and Boyatzis, 2008). It is important for supervisors to reflect on the impressions they create about themselves, whether they are viewed as likable or not.

The elements of likability are these. First, be friendly, positive, and happy to see and meet colleagues. The idea is to create in others a feeling of safety and warmth in being in your company. Next, seek to be relevant to the other person's life. On what issues do we connect, and how can we help one another both professionally and personally? Empathy now comes into play—the ability to understand other people and feel what they are feeling. Finally, likability comes from being real, genuine, and authentic. People easily see through the facade of disingenuous social affability and forced comradery.

Astute political players are conscious of the impression they create and engage in strategies that positively influence others' assessment of them. The most effective impression-management strategy is one of ingratiation, in which people make themselves more attractive to others. This is accomplished by complimenting others and making them feel good about themselves, aligning your opinions with those of others, praising others, doing favors for them, and taking an interest in others and their activities. The point is to recognize that you can make a conscious attempt to have people like you and that likability is a political currency that can be used and traded to influence others.

TACIT KNOWLEDGE

Take a quick review of chapter 3, the management overview. Skim the topics. They convey the basic theories and ideas of management. To assimilate this information is to engage in acquiring explicit information. Explicit learning is an active process and for our purposes will be considered the traditional, academic approach to acquiring information: read the book, take the test, memorize the facts, and understand the theory.

Chapter 3 also presents a sterilized picture of what it is to supervise a group of people. In reality, the process of supervision is messy; people are unpredictable; objectives change, are ambiguous, and conflict with one another; and information is nonexistent or incomplete. Further, this chapter highlights the idea that much of the constraints that impede supervision are hidden, buried in the subconscious of individuals and the misty underground of organizational culture. Also, the calculus of human politics limits possibilities. Who is with us, and who is against us? Will these individuals and alliances change, and in which direction, how quickly, and for what reason?

In learning to swim, one can read the instruction manual as a first step, but actually doing it requires getting in the water. Expertise as a supervisor comes only from practicing the craft of supervision, from making decisions and interacting with people, experiencing the reality of everyday practice. To be successful as a supervisor is to acquire the tacit knowledge, have the practical intelligence, the "street smarts," the common sense to know how to get things done. Each of these—tacit knowledge, practical intelligence, "street smarts," and common sense—vary slightly in their precise definition, but taken together they capture the idea of effectively dealing with the "real world," in this case the world of the supervisor. To have these skills is to be able to solve practical problems in the real world. The ideas in a course like this, and the training one gets in business school, for example, will be helpful in learning to supervise; they may be necessary for the development of a supervisor, but not sufficient.

Tacit knowledge is procedural knowledge that is acquired in a way that is not easily understood. If you ask seasoned supervisors how they learned their job, it would be difficult for them to articulate a clear methodology. Tacit knowledge is acquired through doing, through acting. Oftentimes, tacit knowledge emerges as rules of thumb; for example, only hire people who really need the money. Tacit knowledge may conflict with espoused corporate values. In other words, the company preaches integrity but condones excessive "gift giving" to secure contracts. Tactic knowledge is related to context; for example, position in the hierarchy or the immediate situation. Military officers acquire a different type of tacit knowledge from that of professors. The knowledge of how things work may be deliberately withheld by seasoned staffers who view outsiders or newcomers as a threat.

Tacit knowledge is acquired through experience, more specifically through reflected-on experience. Supervisors have to take the time to assess and understand whether their decisions and behaviors were effective in accomplishing objectives and solving problems. Tacit knowledge requires reflecting on the assessment of the situation; was it diagnosed and read correctly? Was the choice of actions appropriate, and did they work? Next, was that choice implemented in an optimal manner? Finally, what were the underlying assumptions and beliefs that underpinned this sequence? It is through this process, carried out over and over across time and situations, that yields the hard-won lessons of effective supervisory behavior. Unfortunately, tacit knowledge is a trial-and-error process, or muddling through in the search for problem solutions. Supervision is a practice, not a science. Supervisors operate, not in the clean air of the highlands, but in the primeval forest where trails have yet to be blazed.

SUMMARY

This chapter discussed three topics. The first was the idea of organizational culture, or the shared meaning, assumptions, and beliefs that bind an organization together and influence how work is done in the organization. The second was the idea of organization politics, or how power and influence are used in organizational life. The idea that politics at work is not the mark of a defective organization but of all organizations was considered. Finally, the idea of tacit knowledge or practical intelligence was recognized in that supervisors have to learn how to get things done at work. That learning only comes from reflection on experience.

EXERCISES

Summarizing
Write a one-page executive summary of the chapter.
Discuss with your classmates how you would teach this material.
Write a two-page case from your experience on this topic that would be instructional for other students.

What's Important to You in the Chapter?

With several of your classmates, discuss the most important ideas from the chapter. Which ideas do you think will be most useful to you in your career? Which ideas do you think you will remember in six months?

What Do the Practitioners/Others Say?

Discuss with your colleagues or someone at work any of the ideas in the chapter. Alternatively, read an article from any source on corporate culture and politics and be prepared to summarize its message.

Questions

1. Do you spend time at work building networks?
2. At work, do you try to connect with and get to know people with influence and position?
3. Do you have good intuition about what is going on at work?
4. Is it easy for you to develop rapport at work?
5. Do you believe that most people at work like you?
6. Is it easy for you to read people's motives at work?

Think About It

Former president Lyndon Johnson said this about FBI director J. Edgar Hoover: "It's better to have him inside the tent pissing out, than outside the tent pissing in (https://en.wikiquote. org/wiki/J._Edgar_Hoover).

What do you conclude from this statement regarding enemies at work?

Alliances

Develop a matrix, mind map, or diagram of who is allied with one another at work. In other words, who are friends and allies, and who are adversaries?

Relationships

Discuss with your classmates how you would go about "doing business" with someone at work who doesn't like you.

Tacit Knowledge at School

With several classmates, discuss what you have learned about how things get done at your school. Come up with two to three rules that would be helpful to new students.

Thoughts

If you were in Alex's position, what thoughts would be going through your head? How would you handle this situation?

REFERENCES AND WORKS CONSULTED

Casciaro, T., and M.S. Lobo. 2005. "Competent Jerks, Lovable Fools, and the Formation of Social Networks." *Harvard Business Review* (June): 2–8.

Erickson, T.J., and L. Gratton. 2007. "What It Means to Work Here." *Harvard Business Review* (March): 2–9.

Farrell, D., and J.C. Petersen. 1982. "Patterns of Political Behavior in Organizations." *Academy of Management Review* 7 (3): 403–12.

Ferris, G.R., D.C. Treadway, P.L. Perrewe, R.L. Brouer, C. Douglas, and S. Lux. 2007. "Political Skill in Organizations." *Journal of Management* 33 (3): 290–320.

Goleman, D., and R. Boyatzis. 2008. "Social Intelligence and the Biology of Leadership." *Harvard Business Review* (September): 2–8. https://en.wikiquote.org/wiki/J._Edgar_Hoover

Katzenbach, J.R., I. Steffen, and C. Kronley. 2012. "Cultural Change That Sticks." *Harvard Business Review* (July–August): 2–9.

Klaus, P. 2007. *The Hard Truth about Soft Skills*. New York: Collins Business.

Kramer, R.M. 2002. "When Paranoia Makes Sense." *Harvard Business Review*, 62–69.

Kurland, N.B. 2000. "Passing the Word: Toward a Model of Gossip and Power in the Workplace." *Academy of Management Review* 25 (2): 428–38.

McCall, M.W., M.M. Lombardo, and A.M. Morrison. 1988. *The Lessons of Experience*. Lexington, MA: Lexington Books.

McIntyre, M.G. 2005. *Secrets to Winning at Office Politics*. New York: St. Martin's Griffin.

O'Toole, J., and W. Bennis. 2009. "A Culture of Candor." *Harvard Business Review* (June): 2–8.

Sanders, T. 2006. *The Likeability Factor*. New York: Three Rivers.

Schein, E.H. 1984. "Coming to a New Awareness of Organizational Culture." *Sloan Management Review* (Winter): 3–16.

Schein, E.H. 1995. "The Role of the Founder in Creating Organizational Culture." *Family Business Review* 8 (3): 221–38.

Schon, D.A. 1983. *The Reflective Practitioner*. New York: Basic Books.

Sternberg, R.J., G.B. Forsythe, J. Hedlund, J.A. Horvath, R.K. Wagner, W.M. Williams, S.A. Snook, and E.L. Grigorenko. 2000. *Practical Intelligence in Everyday Life*. Cambridge, UK: Cambridge University Press.

Sternberg, R.J., and J.A. Horvath, eds. 1999. *Tacit Knowledge in Professional Practice*. New York: Routledge.

Todd, S.Y., K.J. Harris, R.B. Harris, and A.R. Wheeler. 2009. "Career Success Implications of Political Skill." *Journal of Social Psychology* 149 (3): 179–204.

Vigoda-Gadot, E., and G. Meister. 2010. "Emotions in Managements and the Management of Emotions: The Impact of Emotional Intelligence and Organizational Politics on Public Sector Employees." *Public Administration Review* (January/February): 72–86.

Wagner, R.K., and R.J. Sternberg. 1987. "Tacit Knowledge in Managerial Success." *Journal of Business and Psychology* 1 (4): 301–12.

Yukl, G., C.M. Falbe, and J.Y. Youn. 1993. "Patterns of Influence Behavior for Managers." *Group and Organization Management* 18 (1): 5–28.

Zettler, I., and J.W.B. Lang. 2013. "Employees' Political Skill and Job Performance: An Inverted U-Shaped Relation?" *Applied Psychology: An International Review* 64 (3): 541–77.

Zivnuska, S., K.M. Kacmar, L.A. Witt, D.S. Carlson, and V.K. Bratton. 2003. "Interactive Effects of Impression Management and Organizational Politics on Job Performance." *Journal of Organizational Behavior* 25: 627–40.

9 CHANGE, INNOVATION, AND ENTREPRENEURSHIP

ALEX

Alex walked down the hall with the other department heads, and the mood was despondent. Though no one spoke, everyone was thinking the same thing. In the two years since the new COO arrived, this would be the fourth new program aimed at improving efficiency in the organization. This did not include the two new revised strategic plans. Once a program was announced, the information conveyed, and a few meetings scheduled, nothing ever happened after that. The chief COO would simply declare that the objectives had been met at a meeting and go on to the next program. In fact, nothing really changed in the departments. What was changing was the level of cynicism regarding these efforts among the frontline staff. And now, the responsible department heads were feeling this same level of cynicism. Not only were the department heads cynical, some were angry, as they were now evaluated annually on their change efforts within their departments. Alex walked along thinking.

When would the weather ever change? Late April is too late for snow.

Do these people really know what they are doing?

It would be nice to be able to declare a success without actually doing it.

I don't know why they think these changes happen overnight.

Don't they know change is hard; I've been trying to lose 15 pounds for 15 years.

My oil needs changing.

I just can't stand up and announce another program.

I can see their eyes rolling now.

This stuff is not like changing socks.

I wonder if I should look for a new job.

I would like to lead one of these efforts for the whole company sometime.

I wonder what the other department heads are thinking.

I can see the flow charts on the wall now outlining everything. What a waste of time.

What is wrong with the old way of doing things?

MENTAL MODELS

In the center of the space below, write the word *change*. Next, write the words that come to mind when you think of this topic. Do not edit your thoughts or collaborate with anyone. There is no right or wrong answer.

If things are related, connect them with an arrow. If the relationship is reciprocal (they both affect each other), put arrows at both ends of the line. If one relationship is stronger than another, make the arrow darker and thicker.

The goal is to capture your mental model of what you believe about change. This is the starting point for the discussion on these topics.

LEARNING OBJECTIVES

- Discuss the concept of organizational life cycle.
- Discuss the process of change in organizations.
- Discuss the process of innovation in organizations.
- Discuss the process and impact of entrepreneurship in organizations.
- Discuss the method and process of creative thinking.
- Discuss the attributes of a department or organization that facilitates and encourages change, innovation, entrepreneurship, or creativity.

ORGANIZATIONAL LIFE CYCLE

As with humans, corporations and organizations have a life. Corporations and organizations go through stages similar to that of a human life. There is inception, growth, development, maturity, decline, and then death. This process is termed a corporate life cycle. For most corporations this life cycle is relatively short. According to the Small Business Administration, by the fifth year 50 percent of corporations fail, and by the tenth year 65 percent fail. For a large corporation, surviving for one hundred years at the top without being acquired, merging, failing, or substantially declining in value is relatively rare. From the Forbes 100 of 1917, only a single corporation, General Electric, survives intact. Consider the fortunes of the twelve original corporations in the Dow Jones Index from 1896.

American Cotton Oil: Ancestor of Best Foods, now part of Unilever

American Sugar: Became Amstar in 1970 and subsequently Domino Foods

American Tobacco: Broke up into separate businesses in 1911, expanded beyond tobacco, and renamed itself American Brands; now Fortune Brands

Chicago Gas: Absorbed by Peoples Gas, which replaced it in the Dow in 1898; now part of Integrys Energy

Distilling & Cattle Feeding: After a series of deals, became National Distillers, then sold liquor assets to Diageo and fellow Dow component progeny American Brands; rest of business now part of Millennium Chemicals

General Electric: Still an independent company with diversified assets around the world; was removed from the Dow twice around the turn of the twentieth century but was reinstated both times

Laclede Gas: Still around as the primary subsidiary of the Laclede Group

National Lead: Changed its name to NL Industries in 1971; 83 percent owned by conglomerate Valhi; once known for mining, moved into paints (Dutch Boy brand), pigments, and coatings; sold paint business in 1970s

North American: Dissolved by a federal court in 1938; surviving successor became Wisconsin Electric, part of Wisconsin Energy

Tennessee Coal Iron and RR: During the panic of 1907, was acquired by U.S. Steel, with banker J.P. Morgan playing a key role in arranging the merger

U.S. Leather: The only preferred stock in the original Dow, is also the only company to have vanished with nary a trace since the trust was dissolved in 1911

United States Rubber: Merged first into Uniroyal in 1950s, then with B.F. Goodrich in 1986; resulting company was bought by France's Michelin in 1990 (Dow Jones Indexes, Sylla, Museum of American Finance). (Schaefer, 2011)

The point is that like humans, even corporations have a hard time surviving for as little as one hundred years. This is not to say that there are not businesses and organizations that thrive for an extended period, even centuries; it is just that it is relatively rare. To survive, an organization has to adapt to the changing forces that impact it. In today's environment those forces include commoditization, globalization, and turbulence and disruption in markets. Culturally, organizations are confronted with the rise of the digital revolution and social media. Politically, the emergence of China and changing immigration patterns are influencing change. And demographically, global aging and the rising impact of millennials are influences. The message to be extracted from this brief review is that in order to survive, organizations must change or risk being made redundant.

CHANGE

Organizations are designed to instill routine, to control, to promote efficiency and predictability, and ultimately to maximize profits. Routinization leads to efficiency. People know what to do and know what is expected. However, as suggested above, an unthinking adherence to the past leads ultimately to being put out of business. Supervisors need to understand the process of change at the individual, departmental, and corporate level.

Unfortunately for many people, change is difficult. People drag their feet, resist, and may even sabotage change. The reasons for this include the following:

- Uncertainty: no one really knows where a change program will end up.
- Loss of control: people no longer feel as if they are in control.
- More work: change may result in more work.
- Relationships: old and established networks are altered.
- Job loss: change may result in losing a job or having an altered job.
- Habit: people get comfortable with certain behaviors.
- Fear: change is scary.

Under the pressure and threat of change, other behaviors and patterns emerge in organizations characterized as a threat-rigidity response. People become self-protective; they revert to old and comfortable behaviors. The cry is for conservatism and getting back to "what made us great" in the first place. Under this pressure, people may take a short-term perspective, have a diminished sense of loyalty to the organization, lose trust, engage in more conflict, decrease levels of teamwork, talk to one another less, get more political, become demoralized, try to overcontrol and centralize, lose a sense of innovation, and scapegoat the leaders responsible for this mess. Under the threat of impending change, less work gets done and more energy is devoted to handicapping the future and its implications for all involved.

The process and mechanics of change in an organization are relatively straightforward and understood. The steps to transforming an organization include the following:

- Create a sense of urgency. People need to understand the necessity and pressure for change.
- Form a guiding coalition. Assemble a team with the requisite power to facilitate this change.
- Create a vision. People need to know where they are going and why.
- Communicate the vision. Get the message out. Teach the new behaviors.
- Empower those who buy in to the change. Get rid of obstacles, change the systems that impede the change, and encourage risk taking.
- Create short-term wins. People need to see progress for their efforts, and the sooner the better.
- Consolidate improvements. Use credibility gained in the effort to effect more change.
- Institutionalize the change. The change now becomes the accepted way of doing business (adapted from Kotter, 1995).

There are two distinct theories or approaches to change. Theory E is change based on economic value. This approach emphasizes economic return and is "hard" in its approach in that it seeks to boost economic returns through economic incentives, drastic layoffs, and restructuring. This approach to change is guided from the top down. Theory O is change based on organizational capability and is softer in its approach. Theory O focuses on changing corporate culture and developing human capability and encourages participation from the bottom up. Effective change involves successfully interweaving and combining both approaches in a symbiotic progression. Being able to do this is no guarantee of success as, Beer and Nohria note: "The brutal fact is that 70% of all change initiatives fail" (as cited in Harvard Business Review Press 2011, 137).

The most difficult task in any change effort is to surmount the cognitive hurdles that individuals hold. It is often difficult to get people to agree on the causes of the current situation and the need for change. An approach to surmounting this cognitive hurdle based on numbers and statistics is generally ineffective. Those from performing departments are likely to dismiss this information as not pertaining to them; while those from underperforming groups will feel put upon and be likely to start to protect themselves and their career. A second, cognitive issue that impedes change involves the competing commitment that individuals hold. A competing commitment is a hidden subconscious goal that conflicts with stated commitments. For example, individuals may openly declare their support for a change initiative while subconsciously resisting this change in order to protect their current relationship with a superior. This competing commitment is anchored to an assumption that if the change is successful and I get promoted, my boss may see me as a rival and no longer support my career progression. Isolating these competing commitments and assumptions requires personal introspection and the testing of assumptions for their usefulness.

If leading change, it is wise to understand that some people will try to slow or stop the change by eliminating the source of the change—you. Recommendations for dealing with this issue include being able to maintain a perspective by moving from the "dance floor to the balcony." It is observing the game and playing it at the same time. Change requires an effort to court the uncommitted, converting adversaries into allies to spread the gospel of change. Continuous pressure in support of the change is necessary up to the limit of overt resistance and conflict. Understand that you cannot do the work of change; it needs to be transferred to the appropriate individuals and departments capable of solving the problem. Avoid the desire to overcontrol the change process and an exaggerated sense of importance by remaining anchored to reality and centeredness. Change management is just a job; and while you might be good at it, lots of people are good at their job.

INNOVATION

Innovation is the process of creating something new that adds value to the corporation by developing new procedures, new products, new services, and new methods. Innovations may be incremental, only slightly advanced, or radical. Radical innovations are defined as those that yield a 30 percent or greater reduction in cost, improve performance features by five times or more, yield an entirely new set of performance features, or completely change the basis of competition. Radical innovations, while completely remaking an industry, also require as much as ten years to produce tangible results. Some innovations are the result of serendipity, a sudden flash of insight by an individual. Most are the result of a purposeful and systematic search for something new. The sources of innovation include the following:

- The unexpected: A chance encounter, a "black swan" once-in-a-lifetime event, an accident in the lab, a new customer with strange requirements, an unanticipated failure, a negative that suddenly becomes a positive. All that is required is the eye to see the potential.

- Incongruities: Something that doesn't make sense; for example, market growth with declining profit or assumptions about cost drivers for an industry and the actual reality.
- Process needs: A deficiency in the method of getting things done coupled with emerging technologies; in other words, adapting a process from one arena to something else.
- Industry and market changes: No industry or market is fixed. There is always change. What was required ten years ago may not be what is working today.
- Demographic changes: Changes in people and their lives and their wants and desires are drivers of innovation.
- Changes in perception: What was once acceptable or unacceptable is no longer considered such.
- New knowledge: New ways of doing things and understanding the world (adapted from Drucker, 2002).

The process of innovation, both at the corporate and the individual level, requires letting go of entrenched ways of thinking and learning to think better. At the heart of effectively thinking about innovation is separating creative thinking from critical thinking. Most supervisors and managers, and Westerners in general, are trained in logical and sequential problem solving along with argumentation and criticism; in other words, evaluative thinking. Will it work, what does it cost, will the market accept it; it is the substance of business case analysis. Innovation requires eliminating criticism, generating as many ideas as possible, and entertaining wild and seemingly foolish proposals. Techniques for generating ideas include wishful thinking, exaggeration, distortion, linking seemingly unrelated words and concepts, asking nonthreateningly the question why, repeatedly. To ask why we do it this way is to challenge the current situation. To question the unexamined assumptions is to challenge the status quo. The idea is to move the thinking along in search of the new and improved.

CREATIVITY

Creativity as a process has been the focus of much research. As a result, certain things are known empirically about creativity, and certain myths can be discounted. First, creativity does not correlate with intelligence. Above the relatively modest IQ of 120, there is no correlation with creativity and intelligence. Second, age is not a predictor of creativity. Creative people have developed an expertise in their field that lets them see patterns that a novice misses. Since it takes about ten years to develop expertise in a field, in this case business, novel solutions are not likely to come from the young. Developed expertise sometimes inhibits creativity in that it becomes difficult to move outside of established patterns of thinking and perception. Third, creativity is not an attribute of only a few people, only those willing to take a risk. In fact, anyone can elevate their creativity. Fourth, some creative people work alone; but many unique and creative solutions are the product of collaboration. Fifth, while creativity can't be managed in the classical sense, a manager can create an environment where creativity is likely to flourish.

It goes without saying that if an organization can hire more creative people, it will get more creative solutions. The organization can also do certain things to enhance creativity. Taking risks has to be acceptable to management. Risks and the attendant mistakes and blind allies are the DNA of creativity. Developing something new can be thought of as reconnaissance of a new territory with only a suspicion of the terrain. Wrong turns are inevitable, but they do eliminate false paths that won't lead anywhere. As long as you don't go down the false path again, it was a piece of information that could not be found any other way. New ideas and suggestions should be encouraged and welcomed. Management's task is to screen those ideas for strategic fit and financial return; but the generation of new ideas should be part of everyday business. Information needs to be shared and accessible and departmental silos breeched. It is impossible to know what information might be adapted for something unanticipated; but if information is never shared, it is guaranteed that nothing new will emerge. People who generate novel solutions need to be rewarded for their contribution through recognition and celebration of their contribution, as well as providing the resources to pursue the idea. Finally, the physical space at work can, by its configuration and decor, encourage and convey that openness, sharing, and uniqueness are honored and ingrained in the culture.

ENTREPRENEURSHIP

Entrepreneurs are the people, and entrepreneurship is the process by which innovations are turned from aspirations to concrete reality. At the heart of entrepreneurship is the ability to recognize and act on opportunities. Corporate entrepreneurship is entrepreneurial activity embedded in a corporation and is termed intrapreneurship. It requires using fundamental management skills to challenge a bureaucracy more interested in consistency than change. Corporate entrepreneurs can mobilize resources and people within the corporation in pursuit of new products, services, or processes.

While there is no entrepreneurial personality, there are certain traits, attitudes, and abilities common to most entrepreneurs, including the following:

- Success orientation: a desire to exceed themselves as they take on greater challenges
- Opportunity and goal orientation: the ability to "sense" an opportunity
- Action orientation: the desire to produce results
- Need to achieve: a personal desire to accomplish
- Self-reliance and self-confidence: a belief in their ability
- Tolerance for ambiguity and uncertainty: thriving on fluid and ill-defined situations
- Moderate risk taking: a willingness to take measurable and predetermined risk

- Tolerance for failure: failure is a chance to learn
- Positive attitude: a belief things will work out
- Persistence: a willingness to keep at it
- High energy and stamina: good health

Many variables go into a successful entrepreneurial venture, such as the right economic circumstances, social networks, team composition, marketing, and finance. "But none of these will, alone, create a new venture. For that we need a person, in whose mind all the possibilities come together, who believes innovation is possible, and who has the motivation to persist until the job is done" (McFadzean, O'Laughlin, and Shaw 2005, 364).

FAILURE

At the personal, supervisory level, the key to change, innovation, and entrepreneurship is a tolerance for failure. Not just any haphazard, careless failure, but an effort that is deliberate, thought out, and will yield information that can be gained in no other way. The first type of failure is not acceptable; the second is to be encouraged. Supervisors and leaders need to accept that failure is an inevitable consequence of any human activity and take both the negative (failures) and the positive (success) in stride. They have a perspective on the process. This assumes that the failure is not life threatening nor will it bring significant hardships. At the heart of the American economy is the idea of competition, of winners and losers. To avoid losing, people withhold information, sabotage, and politic. It is collaboration, not competition, that impacts innovation. Supervisors who send a message that constructive failures are not only acceptable but encouraged—in fact, required—will get the change, innovation, and entrepreneurial spirit that ensures the longevity and viability of the organization.

SUMMARY

Corporations have a life, just as human do. For both, surviving one hundred years is rare. An organizations' life can be extended by changing, innovating, and bringing new products, services, and processes to the market. As a supervisor the task is to understand change at the departmental level and the larger context of change within the organization. A tolerance for failure is a significant contributor to facilitating change.

EXERCISES

Summarizing

Write a one-page executive summary of the chapter.

Discuss with your classmates how you would teach this material.

Write a two-page case from your experience on this topic that would be instructional for other students.

What's Important to You in the Chapter?

With several of your classmates, discuss the most important ideas from the chapter. Which ideas do you think will be most useful to you in your career? Which ideas do you think you will remember in six months?

What Do the Practitioners/Others Say?

Discuss with your colleagues or someone at work any of the ideas in the chapter. Alternatively, read an article from any source on change and be prepared to summarize its message.

Change

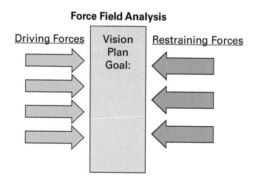

Force Field Analysis

Force field analysis is a method for understanding the forces that drive change as well as thoughts that are restraining change. For some issue about yourself that you have been trying to change, construct a force field analysis of those forces. In addition, rank the magnitude of the forces from 1 to 5 (5 being the strongest and 1 the weakest). If the summed magnitude of the forces for change are greater than those restraining it, the presumption is that the change ought to be possible. This technique can be applied to organizational change as well.

Innovation

Within your industry, research a new product, service, or process as to how it happened, what caused it, who made it happen, and any pitfalls and setbacks on the way. Prepare a one-page summary of the innovation. Do you have of the characteristics of the person who spearheaded the change?

Entrepreneurship

Research the life of a well-known entrepreneur and prepare a one-page summary of his or her life and experiences. What set this person apart from other people? Do you have any of the traits of this entrepreneur?

Creativity

Research the life of someone you admire for his or her creativity. Prepare a one-page summary of this person's life and experiences. What set him or her apart from other people? Do you have any of the traits of this person?

What Exactly Is a Failure?

Check which of these you think is a failure. Discuss your conclusions with a classmate.

You are the world record holder in the marathon; you break your record but come in second. _____

You are the world record holder in the marathon; you win the race but do not break your record. _____

You complete your first marathon, have to walk across the finish line, but finish last in your age group. _____

You are seventy-five years old and finish the marathon, but an eighty-year-old beats you across the line. _____

You are ninety years old and come to the race to pass out water to the runners after they have run the first six miles. _____

You finish the race but are immediately taken to the hospital with chest pains you have been experiencing for the last five miles. _____

REFERENCES AND WORKS CONSULTED

De Bono, E. 1970. *Lateral Thinking*. New York: Harper Perennial.

Drucker, P.F. 2002. "The Discipline of Innovation." *Harvard Business Review* (August): 95–103.

Farson, R., and R. Keyes. 2002. "The Failure-Tolerant Leader." *Harvard Business Review* (August): 65–71.

Foster, R., and S. Kaplan. 2001. *Creative Destruction*. New York: Currency.

Furr, N., and J.H. Dyer. 2014. "Leading Your Team into the Unknown." *Harvard Business Review* (December): 80–88.

Grant, A. 2016. *Originals*. New York: Viking.

Harvard Business Review Press. 2003. *Managing Creativity and Innovation*. Boston: Harvard Business Review Press.

Harvard Business Review Press. 2011. *On Change Management*. Boston: Harvard Business Review Press.

Hurson, T. 2008. *Think Better*. New York: McGraw Hill.

Kanter, R.M. 2003. "Leadership and the Psychology of Turnaround." *Harvard Business Review* (June): 3–11.

Kanter, R.M. 2012. "Ten Reasons People Resist Change." *Harvard Business Review*. hbr.org/2012/09/ten-reasons-people-resist-chang

Kotter, J.P. 1995. *Leading Change: Why Transformation Efforts Fail*. Boston: Harvard Business Review Press.

Krueger, N.F., Jr. 2003. "The Cognitive Psychology of Entrepreneurship." In *Handbook of Entrepreneurship Research*, edited by Z.J. Acs and D.B. Audretsch, 105–140. New York: Springer Science + Business Media, Inc.

McFadzean, E., A. O'Laughlin, and E. Shaw. 2005. "Corporate Entrepreneurship and Innovation, Part 1: The Missing Link." *European Journal of Innovation Management* 8 (3): 350–72.

Pascale, R.T., and J. Sternin. 2005. "Your Company's Secret Change Agents." *Harvard Business Review* (May): 1–10.

Pryor, C., J.W. Webb, R.D. Ireland, and D.J. Ketchen Jr. 2015. "Toward an Integration of the Behavioral and Cognitive Influences on the Entrepreneurial Process." *Strategic Entrepreneurship Journal*. DOK:10.1002/sej.1204.

Schaefer, S. 2011. The First 12 Dow Components: Where Are They Now? https://www.forbes.com/sites/steveschaefer/2011/07/15/the-first-12-dow-components-where-are-they-now/#69fdf48bb032. July 15, 11:44AM.1

Shaw, E., A. O'Laughlin, and E. McFadzean. 2005. "Corporate Entrepreneurship and Innovation, Part 2: A Role- and Process-Based Approach." *European Journal of Innovation Management* 8 (4): 393–408.

Staw, B.M., L.E. Sandelands, and J.E. Dutton. 1981. "Threat Rigidity Effects in Organizational Behavior: A Multilevel Analysis." *Administrative Science Quarterly* 26 (4): 501–24.

Strebel, P. 1996. "Why Do Employees Resist Change?" *Harvard Business Review* (May–June): 86–92.

SECTION III
ORGANIZATIONAL ISSUES

Best Ideas

Best ideas are defined as those ideas from the chapters in this section that you believe will be the most influential in your practice and that you will retain over time. Take a few moments to compile your ten best ideas. Consider these as the residue of the effort and time put into these readings and discussion. In other words, what did you learn?

IDEA ONE

IDEA TWO

IDEA THREE

IDEA FOUR

IDEA FIVE

IDEA SIX

IDEA SEVEN

IDEA EIGHT

IDEA NINE

IDEA TEN

SECTION IV
THINGS TO BE MANAGED

The first section laid the intellectual framework for the book. The second section discussed supervising people. The third section focused on organizational issues. This section considers things to be managed, including money, marketing, operations, quality, and law and ethics.

Chapter 10: Money, Accounting, Finance, Planning, and Budgeting

This chapter is about measuring performance. Specifically, it is about describing the standard metrics for measuring financial performance. The three standard financial statements—income statements, balance sheets, and statement of cash flows—are presented, along with the most often employed financial ratios.

Chapter 11: Marketing and Customer Service

The chapter gives an overview of the basic elements of marketing. It also discusses the issues related to service marketing. The link between effective supervision and customer service is described.

Chapter 12: Operations and Quality and Inventory

This chapter discusses the relationship between operations and performance and also looks at analytics as a tool, technology and its influence, and inventory and supply chain management.

Chapter 13: Law, Ethics, and Stakeholders

Chapter 13 provides a framework for ethical decision making and discusses stakeholder theory and corporate social responsibility. It also discusses employment law.

10 MONEY, ACCOUNTING, FINANCE, PLANNING, AND BUDGETING

ALEX

Alex wanted to honor the staff requests for additional training. Many wanted to study for Board Certified Pharmacotherapy Specialist (BCPS) certification. Others wanted support for other specialty certifications. While the financials had been stable recently, due to reduced reimbursements, gross margins and net contributions to the facility were declining. Also, costs per transaction and per staff hours and salary were creeping up. And some of the first-generation automation that had been installed was reaching the end of its service life. The newer equipment promised at least a 10 percent reduction in processing costs. All Alex had to do was find the money. He looked over the proposed budget for next year and shook his head.

It always comes down to money.

Finally, my student loans are paid off.

How big a hit do the insurance companies think we can take without reducing quality and service?

It's getting easier and cheaper to hire pharmacists.

Training versus automation.

Machines are easier; they always come on time and don't have any personal issues.

I really should get my BCPS. Some of the staff even want time during the day to study.

I need to get my taxes done.

What if we made it one more year with the old equipment?

Let's run the numbers and see what happens.

PRETEST[1]

1. Numbers on accounting statements are precise representations of what is going on in the business.

   True   False

2. If my accounting statement shows a profit, then I have cash in the bank.

   True   False

3. It is possible for a business to have different levels of profit on the books in the same year.

   True   False

4. If profit as a percentage decreases, it is bad for the business.

   True   False

5. Each company can present its books in a way that is most suitable to the company.

   True   False

6. Transactions get recorded in the books when cash changes hands in the accrual system.

   True   False

MENTAL MODELS

In the center of the space below, write the word *money*. Next, write the words that come to mind when you think of this topic. Do not edit your thoughts or collaborate with anyone. There is no right or wrong answer.

---

1   1: false; 2: false; 3: true; 4: false; 5: false; 6: false

If things are related, connect them with an arrow. If the relationship is reciprocal (they both affect each other), put arrows at both ends of the line. If one relationship is stronger than another, make the arrow darker and thicker.

The goal is to capture your mental model of what you believe about money. This is the starting point for the discussion on money, its accounting for, and uses.

LEARNING OBJECTIVES

- Describe the components and use of income statements, balance sheets, and statement of cash flow.
- Discuss the link between profit and cash.
- Discuss the use of financial ratios and list the most commonly used financial ratios.
- Discuss the use of budgeting.
- Reproduce the equations for the income statement and balance sheet.

TERMS TO KNOW

asset: An economic resource that can be used to produce value.

balance sheet: A statement of financial conditions at a point in time reflecting assets, liabilities, and owner's equity.

cost of goods sold (COGS) and **cost of services (COS):** An expense that captures all the costs associated with delivering a product or service.

equity: The owner's share or stake in the company.

gross profit: Sales minus cost of goods sold or cost of services. It is what is left over to cover operating expenses.

income statement: A financial statement that measures performance over a given period of time.

liability: A financial obligation to be paid.

liquidity: The ability to pay the bills in the short term.

net profit, net income: The bottom line. What's left after all the costs have been paid.

operating expenses: Costs not directly related to producing and delivering the product or service.

ratio: Quantified measure of the business's status and performance.

sales: Dollar value of all goods and services provided during a given period of time.

solvency: The ability to pay the long-term financial obligations.

statement of cash flow: Records the inflow and outflow of cash over a period of time.

variance: Deviation from a standard.

METRICS AND PERFORMANCE MEASUREMENT

In many of the professions, the idea that practice should be based on evidence and empiricism rather than intuition, precedent, and tradition is accepted. This is not the case for management. It is hard to find validated and useful evidence that informs management. Much of what passes for "good" management is unverified; it is opinion. Age confers wisdom, or so it is believed. "Experts" from other fields are given a listen, as if success in coaching twelve to fifteen multimillionaire professional athletes is the same as managing minimum-wage employees at a fast-food restaurant. Popular books on management neglect to discuss the limitations of their insights as a research article would. Though validated evidence regarding management is limited, computers can generate massive amounts of data that, if understood and utilized correctly, can inform management.

This chapter on accounting and finance introduces the most basic of financial metrics on managing a business. The most cited metrics to explain value creation for a business are sales, costs, and investments. The metrics presented here are time honored and are the informational currency for all businesses. They are the language of business. Understanding them, and what they convey, is a necessary condition for effective management. A caution is warranted. Being able to quote, for example, the net profit for the business is one thing; getting it to move in the right direction, understanding cause and effect, is quite another.

Certain cautions regarding measuring performance are worth reviewing:

- Measuring performance only against yourself is convenient and customary, but this bypasses the information of a comparison to competitors within the industry.
- Most performance measures compare performance to the past. Beating last year is not the point. Effective performance measures should be instructive for future decision.
- Metrics can be gamed or be of low quality. If a specific metric determines performance bonuses, rest assured some will find ways to manipulate those numbers. The solution is a triangulated approach to metrics where multiple measures are utilized. Though they may be gamed, it will be more difficult.
- The appropriate performance metrics for a business change over time. What's important to a start-up is not the same as what is important to a mature industry leader. Sticking with the wrong metric too long gives a false sense of security. Devising appropriate, useful, persistent, and predictive metrics for frontline supervisors is difficult. It is at the front line of operations where the conflict over the demands to deliver profit, or customer satisfaction, or sales growth, or any other corporate objective plays out. Getting the right metrics, and getting them to move in the right direction, is not easy, but effective supervision and management is never easy.

MORAL ENTERPRISES, NONPROFIT, AND PROFESSIONS

Many professions are moral enterprises aimed at the public good. Education and health care meet this definition. Architecture and design take on aspects of moral enterprise if the impact on the environment and use of resources is factored in. Acknowledging that professionals have an obligation to act altruistically, for the benefit of the client or patient, without regard for personal financial gain, also reflects this perspective.

There are two viewpoints regarding the purpose of a business; one is an exclusive focus on a business generating financial returns to increase shareholder (owners of the company) value. An alternative view includes increasing shareholder value but also recognizes the contributions of other stakeholders to the business (employees, suppliers, customers, government, and so on). A triple bottom line approach to accounting for nonprofits, businesses, and government incorporates three dimensions of performance: financial, economic, and environmental.

As a practical matter, even moral enterprises have to cover their expenses, pay their employees, and save to invest in the future. They may not need to generate a profit in the strict sense of the word, but they must have sufficient cash to operate. Even if a business subscribes to a stakeholder perspective or adopts a triple bottom line approach to accounting, the requirement to generate financial returns remains. In short, moral enterprises and socially conscious businesses and organizations still operate in an environment that mandates financial solvency and responsibility. A physician's practice in an underserved area or a language school for immigrant children is still a business. Thus, those charged with supervising businesses, moral enterprises, and nonprofit operations require certain minimal financial acuity. This requires understanding and utilizing certain metrics, primarily financial indicators grounded in accounting convention.

ACCOUNTING: RULES AND CONVENTIONS

Accounting is the language of business. It is a language mostly expressed in numbers. Just as words have definitions and languages have grammar and syntax, allowing everyone to understand one another, accounting has rules and conventions that allow everyone to understand one another—mostly. There are powerful financial and economic incentives for companies to present their financial status in the most favorable light. Individual bonuses and personal fortunes can be made or lost based on financial reports. To minimize this temptation, the compiling and presenting of financial and accounting information is governed by Generally Accepted Accounting Principles (GAAP). These rules set the standards and establish governing precedents and principles. Other controlling entities include the Financial Accounting Standards Board (FASB), Accounting Standards Codification (ASC), and for international concerns, the International Accounting Standards Board (IASB).

The following concepts are the guiding policies that underlie all accounting reporting:

- **The entity:** Accounting reports focus on a specific entity, from a single small grocery to a multibillion dollar conglomerate.
- **Cash vs. accrual:** Cash accounting is based on the idea that transactions are only recorded when actual cash changes hands. Accrual accounting records the transaction when an activity takes, place rather than when the cash changes hands. For example, wages become an expense when someone actually works, even though the person is not paid until the end of the month.
- **Objectivity:** There must be verifiable evidence to support an accounting transaction. A utility bill is objective; the good feeling a customer has after an interaction is not.
- **Conservatism:** When in doubt, be conservative in recording measurable and verifiable properties, debts, sales, and costs. Conservatism also mandates that transactions be recorded at their historical costs.
- **Going concern:** This recognizes that the value assigned to items is that of an operating, going concern at historical costs, not, for example, at fire sale valuations.
- **Consistency:** Consistency demands that the entity use the same rules year after year. In this way historical comparisons can be made.

- **Materiality:** Financial statements are not exact to the penny. They are materially correct and convey a fairly stated view of the firm. Nobody knows to the exact penny exactly how much inventory Walmart owns, for example.

Taken together, the GAAP rules and the conventions detailed above provide assurances that the financial statements produced by any single entity are accurate and can be utilized to compare one financial entity with another. There are also conventions as to how accounting statements are prepared involving double-entry bookkeeping conventions. This involves the posting of entries to various journals, the tabulation and reconciliation of those entries, the closing of those journals, and a final compilation of those summarized journals into the specific accounting statement. As a supervisor, understanding this methodology and the nuances associated with it is not required. Think of a computer; in order to operate it, it is not required to understand the "backroom" movement of electrons around silicon wafers. The same holds true for accounting. It is understanding the information provided in the compiled statements that is important.

ACCOUNTING STATEMENTS

The Income Statement

There are three accounting statements that are routinely used and referred to: the income statement, the balance sheet, and the cash flow statement. At the supervisory level, the income statement is the most common. Income statements convey whether a department has been profitable for a given period of time. At its most basic level, did the department generate revenues (sales) in excess of the expenses required to generate those revenues? If revenues exceeded expenses, the department generated a profit; if expenses exceeded revenues, the department operated at a loss. Income statements are compiled for a specific period of time, most often for a month, quarter, or year. Income statements are presented based on a standard convention. See below.

1. All revenue and income is tabulated and listed on the first line, or lines if there are multiple sources of income.
2. Next expenses are separated into categories and tabulated; for example, salaries, rent, and utilities. If the business involves inventory, an expense termed *cost of goods sold* is included. Cost of goods sold is the dollar value of all inventory used to generate sales.
3. Total expenses are subtracted from revenues, yielding in this case $10,000.00 of operating profit. Next taxes and interest are subtracted yielding $5,000.00 in net profit. Sometimes profit is referred to as net profit or net income. Losses are generally presented in parentheses.

Income Statement: Jan. 1, 2015 to Dec. 31, 2015

INCOME	$100,000.00
EXPENSES	
Cost of goods sold	$60,000.00
GROSS PROFIT	$40,000.00
EXPENSES	
Salaries	$10,000.00
Utilities	$10,000.00
Rent	$10,000.00
TOTAL EXPENSES	$90,000.00
OPERATING PROFIT	$10,000.00
Taxes, Interest	$5,000.00
NET PROFIT	$5,000.00

The statement of income is based on the simple accounting equation:
Income = Revenue – Expenses

This formula holds from the smallest business to the largest corporation.

Balance Sheet

The balance sheet is derived from the following equation:

Assets = Liabilities + Owner's Equity

Think of the equation from this perspective. If I buy a house for $250,000 cash, I have an asset worth $250,000. However, if I put $50,000 down and borrow the other $200,000, I still have an asset worth $250,000 but have a liability of $200,000 in the mortgage that I owe, and my equity in the property, the part that I own, is $50,000. Thus, the equation would be filled in as $250,000 (Assets) = $200,000 (Liability) + $50,000 (Owner's Equity). For a business a balance sheet is a snapshot of what a business actually *owns* and what it *owes* at any particular time. Thus, what a company owns is its *assets*, what is owes is termed its *liabilities*, and what it is actually worth is termed its *owner's equity*.

As the income statement has a convention regarding its presentation, so does the balance sheet. The left side of the balance sheet lists the assets. The right side of the balance sheet contains the liabilities and owner's equity. On the left side the assets are divided into the current assets and the fixed assets. Current assets are cash or those items that can be converted to cash in the short term, within the next twelve months. Near cash items include savings accounts, bank certificates, money market accounts, and other short-term investments. The important thing is that they can be converted to cash almost immediately. Other items under current assets include accounts receivable—money that is owed to the business in the short term, inventory—that will be converted to cash within the short term. These items are summed and reported as total current assets. Next on the balance sheet is the fixed assets. These assets are not held for sale and are used over an extended period of time and include items such as land, buildings, equipment, computers, trucks, and so on. Generally, they can't easily be converted to cash. A general catch-all category of other assets is listed. Once current assets, fixed assets, and other assets are summed, the total assets of the business are reported. Next, on the right side of the balance sheet, the current liabilities are reported. Current liabilities include money payable in the next year and capture items termed accounts payable, accrued payroll, income taxes payable, and short-term notes payable. Below current liabilities, long-term liabilities are listed and include money required to be paid back over an extended period; in other words, any monies that will be paid back over time. Current liabilities and long-term liabilities are subtracted from current assets and fixed assets, giving value for owner's equity or the portion of the business actually owned. Owner's equity and total liabilities must equal or balance with total assets, just as in the opening example regarding the house.

Balance Sheet

ASSETS

Current Assets

Cash and equivalents	$10,000
Accounts receivable	$5,000
Inventory	$5,000
Total Current Assets	$20,000

Fixed Assets

Building	$10,000
Computers	$5,000
Total Fixed Assets	$15,000

Other Assets

Long-term investments	$5,000
TOTAL ASSETS	$40,000

LIABILITIES

Current Liabilities

Accounts payable	$5,000
Accrued payroll	$5,000
Total Current Liabilities	$10,000

Long-Term Liabilities

Long-term debt	$10,000
Total Liabilities	$20,000
Owner's Equity	$20,000
TOTAL LIABILITIES AND EQUITY	$40,000

Statement of Cash Flow

The statement of cash flow, as the name implies, reports the source and amount of cash coming into the business and the uses and amount of cash exiting the business. The statement of cash flow reports cash inflows and cash outflows. There are three categories of inflows and outflows reported in this document.

- **Cash from or used in operations:** This is cash generated or used by the actual operation of the department or business and is exemplified by cash in when customers pay their bills or cash out when employees are paid. Cash from operations is the most important metric in indicating the health of a business.
- **Cash from or used for investing activities:** This is cash from or used for the buying or selling of any company asset. For example, cash may be used to buy a new computer, or cash may be generated by selling a company-owned building.
- **Cash from or used in financing activities:** This is cash generated from borrowing or cash used to pay back borrowed money. For example, cash is generated from a loan or additional equity from a new shareholder, or cash is used to pay off a loan, buy back stock, or pay dividends to shareholders.

A telling metric for a corporation as a whole is free cash flow. Free cash flow is cash available from operations less any expenditures for capital investments (property, plants, and equipment). The value in this metric from an outsider's perspective is that it is devoid of the assumptions and estimates of the income statement, and cash balances are easily audited. In other words, free cash flow is difficult to manipulate. Free cash flow gives a company the option to make investments in new operations, new businesses, and new plants or pay down liabilities without the constraint of dealing with outside lenders or investments. In short, cash is king.

PROFIT DOES NOT EQUAL CASH

Income statements reveal that there are several forms of profit, as follows:

- Gross profit is revenues minus the cost of goods sold. It is revenues taken in minus the expense associated with delivering the product or service. In the retail industry it is the cost of inventory. It is the amount available to the business to pay all its other expenses.
- Operating profit is the gross profit less the operating expenses. It is the profit left after subtracting the expenses required to run the business.
- Net profit is the bottom line of the income statement and is what is left after all costs and expenses have been subtracted. It is operating profit less interest expenses, taxes, any one-time charges, or anything else not included in operating profit.

It is easy to make the assumption that if there is profit on the books then there will be cash in the bank. This is not necessarily the case, due to the discrepancy in booking revenues and expenses from actually collecting those revenues or paying those expenses. In accrual accounting revenues are matched with the expenses required to generate those sales. If I ship an order today, I may not get paid until some later date. I now have revenues on the books without the associated payment being collected. Any expenses used to generate the order are booked now during the accounting time period. Expenses paid in this month may in fact be for orders shipped the previous month. Reported profit and cash in and out move in asynchronous waves; hence, profit does not equal cash.

Lack of cash even though there is profit on the books is due to the following reasons:

- Cash can be used to pay down the bills. As an individual if you run a balance on your charge cards and pay more than your customary payment, you are obviously diminishing your personal bank account. For a business you are paying down your accounts payable.
- Payments may be delayed from customers. If significant customers have a financial crisis, they may not be able to pay their bill on time; in this case accounts receivable have increased.

- Cash could be used to buy things such as inventory, computers, training sessions, and so on.
- Theft or embezzlement will obviously diminish cash.

RATIOS

Having an understanding of income statements, balance sheets, and statement of cash flow is a good beginning to financial literacy. However, more is required to make sense of them and to make them useful tools in the management of a department or organization. The metrics that make these statements useful are financial ratios. Ratios can be made of any two numbers from any of the accounting statements. A Major League batting average is a ratio. Ratios allow a company to compare performance over time, to an industry average, to other competitors, or to what was projected. Without these anchors it is hard to know if $10 million is an acceptable profit for a company.

Certain types of ratios and certain specific ratios are typically used by most businesses. The typical categories of financial ratios are as follows.

Profitability Ratios
These ratios convey whether a company or department has the ability to generate profits.

$$\text{Gross margin}\ \% \ = \ \frac{\text{gross profit (\$)}}{\text{revenue (\$)}} \ = \ \frac{\$40,000.00}{\$100,000.00} \ = \ 40\%$$

$$\text{Operating profit}\ \% \ = \ \frac{\text{operating profit (\$)}}{\text{revenue (\$)}} \ = \ \frac{\$10,000.00}{\$100,000.00} \ = \ 10\%$$

$$\text{Net profit}\ \% \ = \ \frac{\text{net profit (\$)}}{\text{revenue (\$)}} \ = \ \frac{\$5,000.00}{\$100000.00} \ = \ 5\%$$

$$\text{Return on assets} \ = \ \frac{\text{net profit (\$)}}{\text{total assets (\$)}} \ = \ \frac{\$5,000.00}{\$40,000.00} \ = \ 12.5\%$$

$$\text{Return on equity} \ = \ \frac{\text{net profit (\$)}}{\text{equity (\$)}} \ = \ \frac{\$5,000.00}{\$20,000.00} \ = \ 25\%$$

Liquidity Ratios
Liquidity ratios indicate whether a company has sufficient liquid resources (cash or near cash) to pay its bills in the short term.

$$\text{Current ratio} \quad = \quad \frac{\text{current assets (\$)}}{\text{current liabilities (\$)}} = \frac{\$20,000.00}{\$10,000.00} \quad = \quad 2.0$$

$$\text{Quick ratio} \quad = \quad \frac{\text{current assets (\$)} - \text{inventory (\$)}}{\text{current liabilities (\$)}} = \frac{\$20,000.00 - \$5,000.00}{\$10,000.00} \quad = \quad 1.5$$

Solvency Ratios

Solvency ratios measure how much debt a company uses to finance its operations. They are a measure of the long-term viability of the company.

$$\text{Debt to equity} \quad = \quad \frac{\text{total liabilities (\$)}}{\text{owner's equity (\$)}} \quad = \quad \frac{\$20,000.00}{\$20,000.00} \quad = \quad 1.0$$

Efficiency Ratios

Efficiency ratios indicate how efficiently a company uses its assets to generate income. Efficiency ratios are often unique to specific departments or organizations dependent on the specifics of their product or service and operations.

$$\text{Inventory turnover} \quad = \quad \frac{\text{annual cost of goods sold (\$)}}{\text{average inventory (\$)}} = \frac{\$60,000.00}{\$5,000.00} = \quad 12.0$$

$$\text{Average collection period} \quad = \quad \frac{\text{ending accounts receivable (\$)}}{\text{revenue/day (\$)}}$$

The manager's task is to manage in such a way as to move the ratios in a desired direction. It is generally desirable for net profit as a percentage to be increasing. Any trend in the ratios must be viewed in light of the strategic objectives of the firm and common sense. If a business has made a strategic choice to trade profit margin for market share, the appropriate trend for net profit may be down. In other words, is a retailer prepared to lower profit margin to sell more items across a larger market? If this is the case, the expected trend for profit margin percentage is down, with the recognition that total dollars of net profit will increase. A 3 percent profit on $100 million in sales is better than 10 percent profit on $1 million. Similar logic will hold for any financial ratio. The context for the business needs to be understood before the movement in a financial ratio can be judged as positive or negative.

BUDGETING

A budget is a planning and analysis document. It allows a manager to predict and control. It is based on an estimate of revenues for the next period. From this estimate, the expenses required for their support are estimated. There are two types of budgets: an operating budget and a capital budget. Supervisors are most typically involved with developing an operating budget and monitoring performance relative to the budget. Budgets are ubiquitous across all departments. The budgeting process is where priorities are established and organizational politics play out. There will be winners and losers in this process, in that certain departments will get more of their budget requests funded.

The key assumption in the budgeting process is the estimate of revenues. Forecasts and predictions with any degree of certainty are difficult. A prudent manager will develop two or three versions of a budget ranging from the most optimistic scenarios to the most negative. The value in this approach is that surprises are minimized. Nevertheless, one budget will be required to be adopted and will become the standard against which performance will be measured. The budgeting process is valuable in that it helps create cost awareness, productivity, and profitability; it can be measured; it can produce cost savings, reduce waste, minimize operational surprises, provide an organization-wide standard for evaluation—conformance to budget—and motivate employees.

A capital expenditure budget forces management to anticipate the monies that will be required to fund future capital acquisitions. For example, if a plant is becoming obsolete, a capital budget will help determine how much will be required for a new plant and how it will it be paid for or financed.

For either budget a supervisor's primary role is to deal with variance from the projections. In other words, what should happen if an item on the budget is over or under the budgeted amount? A key aspect of this issue is to determine why it occurred. Was the variance due to less-than-effective internal management or was it due to extraneous events beyond anyone's control? When the economy collapsed in 2008, all budget predictions went out the window. Only the completely prescient could have predicted this circumstance; for everyone else the task was to make the appropriate adjustments. Having determined the why of the variance, the next and most difficult issue is to determine what to do. The answer varies by circumstances, department, and organization and is the essence of what a supervisor's job is about. Finally, a variance in the budget and the response contains powerful information about developing the next year's budget.

The power in the budgeting process is that it forces a supervisor to think in a strategic and disciplined manner about the future. Though the budget estimates may be off, they are better than running a department or organization by "the seat of the pants." With time, and given management that is professional in its orientation, it should gradually produce more finely grained and thus more useful budgets and response to variances.

INCREASING PROFIT

Profits for a business are increased by (1) increasing sales, (2) raising prices on the same level of sales, or (3) reducing expenses on the same level of sales. Each choice has its risk. Increasing sales usually requires inducements or expenses of some kind. The amount of the increased sales must offset the costs incurred to gain them, and more. Raising prices has the greatest impact on profit. In the long term raising prices may limit sales and growth. Reducing expenses usually requires eliminating something and may result in diminished service levels. In the long term sales and growth may suffer.

THINK LIKE AN OWNER

A business is a moneymaking operation. There is no reason to apologize for it. It is a professional obligation to make money. Understanding whether a business is making money or not is relatively simple. That information is conveyed in the following metrics:

- **Sales growth:** Increased revenues are a healthy indicator as long as they are profitable and sustainable. Growth for its own sake is not an objective.
- **Cash generation:** Cash is a business's lifeblood. Cash is required to continue to operate. Companies extend and receive credit. Balancing the relationship between accounts receivable (what is owed us) and accounts payable (what we owe) is the determinant for cash balances.
- **Return on assets:** Assets represent the value of the monies invested in the business. Return on assets (ROA) is the ratio of net profit from the income statement to assets from the balance sheet. Obviously, the higher the ROA, the better the business does. And fewer assets used to generate that return signals superior performance and more efficient operations.

Most supervisors only see income statements for their departments. They operate in a silo. With only this perspective, it is difficult to see how the decisions they make impact the company as a whole. A broader perspective for a supervisor, a perspective of an owner, improves operations. For example, missing budgeted salary expenses for a single store by 1 percent may not be significant; realizing that if it happens for all six thousand stores, the cash drain will be significant and result in layoffs and diminished service. Such a business-wide perspective by all supervisors reinforces the idea of their obligation to deliver results and sharpens their focus.

CAUTIONS ABOUT FINANCIAL STATEMENTS

Financial statements convey only part of the reality of a department or a business. They are not precise, as they are built on assumptions and estimates. No one knows to the penny at any given time what the true value of inventory is for a business; there is a good idea, but not a precise figure. Financial statements vary in the methods that accountants construct them. Within the guidelines there is latitude on what is permissible. More than that, financial statements are subject to outright manipulation and fraud. Supervisors and managers are tempted to shade financial statements to present themselves in the best light or to hide theft and embezzlement.

Financial statements do not capture or present that state of a business's nonfinancial health. Financial statements do not pick up significant deficiencies in security and safety or in any if the systems that a business operates that have the potential to impact the business. Nor do financial statements reflect what customers are thinking or whether they are satisfied, only buy once, or are starting to shift their loyalties to other choices. Finally, financial statements do not reveal what competitors are doing or planning that may diminish the business. Or which little-noticed competitor is about to rewrite the rules of competition for the industry. Financial statements are essentially backward-looking documents; they are valuable, but they have their limitations. The true picture of a business is only possible if taken from multiple perspectives. Even this is limited. Some aspects of the business can only be felt, as businesses are living, breathing entities. Some aspects of the business can only be understood by "walking around," by being there.

SUMMARY

This chapter presented the basic metrics of accounting and the three most common financial statements, along with the idea of financial ratios. It also discussed the relationship between profit and cash. Budgeting and the basics of money were also considered.

EXERCISES

Summarizing
Write a one-page executive summary of the chapter.
Discuss with your classmates how you would teach this material.
Write a two-page case from your experience on this topic that would be instructional for other students.

Develop a mental model for this chapter based on the mind mapping technique.

What's Important to You in the Chapter?
With several of your classmates, discuss the most important ideas from the chapter. Which ideas do you think will be most useful to you in your career? Which ideas do you think you will remember in six months?

What Do the Practitioners/Others Say?
Discuss with your colleagues or someone at work any of the ideas in the chapter. Alternatively, read an article from any source on accounting and finance and be prepared to summarize its message.

Professionalism and Money
Chapter 2 presented a content and process model of professionalism and the following matrix combining both aspects of this conceptualization. Utilize this matrix to deal with the following case that links judgment and accountability.

Content/Process	Sensitivity	Motivation	Judgment	Action
Accountability			XXX	
Altruism				
Duty				
Honor				
Integrity				
Excellence				
Respect for others				

Your department has had a great year. Every metric (on-time delivery, quality, and customer service) for your department has improved over the past year and exceeded projections. The financial reports for the first three quarters were just barely meeting goals. It was your belief that the final quarter would come in strong and easily raise your financial results above goal. As the initial financial results for the final quarter were delivered to your office, you were stunned. They were close, but your department did not meet your goals. As you glanced at the financials, it was clear that revenues had declined in the last six weeks of the quarter, overtime had increased due to hiring temps to cover unexpected sickness for two key staff, pro-bono work was more than you had allowed for, and there was a charge back to the department from a lawsuit from an incident four years ago that had finally settled. You knew you had to go to the executive meeting, with all the other department heads, to discuss and justify last year's performance.

Any metric, financial or operational, is an objective measure of the supervisor's performance; it is a measure of excellence. Though it is not likely that financial and operational excellence can be achieved without being technically or clinically excellent, the financial metrics do not explicitly capture this dimension. If supervisors aspire to be a professional in this aspect of their job, to aspire to excellence, then they have to confront that they failed to meet the standard. For supervisors, it is not a defense to say that we operated at the highest level of quality. Supervisors' task, their professional obligation, is to win, to deliver all the metrics while meeting financial projections. For a basketball coach, it is not a defense to say we made more 3-point shots than the opposition. Excellence for a basketball coach is winning the contest.

1. Not meeting a standard evokes certain emotions and engages certain psychological defenses. Consult with two to three of your classmates as to what those emotions might be and how to deal with them.

    To address this shortfall, you meet with a key client who is about to sign a new retainer agreement at a higher rate. In other words, the client's payment to your department will go up once this document is signed. Also, the client has certain discretionary work that can be moved up or delayed. Typically, you would hold this work for slack periods during the year. You meet with the client and offer to provide a bonus of extra hours worked that won't be billed if the client will sign the new agreement now, throwing the added revenues into this quarter's financial report. You also plan to move the discretionary work into this fiscal year to help pad revenues. Neither of these is illegal, though it is not clear you have the authority to offer extra hours at a nonbillable rate. You plan on hiding these hours by increasing the workload on the staff. If you meet your numbers, you will most likely be promoted, and the next supervisor will have to unravel your accounting machinations.

2. In your professional judgment, is this appropriate? Remember, it is all work that would have been done anyway, and at a rate that was going to happen. You are just moving things forward. Consult with two to three of your classmates.

3. Rather than engaging in accounting and financial manipulations, devise a solution for dealing with this issue that meets the test for accountability. Be specific in stating what you would say and do in the executive meeting regarding this issue.

4. Consider the question of what your duty is to the company to deliver accurate information versus your duty to your family regarding their financial well-being and the opportunities derived from a successful career. In other words, what is your motivation in this issue?

Income Statements

Develop your personal income statement using this sequence. It is not necessary to know amounts to the penny. Estimates will suffice.

1. Tally any income you have for the month.

    INCOME

Salary:	_____
Loans:	_____
Gifts:	_____
Other:	_____
TOTAL:	_____

    EXPENSES

Rent:	_____
Food:	_____
Utilities:	_____
Entertainment:	_____
Other:	_____
TOTAL:	_____

    INCOME: _____ – EXPENSES: _____ = SAVINGS: _____

For your personal income statement, savings is used as a proxy for net profit. If your expenses exceed your income, savings would be negative, and the shortfall is made up by borrowing money or selling something.

More than likely, you used a cash basis for your personal income statement. On an accrual basis, you would record under salary the amount worked this month even though payment is not forthcoming until next month, and utilities are recorded for those used this month even though they will not be paid until next month.

2. Calculate the following financial ratios from your personal income statement:

$$\frac{\text{Savings}}{\text{Income}} =$$

$$\frac{\text{Savings}}{\text{Salary}} =$$

$$\frac{\text{Total Expenses}}{\text{Total Income}} =$$

$$\frac{\text{Entertainment}}{\text{Total Income}} =$$

While the calculation of these ratios is instructive, they are more useful if you could compare these calculations to your historical numbers and also with those of your classmates. This is similar to what any business does.

3. All companies that are publicly traded will post their financial statements online. Review the *income* statements for two to three of those companies. Though they are more complicated and may be embellished with footnotes, the basic format of the simple income statement from above holds.

Balance Sheets

Develop your personal balance sheet using this sequence. It is not necessary to know amounts to the penny. Estimates will suffice. For the value of your assets, use the price you paid for them, no matter how long ago or what has happened to their value over time.

Tally your current assets, cash, savings accounts, and any stock or bonds that you could convert to cash in the short term.

CURRENT ASSETS

Cash: _____
Savings: _____
Stocks: _____
Bonds: _____

TOTAL   _____

FIXED ASSETS

House: _____
Car: _____
Furniture: _____
Other: _____

TOTAL
ASSETS   _____

CURRENT LIABILITIES

Charge Cards: _____
Other: _____

TOTAL   _____

LONG-TERM LIABILITIES

Mortgage: _____
Student loan: _____
Other: _____

TOTAL   _____

Calculate your personal net worth using this formula. Your personal net worth is the equivalent of owner's equity for a corporation.

Assets   –   Liabilities   =   Net worth

Many of you may have a negative net worth. As an exercise, calculate your projected life-time earnings for your degree. Add that total to your fixed assets and recalculate.

Calculate the following ratios from your personal balance sheet:

$$\frac{\text{Current Assets}}{} =$$

Current Liabilities

$$\frac{\text{Total Debt}}{\text{Net Worth}} \qquad =$$

(Calculate net worth both including and not including your career earnings.)
What does the ratio of total debt to net worth with future salary included say about your ability to be solvent over the long term?

4. All companies that are publicly traded will post their financial statements online. Review the balance sheet statements for two to three of those companies. Though they are more complicated and may be embellished with footnotes, the basic format of the simple income statement from above holds.

REFERENCES AND WORKS CONSULTED

Berman, K., J. Knight, and J. Case. 2013. *Financial Intelligence*. Boston: Harvard Business Review Press.

Jain, P., P. Sharma, and L. Jayaraman, eds. 2015. *Behind Every Good Decision*. New York: American Management Association.

Likierman, A. 2009. "The Five Traps of Performance Measurement." *Harvard Business Review* (October): 96–101.

Mauboussin, M.J. 2012. "The True Measures of Success." *Harvard Business Review* (October): 46–56.

Pfefer, J., and R.I. Sutton. 2006. "Evidence-Based Management." *Harvard Business Review* (January): 2–12.

Rundio, A. 2012. *The Nurse Manager's Guide to Budgeting and Finance*. Indianapolis, IN: Sigma Tau Theta International.

Siciliano, G. 2015. *Finance for Nonfinancial Managers*. New York: McGraw-Hill.

11 MARKETING AND CUSTOMER SERVICE

ALEX

Sometimes the lunches with the other department heads are great fun. Other times they take on a confrontational tone. Yesterday was one of those times. Alex was essentially blindsided by the director of nursing (DON) about the level of service the pharmacy was providing to the floors. According to the DON, there had been a spike in complaints from the nursing staff regarding the pharmacy, ranging from delays in medications reaching the floor to the attitude of some of the pharmacy staff. Needless to say, Alex immediately lost his appetite and did his best not to become defensive. He promised to check into the complaints and get back to the DON. At this point they both agreed to deal with these issues informally. Alex recognized that the DON was implying she would make the complaints formal if the issues were not resolved. Alex headed back to the pharmacy, thinking to himself.

Wow!

I need a Pepcid.

Don't they know we are short staffed?

Don't they know the census is up?

Don't they know that the pressure to generate profits continues to increase?

It's not like nursing is easy to work with.

I hear it every morning when I come in; "Guess what nursing did last night."

I noticed the flowers are starting to bloom in the front yard; I hope it doesn't freeze.

I need to send my nieces Valentine's Day cards.

It's not like we work for nursing.

Maybe I should open a complaint department.

Some of the nurses are really good. I wouldn't want their job.

The patient is the real customer.

Alex walked into his office and closed the door.

MENTAL MODELS

In the center of the space below, write the word *customer*. Next, write the words that come to mind when you think of this topic. Do not edit your thoughts or collaborate with anyone. There is no right or wrong answer.

If things are related, connect them with an arrow. If the relationship is reciprocal (they both affect each other), put arrows at both ends of the line. If one relationship is stronger than another, make the arrow darker and thicker.

The goal is to capture your mental model of what you believe about money. This is the starting point for the discussion on marketing, marketing services, and customer service.

LEARNING OBJECTIVES

- Discuss the marketing concept.
- Discuss the marketing mix including service (the seven Ps).
- Discuss the idea of segmentation and target markets.
- Describe the gap model of service quality.
- Describe the basics of relationship marketing.
- Discuss the link between effective supervision and customer service.

The Marketing Concept

Marketing is a discipline that focuses on understanding what the customer wants and then delivering a product or service that the customer finds valuable, while generating sufficient financial returns. It is a simple concept. Just give customers what they want. In reality, effective marketing is difficult. Sometimes customers don't know what they want. Or convenience trumps conscience, as everyone declares they want to protect the environment while disposable diapers continue to sell. Much is written and researched about marketing and consumers, but at the core of those efforts is this simplest of ideas—give them what they want.

The Marketing Mix

The marketing mix is the set of factors that can be manipulated to sell a product to the customer. There are four elements in the marketing mix:

- The **product** is the tangible good to be sold. The features can be changed in response to consumer requirements. When thinking of a product, there are different bundles of satisfaction that consumers receive in return for their money.

  The *core* benefit is the most fundamental reason for people buying a product. Cars are bought for transportation. The *generic* level of satisfaction is the configuration and elements of the product itself. For a car it is the steel, plastic, and glass. The *expected* product is the benefits the consumer assumes will be there; the seats, steering wheel, and so on for the car. The *augmented* product is added benefits or options for the product. A superior sound system is an augmented benefit. The *potential* level of benefits is the improvements and enhancements to come.
- The **price** is the dollar value charged for the product.
- **Place,** or distribution, is the choice of how to deliver the product to the customer. Is it via mail, direct sales, retail stores, or another means?
- **Promotion** consists of the methods of providing information about the product to the consumer, including advertising, public relations, word of mouth, choice of media, and so on.

Segmentation

There are approximately 320 million people in the United States. No single product or service is likely to satisfy all 320 million. If everyone wanted to shop based on price, then Walmart would soon be the only store in the United States. Some people shop based on convenience, some on quality, some on novelty, and some on another dimension. Effective marketing involves segmenting the market; that is, grouping or dividing the market into smaller clusters of people with similar wants and needs and then designing products to meet the wants and needs of each segment. Segmentation recognizes that AARP members buy different things than college students. Smaller than a market segment is a market niche. This is a very specialized set of consumers with very specific needs and wants. If the market is not segmented, then a mass-marketing approach is being used. In this approach, a product is designed, priced, delivered, and promoted to appeal to the broadest possible number of people.

Markets can be segmented on the basis of demographic variables such as age, gender, or ethnicity. They can be segmented based on geography. This might include urban versus rural or sections of a country. Psychographic segmentation is based on lifestyle, where people are grouped based on their attitudes, behavioral characteristics, or opinions. For example, markets could be segmented based on political orientation—liberal versus conservative. Markets can also be segmented on usage, whether one is a frequent or casual user of a product. Finally, markets can be segmented on why people use a product. Do they, for example, buy toothpaste based on taste, whitening, or decay prevention?

Target Market

The target market is the specific set of consumers that a company wishes to attract and entice to buy its products. An expensive, high-fashion boutique is targeting the wealthy, status conscious, and fashionably inclined. It has no interest in satisfying or attracting working, blue-collar mothers.

Brands

A brand is a name, logo, or symbol that distinguishes one product from another. The five most valuable brands in the world in order are Apple, Google, Microsoft, Coca-Cola, and Facebook (*Forbes* 2017). To consumers, a brand simplifies their choice about products. Through advertising or past experience, consumers have a relationship with the product. Instead of shopping and having to choose, consumers buy based on brand. For unsophisticated consumers, the Apple brand helps simplify their choice of computer or electronic device. For this security, the manufacturer charges a premium. Due to the ability to charge a premium, brands have value termed brand equity. If consumers are satisfied with the branded product, brand loyalty drives future and continued purchases.

Positioning

The object of positioning is for a product to occupy a distinct position in the consumer's mind relative to the competition. Marketers emphasize certain features or benefits of their brand to claim a position in the consumer's mind, or their relationship to other offerings. In the retail world Walmart occupies the low-cost position, Target occupies a position based on style, and Nordstrom's might occupy a position based on service. Select positions in the consumer's mind are valuable and fought for by marketers.

Consumer Behavior

Whereas segmentation and targeting are an attempt to understand who is going to buy, the attempt to understand consumer behavior is to understand why the consumer buys. Consumers don't buy products and services, they buy solutions to their problems. In seeking out these solutions, they search for information about the product or service, evaluate alternative options, make the purchase, and then evaluate their choice afterward. This decision process is subject to internal influences that include their beliefs, values, attitudes, motives, needs, personality, lifestyle, perceptions, and learning. This decision can be stimulated or influenced by manipulating the four Ps of the marketing mix (product, price, place, promotion). The decision is also influenced by consumers' demographic characteristics, economic situation, social and lifestyle profile, and certain situational variables. Consumers are either satisfied with their purchase or may suffer buyer's remorse regarding their choice.

MARKET GROWTH STRATEGIES

A strategy is a plan; it is a statement of intention for achieving goals in the future, generally more than a year. The options for market growth include market penetration (increasing the sales of current products and services to the present markets, selling more to the same consumers); market development (selling current products or services to new markets); product development (selling new products to the same markets); and diversification (selling new products or services to new markets).

SERVICES

Delivering a service is different from manufacturing a product. That difference is due to several factors:

- The customer is a participant in the service.
- Many services are produced and consumed simultaneously, making quality control difficult.

- Services are time perishable; an hour of a dentist's time without a patient is wasted.
- Service locations tend to be close to consumers.
- Services are limited economies of scale; many services are customized for an individual.
- Services are labor intensive.
- It is difficult to measure output—some service consumers just take longer, and thus the number of transactions may not accurately capture true productivity.

The chief distinction for services is they are intangible. The workings of an architect's brain can't be captured.

MARKETING MIX FOR SERVICES

The marketing mix for services includes the four elements of the marketing mix for products detailed above, plus the following three elements; thus, the seven Ps for service marketing.

- **People:** People are integral and inseparable from the delivery of a service. Their appearance, attitude, and competency are a significant marketing variable.
- **Process:** The procedures and mechanisms of delivering a service, its replicability, its responsiveness, and its flow constitute a significant variable.
- **Physical evidence:** Being intangible, the tangible aspects of the service encounter and environment are significant markers for the consumer in assessing services.

SERVICE QUALITY

Research has identified the following five dimensions that consumers use to judge service quality:

- **Reliability:** the ability to perform and deliver the promised service dependably and accurately
- **Responsiveness:** the willingness to help in a timely and prompt manner
- **Assurance:** the knowledge and courtesy of employees and staff and the degree to which consumers believe they can trust and are confident in the service providers
- **Empathy:** caring, individualized attention to specific consumer problems and requests
- **Tangibles:** the sounds, smells, feel, and ambience of the physical facilities, staff, and promotional materials

The fact that many services are intangible creates a problem for consumers in judging the quality of output. In services, quality is assessed by consumers as the gap in their expectations relative to the perceptions of the service encounter. Consumer expectations of a service are reference points, or expectations, of what a consumer believes should happen in the service encounter. These expectations derive from explicit service promises delivered via both personal and nonpersonal sources; implicit service promises delivered via various cues, such as price and the tangible aspects of the service; word-of-mouth advertising; and past experiences. Other factors influencing consumer expectations are the physical, psychological, social, and functional needs of the consumer; the service philosophy of the consumer—having been wait staff in a restaurant impacts the assessment of what constitutes acceptable service; certain service intensifiers, such as an emergency situation or a hard deadline, are impactful; the availability of service alternatives—if there is only one provider for a service, then that is the service standard. It makes sense that an effective strategy regarding consumer expectations is to underpromise and overdeliver. The risk in this approach is that competitors may win customers by making inflated service promises. Expectations for service tend to escalate over time as competitors vie for consumers.

The level of consumer expectations is variable. Consumers have a range of expectations that progress from minimum tolerable expectations to acceptable expectations, expectations based on experience, expectations of what should happen, and expectations of a desired or ideal service. This suggests that there is a zone of tolerance for services bracketed by adequate service and desired service. This zone of tolerance may vary, based on the service dimensions. In other words, the zone of tolerance for reliability in a pharmacy may be extremely tight and relatively loose for the tangible dimensions. The zone of tolerance varies by consumer. For a working professional the zone of acceptance for a scheduled home service delivery is different than for a retiree.

Consumer perceptions of a service are influenced by the features of the service itself (the seven Ps); the consumer's emotions, both stable and transient; the attribution for service failures, whether it was within or beyond the control of the service provider; perceptions of equity and fairness regarding the level of service relative to other consumers; and finally other consumers, family members, and coworkers. Some dimensions of the management of the service quality gap from the consumer perspective are amenable to influence by marketers, while others are beyond their influence.

In addition to the customer gap in services, there are provider gaps. Those gaps include the following:

- The provider gap—the difference in what consumers want versus what the provider believes they want
- The service design and standards gap—poorly designed or developed services that do not meet the consumer's desires
- The service performance gap—the difference between what a well-designed service should deliver and what it actually delivers
- The communication gap—the difference between what is promised and what is delivered

A layman's understanding of marketing usually focuses on advertising, promotion, and sales. At the core of true marketing is a focus on the customer. Everyone in an organization is in the marketing department. The housekeeping staff in a hospital is in the marketing department, as consumers evaluate the quality of their experience based not only on the interactions with staff but the cleanliness of the bathrooms. A young parent with a baby's diaper to change is profoundly interested in a sanitary changing station. Even the support staff within an organization is in the marketing department through this linkage. If a frontline employee has issues regarding his or her benefits, and human resources alleviates the problem, resulting in a satisfied employee, that employee's good feelings will be expressed in encounters with consumers. Conversely, a disgruntled frontline employee will be hard pressed to be an effective service provider. Thus, supervisors interested in improving service quality for their department should recognize that the quality of their management of individuals and staff is significant and impactful.

RELATIONSHIP MARKETING

The "moment of truth" in services is the service encounter when the consumer and firm interact. Each specific interaction is evaluated by the consumer, as are the sum of all interactions. Marketing has moved from a focus on specific transactions to a realization that building long-term relationships with customers is a superior approach in that acquiring and servicing new customers is more expensive than servicing and maintaining relationships with current customers. Customers begin as strangers to the firm, move to acquaintances, then friends, and finally partners with the firm. The benefits to consumers of the relationship are that they develop enhanced confidence in the service, may develop social relationships with the service providers, and may get special benefits as a result of the relationship. The benefits to the firm are economic, more and more profitable purchases, enhanced word-of-mouth advertising, and the expedited workflow from repeat customers as they understand what the requirements are and how the systems work. In other words, the customers are trained. Relationship marketing recognizes that a retained customer is a potential lifetime annuity of cash flows to the business. Some customers are termed platinum tier, in that they are heavy users and are not very price sensitive; gold tier customers tend to be heavy users but want price discounts; iron tier customers provide the volume to justify a firm's capacity but are not loyal or profitable enough to justify special treatment; and lead tier customers cost the firm money due to required special attention and problems they cause.

CUSTOMER SERVICE

Customer service is a function of the following: the response to service failures, the employee response to customer needs and requests, unprompted and unsolicited employee actions, and employee response to problem customers (Zeithaml, Bitner, and Gremler 2009).

Customer service is about one-on-one interactions; it is marketing at the individual level. As an interaction between individuals, the attributes of the service provider are critical. The attributes of service providers include their attitude, appearance, verbal and vocal skills, listening skills, and overall attention and promptness in dealing with the unique demands of the entire array of customers and their requests. Customer service is about taking the pain and anxiety out of the experience. Customer service is about enhancing the customer's experience.

The Walt Disney Company is noted for the level and sophistication of its customer service. Its superior customer service is driven by the following guidelines: make eye contact and smile, greet and welcome everyone, seek out customer contact to offer assistance, provide an immediate attempt to correct any service failure, display body language that is approachable, thank each customer, and preserve the "magic" of the experience by focusing on the positive rather than rules and regulations (Kinni 2011).

Much of customer service can be scripted, or standardized. However, there are customers and circumstances requiring a customized response such that if customer satisfaction is the goal, their requests may be outside the announced protocols. In other words, if excellent customer service is the desire, then service employees need to be able to "break" the rules when required. The gold standard for empowering staff to provide customer service is Nordstrom. The company's approach is conveyed in its brief statement to new hires.

Welcome to Nordstrom.

We're glad to have you with our Company. Our number one goal is to provide outstanding customer service. Set both your personal and professional goals high. We have great confidence in your ability to achieve them.

Nordstrom Rules: Rule #1: Use best judgment in all situations. There will be no additional rules.

Please feel free to ask your department manager, store manager, or division general manager any question at any time. (Spector and McCarthy, 1995)

This statement conveys to staff that any reasonable service request is to be honored. Stories abound of Nordstrom acquiescing to service demands that would appear to be unreasonable, such as returning tires for a confused customer, even though Nordstrom does not sell tires. The point is that Nordstrom allows its employees to service customers, whatever their requests, rather than unthinkingly adhere to some limiting policy or procedure. Nordstrom's Rule # 1 is an example of a mindset and illustrates the power of such a simple declaration.

Emotional Labor

Consumers evaluate service encounters based not only on the reliability and timeliness of the service, but also on the emotions displayed by the service provider. Was the waitress friendly or the ticket taker pleasant? When I conveyed my situation, was the reaction appropriate, was it genuine? For a few moments, could I feel that the practitioner cared about me, or did I sense I was an interruption? Did she smile where appropriate, furl her eyebrows at the right point, and seem saddened by my situation? Service jobs require providers to regulate their emotions to fit the circumstances. The original work in this field captured this idea: *The Managed Heart*. This emotional requirement is termed emotional labor. Emotional labor is when feelings are changed or masked based on specific organizational requirements.

Service Recovery

Services are performances, and sometimes they go wrong. When services are deficient, the consumer may or may not complain. A complaint from a consumer should be considered a gift in that the consumer is giving the company a chance to correct the problem rather than switching providers; since most consumers don't complain, a complaint is notification of a much larger problem with the service delivery. An effective response to a service failure is a powerful variable impacting customer satisfaction, loyalty, and relationships. There is an apparent paradox associated with service recovery in that if a service failure is handled satisfactorily, the consumer is more satisfied than if the service had been done correctly the first time. The mechanics of service recovery involve correcting or fixing the service deficiency, reimbursement for any costs associated with the failure, and providing a free service experience in the future. There are hard dollar costs associated with these remedies. Consumers also want an explanation for what happened, an assurance it won't happen again, a thank-you for their business, an apology, and the opportunity to vent their frustrations. Consumers want outcome fairness, procedural fairness, and interactional fairness.

PRICE AND QUALITY

As an intangible good, quality is difficult to assess in services. Many service consumers equate price as the only tangible element available to them to determine quality. Price as a proxy for quality is particularly important in services associated with high risk or if there is wide variety in quality and price within a specific service segment.

COMMUNICATION IN SERVICES

Recall that the consumer assesses quality in services as the gap between expectations of the service and perceptions of the service. Much of external communication in services focuses on setting those expectations. Therefore, promises made regarding services need to be appropriate and deliverable. Announcing a service promise through the media is a marketing choice; it is also an operational issue regarding the ability to actually deliver on the promise. External service communication can also be an exercise in customer education as to what the service is, how it will be provided, what the customer's role in the process is, and how to actually evaluate the service. Customer education can also be used to smooth out demand and alert consumers to the specific times for optimal service.

GETTING THE SERVICE RIGHT

Supervisors generally overestimate the quality of the service they provide and the degree to which it satisfies the customer. The first step in service marketing is to get the service right; it is to create and deliver services that consumers love, that delight them, that are positively outrageous. Doing this, the need to market in the traditional sense will be nearly eliminated. Getting the service right means getting the people who deliver the service to get it right. It means arming them with the appropriate mental models, establishing specific markers of expected service, and simplifying expectation to specific mindsets that are a residue of supervision and management's efforts and then continuously reinforcing expectations.

People deliver services and customer service. Consequently, their well-being is a direct and powerful influence on the level of service they deliver, and thus on consumer satisfaction and profitability (Zeithaml, Bitner, and Gremler 2009). All people at work have an inner work life of a constant stream of perceptions, emotions, and motivations as they react to and make sense of what happens to them at work. The two most influential factors on a positive versus a negative work life are management facilitating progress at work and treating employees decently as human beings (Amabile and Kramer 2007). Marketing a service, at the core, is getting the supervision right.

The first task of any supervisor is to set a mood that galvanizes staff to want to serve. Goleman, Boyatzis, and McKee write, "The leader's moods and behavior drive the moods and behaviors of everyone else ... an inspirational, inclusive leader spawns acolytes for whom any challenge is surmountable" (2001, pg. 44). Twenty-five percent of staff reported that they take the frustrations of a workplace characterized by incivility out on customers

(Porath and Pearson 2013). It is a straightforward link; effective supervision produces satisfied staff who deliver good customer service.

SUMMARY

This chapter gave an overview of the basic elements of marketing. It also discussed the issues related to service marketing. The link between effective supervision and customer service was described.

EXERCISES

Summarizing
Write a one-page executive summary of the chapter.
Discuss with your classmates how you would teach this material.
Write a two-page case from your experience on this topic that would be instructional for other students.
Develop a mental model for this chapter based on the mind mapping technique.

What's Important to You in the Chapter?
With several of your classmates, discuss the most important ideas from the chapter. Which ideas do you think will be most useful to you in your career? Which ideas do you think you will remember in six months?

What Do the Practitioners/Others Say?
Discuss with your colleagues or someone at work any of the ideas in the chapter. Alternatively, read an article from any source on marketing and be prepared to summarize its message.

Customer Service
Recall your best and worst customer service experience. What words would you use to describe each experience? For the negative experience, if you were the supervisor, how would you correct the situation?

Consumer Behavior
For your particular profession or industry, what do you believe the core expectations of most of the consumers are?

Professionalism

Discuss how the professional obligation to be altruistic translates into good marketing.
Discuss how the professional obligation for integrity translates into good marketing.
Discuss how the professional obligation to respect others translates into good marketing.

Difficult Customers

Discuss with several of your classmates how to deal with the following potentially difficult customers.

- Customers with language or cultural barriers
- Elderly customers
- Impatient customers
- Angry customers
- Customers with special needs
- Price-complaining customers

Markers and Mindsets

With your classmates, develop three specific markers for superior customer service and three mindsets that will reinforce these markers.

Segmentation

For your industry or profession, develop a segmentation plan based on either psychographic or usage criteria.

Your School

The school you attend is a business with the same obligation to deliver a product or service that the consumer finds valuable and generate sufficient revenues to cover its expense. With several of your classmates, work through the following analyses.

1. What is the core, expected, augmented, and desired product?
2. How would a change in price (tuition) change enrollments in the school? How much would price have to change to impact enrollments?
3. Comment on how the school promotes itself to students. How does this compare to other competitor schools?
4. Who is the target market for your school?
5. Comment on your school's brand. What does it signify? How valuable is it?
6. What influences consumers (students) to choose your school?
7. How would you measure quality for your school?

8. Is customer service a variable that influences students to choose your school?

REFERENCES AND WORKS CONSULTED

Amabile, T.M., and S.J. Kramer. 2007. "Inner Work Life." *Harvard Business Review* (May): 72–83.

Bateson, J.E.G., and K.D. Hoffman. 1999. *Managing Services Marketing*. Fort Worth, TX: Dryden.

Broderick, M. 2011. *The Art of Managing Professional Services*. Upper Saddle River, NJ: Prentice-Hall.

Clark, N., ed. 2015. *Professional Services Marketing Handbook*. With C. Nixon. London: Kogan Page.

Evenson, R. 2012. *Powerful Phrases for Effective Customer Service*. New York: AMACOM.

Forbes. 2017. "The World's Most Valuable Brands." http://www.forbes.com/powerful-brands/list/

Goleman, D., R. Boyatzis, and A. McKee. 2001. "Primal Leadership." *Harvard Business Review* (December): 42–51.

Harris, E.K. 2013. *Customer Service*. Boston: Pearson.

Kinni, T. 2011. *Be Our Guest*. New York: Disney Editions.

Parasuraman, A., V.A. Zeithaml, and L.L. Berry. 1988. "SERVQUAL: A Multiple-Item Scale for Measuring Consumer Perceptions of Service Quality." *Journal of Retailing* 64 (1): 12–40.

Porath, C., and C. Pearson. 2013. "The Price of Incivility." *Harvard Business Review* (January–February): 115–21.

Ries, A., and J. Trout. 1981. *Positioning: The Battle for Your Mind*. New York: McGraw-Hill.

Schultz, M., and J.E. Doerr. 2009. *Professional Services Marketing*. Hoboken, NJ: Wiley.

Spector, R. and McCarthy, P. D. 1995. *The Nordstrom Way*. New York: John Wiley and Sons.

Zeithaml, V.A., M.J. Bitner, and D.D. Gremler. 2009. *Services Marketing*. Boston: McGraw-Hill Irwin.

12 OPERATIONS AND QUALITY

ALEX

There the numbers were, right in front of all the department heads. With four months to go in the fiscal year, it was clear that the organization would not meet its financial projections for revenue. Now each department head was being asked to reduce costs, labor, and nonlabor by 10 percent for the rest of the fiscal year. Since this was the second year in a row this had happened, the CEO declared that rather than attack the problem piecemeal, each department would be asked to go back to a blank piece of paper and reexamine all their processes, all their assumptions about how work was done. The CEO made it clear that if sufficient efficiencies and cost savings could not be found, layoffs would begin. She also made it clear that some departments could be consolidated with others and some department heads would likely be terminated. That evening while absent-mindedly clicking the remote in front of the TV, Alex pondered.

Great, I still have student loans to pay off.

What if I lose my job?

I can't believe they will just let people go like that!

I should start checking with friends about other positions.

I'll be glad when the election is over... I'm tired of these people.

Lunch was really good today.

I need to call my dad; it's his birthday.

How am I going to cut expenses? We don't have enough people now.

I can't believe how much they take out of my check each period.

If I could automate the call-ins, it would save money.

My niece just got engaged; I hope her fiancé gets into grad school.

If I get fired, can I collect unemployment?

I wish I could get rid of this cough.

The sun's out. I'm going for a walk to get some ice cream.

Service Blueprints

For your particular industry, construct a service blueprint for a typical operation. Capture the typical functions and their sequencing. Where do the clients/patients/customers enter? Where are phone calls handled? Where does the actual work take place—in a back room, in front of the client? Who are the people involved? What is each of their roles? Who makes the decisions? Who checks the output? Is the service/product delivered in real time, or is it asynchronous? In other words, if you looked down from the balcony, what would you see going on, and who would be doing it? Also, record the length of time a typical client is in the system.

LEARNING OBJECTIVES

- Discuss the idea of operations management on increasing organizational performance.
- Discuss the emergence of analytics as a tool for increasing productivity.
- Discuss the influence of technology on increasing performance.
- Discuss the concept of quality and quality management.
- Discuss ideas related to inventory management and supply chain management.

OPERATIONS

At its simplest, operations management is concerned with the design and control of the transformation process by which organizations convert inputs into outputs. A process is a set of steps, activities, and tasks performed in sequence to yield an output. The service blueprint constructed above captures the elements of a process. The inputs into any business are people, information, materials, technology, capital, and equipment, while the outputs are goods and services. All organizations are concerned with productivity, which is the ratio of output, or goods and services, to inputs; the higher the ratio, the higher the productivity.

Inputs	Operations	Outputs
People Information Materials Technology Capital Equipment	**Transformation**	Products Services

The supervisor's role in productivity is as follows (adapted from Langabeer and Helton, 2016):

1. To reduce costs via standardization, optimization, and resources tracking systems
2. To reduce variability and improve logistical flow by integrating service delivery and utilizing analytics and supply chain management
3. To improve productivity through information technology and tracking systems
4. To provide higher-quality services through evidence-based practices and Six Sigma management
5. To improve business processes through outsourcing and globalization

Operations management is a rigorous and scientific approach to productivity in management that emerged out of World War II and the need to coordinate vast global operations. In dealing with productivity issues, quantitative and analytical techniques are applied. Specific techniques and tools are available for specific productivity issues. Specific techniques to reduce costs include optimization, location analysis, minimization models, break-even analysis, and sensitivity analysis. Techniques to reduce variability and improve logistical flows include process engineering, forecasting, capacity analysis, simulation, and control charts. Tools to increase productivity include time and motion studies, staffing models, and queuing models. Tools to improve quality include business planning, statistical process control, root cause analysis, and Six Sigma. Tools to streamline business processes include process engineering and flowcharts (adapted from Langabeer and Helton 2016).

It is not required that a supervisor be expert in the various techniques; these are the realm of specialists. What is critical is to understand that problems of productivity and quality can be approached rigorously and analytically, and that consulting such specialists is appropriate when warranted. Also, it is important to understand that expertise in operations, the ability to transform inputs more efficiently at lower cost and more effectively, is a source of competitive advantage over competing firms. The standard for survival is that the firm must be at least as good as the competition on this point, or over time the negative financial implications of higher cost and lower quality will result in closure, bankruptcy, acquisition, or major reorganization. The fundamentals of operations management are these: (1) Can it be done faster, (2) can it be done better, (3) can it be done cheaper, and (4) can it be done differently?

Operations management is the scientific method applied to business. The same steps apply. A research question is generated from a current business need; for example, the need to buy a component product cheaper. A hypothesis is generated; supplier X will provide the required product at a reduced price. Data are collected regarding costs of the required product as well as the impact on ultimate quality and customer satisfaction. The data are analyzed, and the hypothesized solution (supplier X will meet the need) is either accepted or rejected. The process is repeated until the original issue is resolved and a new research question emerges.

ANALYTICS

Analytics, the ability to collect and analyzes huge amounts of statistical data, is revolutionizing the way that organizations manage their operations. Organizations employing analytics use sophisticated information systems and rigorous analysis and modeling to wring the greatest efficiencies from their operations. Analytics supports fact-based decision making rather than relying on managerial hunch or intuition. Analytics can be used to (1) optimize supply chain flows and reduce inventory and stock outs, improving customer service; (2) identify customers with the greatest profit potential and retain their loyalty; (3) identify the price that yields maximum profit; (4) select the best employees at a specific compensation level; (5) detect quality problems; (6) understand the drivers of financial performance as well as the nonfinancial drivers factors; and (7) improve the quality and efficacy of the research function. Analytics can also be extended to analyze the human capital (employees) of an organization and can measure and analyze factors such as individual performance, departmental performance, which actions have the greatest impact on business performance, turnover predictions, succession planning and excesses, shortages in the workforce, and how the workforce should change with changes in the business environment. As with the operational techniques detailed above, supervisors need not be expert in analytic methodology but should be aware that the trend is to use analytics and that they should be able to use the available data to enhance productivity. Supervisors should also expect to be evaluated on ever-finer-grained metrics for performance. Simple profit is not likely to remain the standard for performance assessment.

QUALITY

In manufacturing, quality is the absence of defects, deficiencies, and significant variation from one product or service to the next. Quality in services is the degree to which consumer expectations are matched by consumers' perception of the service. Quality is meeting the needs and expectations of the customer regarding performance, appearance, availability, delivery, reliability, maintainability, cost, and price. Quality is the conformance to requirements or specifications. In other words, does the product or service do what is intended?

In the 1980s American industry was falling behind the Japanese regarding the quality of the products being manufactured. This spurred a focus on quality management and quality improvement. The dominant framework for quality was developed by Edward Deming. Deming proposed the following fourteen points of quality as a philosophy of management (http://asq.org/learn-about-quality/total-quality-management/overview/deming-points.html).

1. Create constancy of purpose toward improvement of products and service.
2. Adopt the new philosophy. We can no longer live with commonly accepted levels of delay, mistakes, and defective workmanship.
3. Cease dependence on mass inspection. Instead, require statistical evidence that evidence is built in.
4. End the practice of awarding business on the basis of price.
5. Find problems. It is management's job to work continually on the system.
6. Institute modern methods of training on the job.
7. Institute modern methods of supervision of production workers. The responsibility of forepersons must be changed from numbers to quality.
8. Drive out fear so that everyone may work effectively for the company.
9. Break down barriers between departments.

10. Eliminate numerical goals, posters, and slogans for the workforce asking for new levels of productivity without providing methods.
11. Eliminate work standards that prescribe numerical quotas.
12. Remove barriers that stand between hourly workers and their right to pride in their work.
13. Institute a vigorous program of education and training.
14. Create a structure in top management that will push on the above points every day.

Others besides Deming developed their own approaches to quality-management and quality-improvement initiatives that may have other names; for example, TQM—total quality management; Kaizen—a Japanese approach based on continuous improvement; and BPR—business process reengineering. A key aspect of all quality-improvement programs is the idea of prevention, eliminating errors before they happen. All are based on analyzing the process of production and then through statistical control and analysis optimizing the system. Quality-improvement plans are most effective if they align with the strategic and financial goals of the organization. Successful quality-improvement programs require a long-term commitment from management and the development of a culture of quality and increased employee ownership of the process.

A QUALITY-MANAGEMENT TOOL

In dealing with quality issues within a department, certain techniques and tools are useful for the supervisor. One useful diagrammatic tool termed a cause-and-effect diagram or a fishbone diagram was developed by Kaoru Ishikawa. If there is a quality issue or problem, it is filled in at the "head" of the fish. Then for each of the dimensions on the diagram, causes for that issue are recorded. The idea is to present simply and diagrammatically the assumed cause for the deficiency, which can then be tested, confirmed, or rejected, and then corrected if necessary.

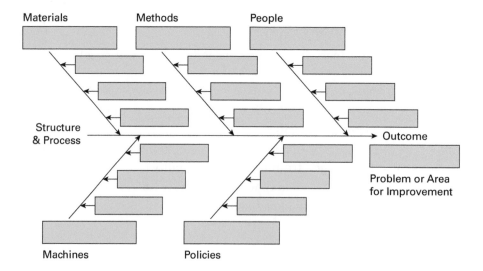

OPERATIONS AS PLANNING

Utilizing analytics and undertaking quality initiatives are typically large and complicated organizational undertakings. At the departmental level, supervisors are confronted with the more mundane but just as important task of actually getting the work done. To that end, certain types of day-to-day planning are required. The types of planning that a supervisor is likely to engage in include the following:

- **Capacity planning:** Ensuring that the department has sufficient human and physical resources to meet current demand and also any changes in future demand to include the possibility of downsizing or capacity upgrades.
- **Process planning:** Evaluating the various options for transforming inputs into required outputs. What combination of technology, automation, and human resources are required, and in what proportion? Is the objective maximum efficiency, ultimate customer service, or flexibility of output? Can a production line be developed, or is all output essentially one-off and customized? Are economies of scale possible?
- **Layout planning:** Exactly how will the process be configured within the allotted space?
- **Aggregate or time-based planning:** What is the cycle time for production? When are the peaks and slack seasons? How does this impact buying supplies, inventory, cash flow, and scheduling? How does the department fit within the larger cycle of organizational demand?

From this planning, budgets and schedules are developed that serve as standards for compliance and variance reconciliation. In this process it is beneficial to benchmark the process under consideration relative to other providers and competitors. A benchmark is a comparison. It gives a department or organization a standard to which to aspire, a way to keep score. In thinking of how to improve the process within a department, the following questions serve as evaluative targets (adapted from Brennan, 2011):

1. Keep it simple. Design for the majority of the cases with provisions for exceptions, rather than a system designed for every contingency.
2. Is value added in each step? Any step or resource that does not add value for the consumer is wasteful and should be eliminated.
3. Are the handoffs minimized? Transitions and handoffs do not add value and are potential sources of dissatisfaction, often inconveniencing the consumer. Think of dialing in to any customer service department and the number of people you are likely to go through to resolve a problem.
4. Are individual steps and responsibilities clearly defined? The more people understand their roles, the cleaner the process.
5. Are there controls and failsafe points built into the process?

6. Is technology leveraged for maximum value and efficiency?
7. How is throughput and variability monitored throughout the process?
8. It is supervisors' role to address and resolve these issues as they consider the process within their department.

INVENTORY

For many businesses, inventory is the single largest financial investment. The acquisition, storage, distribution, and financing of inventory constitute a critical operational variable. Managing inventory can be thought of as a problem similar to buying food for a family of seven, two adults and five children. The problem is to balance the variables associated with feeding the family; specifically, buying food at the best price and the right time, while being cognizant of individual tastes, nutrition, spoilage, and costs of acquiring the food. The economic order quantity (EOQ) model seeks to balance the four costs associated with ordering and carrying inventory. Those costs are the purchase costs—purchase price plus delivery, less discounts; ordering costs—paperwork, follow-up, and any other processing costs; carrying costs—storage, insurance, taxes, money tied up in inventory; and stock out costs—lost profits, dissatisfied consumers, and expenses incurred to deliver late orders. The EOQ is expressed algebraically as

$$EOQ = \sqrt{\frac{2 \times \text{Annual Consumption} \times \text{Ordering Cost}}{\text{Storage (holding) Cost per Unit}}}$$

Storage (holding) Cost per Unit = Cost per Unit × Storage Cost (%)

The goal of the EOQ model is to minimize the ordering costs and the carrying costs. As inventory orders increase in size, the ordering cost per unit declines while the carrying cost per unit increases. At some order quantity, both ordering and carrying costs are minimized. It is not likely that a supervisor will precisely calculate the EOQ for all the items required to run the department. What is important is to understand the trade-off between ever larger orders and the greater costs of paying for, storing, and dealing with dated merchandise that negates the cost savings. Back to the example of feeding a family of seven, no matter how great the bargain, a supply of milk longer than the expiration date or an item the family won't ever eat is no bargain. Families tend to work out intuitively their own economic order quantities for various food items.

SUPPLY CHAIN MANAGEMENT

Goods and services move through a supply chain. A supply chain is composed of those organizations required to facilitate the movement of raw product to the ultimate consumer. A typical supply chain is composed of a supplier, manufacturer, wholesaler or distributor, retailer, and consumer. For some products one or more of the intermediaries may be eliminated in the movement of product from raw material to consumer. Along with the product supply chain, there is also a supply chain that includes the flow of information and money. Managing the supply chain involves driving inefficiencies from the system and adding value for the consumer. This comes from integrating the various business functions within a business and across the linked businesses. For example, payment may be deducted from an account on the day an order is shipped, or an item out of stock in a retailer ripples back through a distributor to the manufacturer in an automated and automatic restocking progression. Effectively managed supply chains seek to reduce the time for moving product from manufacturer to consumer while seeking greater consistency in quality, a tighter coupling with consumer preferences, greater flexibility in responsiveness, and increased innovativeness. One approach to managing the supply chain is that of just in time. Just in time inventory means that minimal amounts of inventory are kept on hand, and what is required is delivered right before it is needed, or just in time. This approach minimizes inventory holding costs. Writing a paper for class can be considered a just in time approach to delivering inventory. An alternative approach is termed supply to stock, where larger quantities, acquired at discounted prices due to bulk purchase, are kept in-house. This approach relies on economies of scale to hold down costs.

Typical Supply Chain

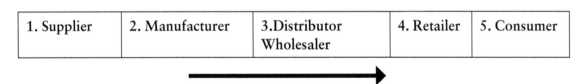

1. Supplier	2. Manufacturer	3.Distributor Wholesaler	4. Retailer	5. Consumer

The rubric for supply chain management is optimizing the "six rights": right goods, in the right quantity, in the right condition, to the right place, at the right time, and at the right price.

TECHNOLOGY IN OPERATIONS

Technology is constantly changing. Discussions of a specific technology applied to a single industry would be pointless in that the information would most likely be dated prior to the publication of this book. Rather, a discussion of how technology impacts operations ensues. Technology can be considered as the physical manifestation of knowledge and can be applied to the product, the process, or information technology. Changes in technology are the drivers of continuous improvement for the organization. Technology has profound impacts on how work is done and how inputs are converted to desired outputs. Those impacts include the following:

- Creating access and immediacy in reaching customers, suppliers, and employees
- Shrinking the globe, allowing processes to be distributed to offshore locations
- Transform unstructured processes into routine transactions
- Replace human labor in a process
- Permit complex analytical methods to be applied to the process
- Collect and disseminate vast amounts of data
- Altering the sequencing of tasks
- Permitting the tracking of tasks, inputs, and outputs

More specifically, technology enables the supply chain to be managed as a single integrated system, rather than a series of distinct operations; allows for more effective management of enterprise-wide operations; allows for improved customer relationship management; and allows for a more efficient utilization of the intellectual capital of the organization.

SUMMARY

This chapter gave an overview of the ideas related to supervision and operations management, productivity, and quality. Ideas related to analytics, the influence of technology on operations, quality, quality improvement, and inventory and supply chain management were also considered.

EXERCISES

Summarizing
Write a one-page executive summary of the chapter.
Discuss with your classmates how you would teach this material.
Write a two-page case from your experience on this topic that would be instructional for other students.

What's Important to You in the Chapter?

With several of your classmates, discuss the most important ideas from the chapter. Which ideas do you think will be most useful to you in your career? Which ideas do you think you will remember in six months?

What Do the Practitioners/Others Say?

Discuss with your colleagues or someone at work any of the ideas in the chapter. Alternatively, read an article from any source on operations management and be prepared to summarize its message.

Watch the move *Moneyball* movie with Brad Pitt and consider the impact of analytics and statistics on the building and performance of the Oakland Athletics baseball team. Prepare a one-page summary on this point.

Find an article on the coming generation of robots. Discuss with several of your classmates the implications, if any, for your industry.

With several of your classmates, look up definitions and descriptions of the following operational tools and techniques. Use a computer or your phone to access the information. The objective is to get a "feel" for some of the techniques available.

- Optimization
- Location analysis
- Minimization models
- Break-even analysis
- Sensitivity analysis
- Process engineering
- Forecasting
- Capacity analysis
- Simulation
- Control charts
- Time and motion studies
- Staffing models
- Queuing models
- Statistical process control
- Six Sigma
- Process engineering
- Flowcharts

Design a production system to deal with the following problem. The system needs to make peanut butter and jelly sandwiches that are wrapped and that will produce one thousand sandwiches in an hour. To satisfy the market, there are two types of peanut butter, four varieties of bread, and ten varieties of jelly. What numbers do you need to consider? How will the system be laid out? What about spoilage? Buying in bulk? Most popular sandwiches? Assume that some processes can be automated.

REFERENCES AND WORKS CONSULTED

Barton, D., and D. Court. 2012. "Making Advanced Analytics Work for You." *Harvard Business Review* (October): 79–83.

Brennan, L.L. 2011. *Operations Management*. New York: McGraw-Hill.

Davenport, T.H. 2006. "Competing on Analytics." *Harvard Business Review* (January): 1–9.

Davenport, T.H., J. Harris, and J. Shapiro. 2010. "Competing on Talent Analytics." *Harvard Business Review* (October): 2–6. http://asq.org/learn-about-quality/total-quality-management/overview/deming-points.ht

Langabeer, J.R., II, and J. Helton. 2016. *Health Operations Management*. Burlington, MA: Jones and Bartlett.

Namdev, S., and K.N. Pandagre. 2014. "Artificial Intelligence Robotics: Services and Future Roadmap." *International Journal of Innovation and Scientific Research* 6 (1): 71–74.

Prakash, O., and V. Pandey. 2014. "Reducing the Bullwhip Effect in a Supply Chain Using Artificial Intelligence Technique." *Journal of Production Research and Management* 4 (2): 1–13.

Srinivasan, A., and B. Kurey. 2014. "Creating a Culture of Quality." *Harvard Business Review* (April): 23–25.

13 LAW, ETHICS, AND STAKEHOLDERS

ALEX

Budgets were tightening, that much was clear. The finance people were pessimistic regarding the short-term financial picture for the organization. All the nonlabor expenses were being cut to the bone. Now the task for all the department heads was to decide which employees would need to be released. In the department head meeting, everyone agreed that using seniority would be the easiest criteria. But is it fair? What if the least senior were the most competent or energetic in the department? Why not those closest to retirement, or those who could retire and were still working? How about those who needed the job the most, single parents, or those with special-needs children? Should they get special consideration? How about those with the highest claims against the health plan? What about those who were close to graduating and would be leaving in a year anyway? As far as Alex was concerned, he had two candidates in mind, one extremely competent and one a single parent with no other support. But each had challenged his authority in an open meeting and were hard to work with. Alex thought.

I hate being embarrassed in meetings.

I'd like to fire both of them.

I wonder if we would get sued?

How will the choice impact the other staff, and what will it do for morale?

I can't believe that one of the senior department heads was reassigned back to staff!

What a great hockey game last night, a win in OT.

My sister keeps calling about Dad. He is 90 years old after all.

How do I fire someone with a child? What will they say to the child?

It's not my problem. I need to make the numbers for the rest of the department.

Did she really say that Dad has given up and won't get out of his chair?

I need to go see him.

I'll just flip a coin as to which one.

MENTAL MODELS

In the center of the space below, write the word *ethics*. Next, write the words that come to mind when you think of either this activity or this type of person. Do not edit your thoughts or collaborate with anyone. There is no right or wrong answer.

If things are related, connect them with an arrow. If the relationship is reciprocal (they both affect each other), put arrows at both ends of the line. If one relationship is stronger than another, make the arrow darker and thicker.

The goal is to capture your mental model of what you believe about professionalism. This is the starting point for the discussion on professionalism.

Learning Objectives
- Discuss the frameworks for ethical decision making.
- Discuss stakeholder theory.
- Describe the concept of corporate social responsibility.
- Discuss the legal aspects of employment law.
- Discuss what is acceptable or not acceptable in a job interview.
- Discuss what constitutes sexual harassment.
- Discuss workplace violence, romantic relationships, and progressive discipline at work.

LAW, ETHICS, AND STAKEHOLDERS

Ethics

To be in management is to have power. At the uppermost corporate level, that power is immense. What diseases get targeted for research funding, which factory is closed, moved, or upgraded? How are the world's natural and human resources to be used, expended, or husbanded? What will be the quality and cost of our transportation systems, health care, entertainment? Leaders of nonprofit organizations are just as powerful. What will be the quality of our education, the access to clean water, the vitality of our arts and humanities?

Supervisors, being at the front line, seldom have this level of societal power. They operate in a narrower scope and in a constrained world, typically a single department. But for the individuals in that department and the clients they serve, supervisory power is also immense. Which orders get processed first, how are people treated, is the workday productive and enjoyable or drudgery, what is the quality of departmental output? Supervisors have the power to make a significant number of people's lives better or diminished at an intimate, personal level.

Though powerful, management and supervisors are constrained by broad external forces of competition, globalization, technology, and demographics. They are also constrained by the requirements to meet financial targets and strategic market objectives. Government and the legal system are also constraining factors. This text points out that managers and supervisors are constrained by the obligation to measure themselves relative to declared professional standards and that professionalism embodies context specific moral, ethical, and legal behavior.

Supervisors can take one of three orientations to making ethical decisions. One approach is immoral in that the ethical standard is only minimal or nonexistent. Immoral supervision is ignoring any ethical principles or fair and equitable treatment of individuals. A second approach is amoral. In this perspective, stakeholders and those impacted by decisions are essentially ignored. Willful harm is not intended, but neither is any ethical concern. Decisions are profit oriented or production oriented. People are viewed as instruments to accomplish financial objectives. Finally, moral management values the equitable treatment of all stakeholders and those impacted by a decision. Ethical codes are established and honored on a day-to-day basis. Ethical behavior is the guiding rubric.

Faced with a situation where the professional, moral, ethical, or legal choices are not clear, how is a supervisor to know what is right or wrong? The financial consequences of a choice can be reasonably approximated, as well as the strategic market outcomes. Models and theories exist to approximate those consequences. In the ethical realm, certain ethical frameworks and principles can be applied to tease out the appropriate ethical choice. One approach to an ethical decision is to assess the *utility* of a choice. Utility is defined as the overall good that results from an action or choice. This approach is termed utilitarian and compares the economic, social, and human costs and benefits of a decision. Benefits that outweigh costs are deemed ethical in that they produce the greatest good for the greatest number of people. The weakness in this approach is in the estimation of certain social and human costs; for example, the long-term impact on the environment or the cost of a human life. A second approach is based on *universal human rights* to which we are all entitled; for example, the right to life, safety, freedom, due process, and so on. The dilemma with this approach is in balancing conflicting rights, such as the right to individual privacy versus a corporation's right to protect proprietary secrets as it reads employee e-mails. A third approach asks the question, is it fair or was *justice* served? Are the benefits and burdens of society and the corporation distributed equitably and by a process that was not biased? A fourth approach is linked to *duty* and is based on universal principles such as justice, fairness, and respect. The decision criteria is this: Every person on earth in this same situation would be required to act in the same way. *Virtue ethics* provides a framework for decisions. This approach is grounded in individual character virtues such as truthfulness, honesty, and integrity. Finally, *ethical relativism* holds that there are no universal standards to guide ethical behavior and that individual self-interest and values are the standards for ethical choice. A corollary to this approach is the idea of *cultural relativism*, in that what is right and ethical varies by culture.

Each approach can be applied individually to an ethical analysis or all used simultaneously. The questions then become about a choice; do benefits exceed costs, is it fair, are human rights respected, what is my duty, or what is virtuous? Ideally, each approach would yield the same conclusion. Unfortunately, this may not be the case, complicating the choice. In this case the best that can be done is to prioritize one framework over another. As to which framework to feature, that is a function of the decision itself, the corporate culture, and social and personal values.

STAKEHOLDERS

One view of a business is that its only function is to generate profit for shareholders. An alternative view is that organizations have an obligation to multiple stakeholders. Stakeholders are any group that can affect or are affected by the actions and policies of an organization. "The ethical dimension of stakeholder theory is based on the view that profit maximization is constrained by justice, and that regard for individual rights should be extended to all constituencies that have a stake in a business, and that organizations are not only 'economic' in nature, but can also act in socially responsible ways" (Weiss 2014, 120). Stakeholders can be grouped into two categories: (1) market stakeholders who engage in economic activities with the corporation, composed of employees, stockholders, creditors, suppliers, customers, distributors, wholesalers, and retailers; and (2) nonmarket stakeholders who do not engage in economic activities but are affected by the corporation, composed of government, activist groups, the media, business support groups, the general public, and local communities.

One way of understanding the issues related to the various stakeholders is to conduct an objective appraisal of those interests. This appraisal is termed a stakeholder analysis. The mechanics of a stakeholder analysis begins with a series of questions: (1) Who are our stakeholders; (2) who are potential stakeholders; (3) how does each stakeholder affect us and the organization affect them; (4) what current environmental factors (inflation, financial, public image, and so on) affect both the organization and the stakeholders; and (5) how do we measure the impact of our actions on the stakeholders and keep score? These questions are then followed by the actions listed below:

- Map the various stakeholder relationships schematically.
- Determine and map any coalitions among the stakeholders. For example, employees and local taxing authorities will be interested in a proposed plant closing.
- Assess each stakeholder's responsibilities to themselves and to the corporation.
- Determine the nature of each stakeholder's power. Who stands to win or lose as a result of a decision or policy? Power is reciprocal in that stakeholders impact the corporation and vice versa.
- What are the moral responsibilities of each stakeholder?
- Determine what will be the strategy relative to each stakeholder. Stakeholders will be either indifferent, supportive, or opposed to any specific strategy, contingent on their specific interests.
- Monitor any shifts in stakeholder coalitions and impact of strategic choice.

It is not likely that any strategy will appeal to all stakeholders equally. Some will be dissatisfied. At this stage individual decisions are analyzed utilizing the ethical frameworks detailed above. Ultimately, disputes between stakeholders will have to be negotiated or resolved legally or through a formalized dispute resolution process. Following such a protocol, a firm will be deemed to be exemplifying corporate social responsibility.

CORPORATE SOCIAL RESPONSIBILITY

Corporate social responsibility suggests that corporations be held accountable for their actions and their impact. The argument for this perspective is the immense impact of business on everyday lives and the essential functions that business performs for society. It is argued that in the long run, a lack of social responsibility will result in businesses being deprived of their power and influence. This idea is termed the iron law of responsibility. Corporate social responsibility rests on the idea that businesses are entrusted with society's resources and need to be good stewards of those resources. The arguments for and against corporate social responsibility are (adapted from Lawrence and Weber 2008):

Arguments For
Balances power with responsibility
Discourages government regulation
Improves business reputation and value
Corrects social problems caused by
business.

Arguments Against
Lowers efficiency and profit
Imposes unequal costs among competitors
Requires skills business may not have
Places responsibility on business rather than
individuals.

Sustainability

Sustainability in business involves the idea of managing the triple bottom line. The triple bottom line involves managing the financial, social, and environmental performance of the company. Another version of the bottom line is managing profits, people, and the planet. Sustainable business development meets present-day needs without compromising the future, future generations, and future impacts on the planet. Sustainable business development meets the test for economic efficiency, environmental accountability, and social equity. Linking this idea to corporate social responsibility is to consider future generations and the environment as stakeholders in current corporate behavior. In other words, generating additional profits at the expense of environmental degradation or social neglect is not acceptable and does not meet a test of effective stewardship.

LEGAL

Supervisors are clearly constrained by the legal environment. While many laws impact the corporation in aggregate, supervisors are most likely to be constrained by the laws pertaining to employment and the conditions at work. The following section provides a brief review of the laws related to equal employment opportunities. In the United States using race, gender, disability, age, religion, or certain other characteristics is prohibited. In other words, discrimination is illegal. However, employers may discriminate, or choose among employment candidates based on job requirements and candidate qualifications. The following are the basis for considering individuals in protected classes and thus protection under Equal Employment Opportunity Commission (EEOC) laws and regulations.

Race, ethnic origin, color
Sex/gender/pregnancy
Age (over forty)
Disabilities (mental and physical)
Military experience
Religion
Marital status (some states)
Sexual orientation (some states and cities)

There are two types of illegal employment discrimination: (1) disparate treatment where members of a group are treated differently from others in employment decisions, and (2) disparate treatment where a policy results in different employment outcomes for a group. Some of the significant federal laws relating to employment and the employment-related prohibitions are:

- Title VII, Civil Rights Act of 1964 prohibits discrimination against employees on the basis of race, color, religion, sex, or national origin.
- Age Discrimination in Employment Act prohibits discrimination on the basis of age for employees over age forty.
- Pregnancy Discrimination Act prevents discrimination on the basis of pregnancy or related condition.
- Americans with Disabilities Act prevents discrimination on the basis of disability.
- Immigration and Reform Control Act prevents discrimination on the basis of national origin or citizenship.
- Occupational Safety and Health Act protects employees against unsafe working conditions and prohibits retaliation against employees who report unsafe working conditions.
- Equal Pay Act provides that women must be paid no less than men for equal work unless the difference is due to seniority, merit, or some factor other than gender.
- Genetic Information Nondiscrimination Act makes it illegal to discriminate based on genetic information.

Based on the employment law framework, certain acts are prohibited by employers to include:

- Failure to hire or discharge someone because they are a member of a protected class.
- Deprive a member of a protected class certain employment opportunities regarding working conditions, training, rates, of pay, and opportunities for advancement.

- Retaliate because an individual made a charge or claim under Title VII.
- Print or publish any advertisement that may adversely affect a member of a protected class.
- Failure to post in an obvious place a notice regarding the contents of this law.

Individuals who believe they have been discriminated against have the right to file for redress. Generally, the procedure for this is for the individual to raise the issue within the company and follow whatever administrative mechanisms are in place. If the individual is not satisfied with the outcome, he or she has the right to petition the courts for a remedy.

JOB INTERVIEWS

It is rare that a supervisor will have a new employee assigned to his or her department without the opportunity to conduct an interview, even though the applicant may have been prescreened by the human resource department. The interview itself is subject to the same constraints regarding discrimination under Title VII and EEOC guidelines. Questions that do not focus on job-related issues expose an organization to potential discrimination complaints. It is advisable to ask all applicants the same set of core questions. General questions as to whether the applicant can perform the essential functions of the job are permitted as well as whether the applicant has the required education, skills, and training for the job. It is also to acceptable to ask why someone left a job, if there was any past disciplinary actions, and how much time the person took off in a previous job, but not why. At the pre-job offer stage, you cannot ask candidates whether they need any special accommodations to do the job, questions about any physical or mental impairment, use of medication, or prior worker's compensation claims. If a candidate has been given a conditional job offer, questions regarding any potential disabilities are acceptable, and if warranted the firm must make "reasonable accommodations" such as ramps for a wheelchair-bound individual. This is a requirement of the American's with Disability Act. Post-job offer, the company may also request medical examinations as long as all potential applicants are subject to the same procedures. A job offer may be withdrawn following a medical examination or if it is clear that a disability will preclude candidates from doing the essential functions of the job or pose a significant risk of harm to themselves or others. For example, if a medical examination reveals a history of seizures, then a job offer may be withdrawn if the job requires operating heavy equipment.

Questions about the following are acceptable in an interview: name; age, if a job requirement (must be over twenty-one to serve alcohol depending on the state); if the candidate can meet the posted work schedule for the job; languages that a candidate can read, write, or speak; educational background; work experience; felony convictions; any family currently employed with the company; and physical conditions regarding ability to perform the job. A statement that any misstatements during the interview may result in termination is also permitted. Questions regarding birthplace, religion, race, and arrests are not acceptable. Questions regarding citizenship are permitted to the extent that they determine if the individual is legally employable if a job is offered.

The preferred method of questioning an applicant is a series of competency-based questions. Competency-based questions focus on conveying past job performance and seek to project how a candidate will perform in the new position. Examples of competency-based questions include the following:

- Describe a time when…
- Describe the most significant…
- Tell me about a specific job experience…
- Describe a situation in which you felt_____. What happened?

SEXUAL HARASSMENT

The EEOC provides guidelines to limit sexual harassment in the workplace. Sexual harassment includes actions that are sexual in nature, unwanted, subject a worker to adverse employment conditions, impact work performance, or create a hostile work environment. Generally, sexual harassment involves the harassment of women by men, though cases may be filed by men. Innocent flirtation and horseplay are not generally considered sexual harassment, even if the victim does not like it. Brief, isolated incidents are not considered sexual harassment unless they are extremely serious. There are two types of sexual harassment: (1) quid pro quo—this for that—where a supervisor expects some type of sexual trade-off as a condition of employment; and (2) creating a hostile environment that unreasonably interferes with an individual's ability to do his or her job. A key aspect of sexual harassment is that it must be unwelcome. If everyone at work uses foul language and no one cares, then it is not sexual harassment. The courts utilize a reasonable person standard in determining if something is sexual harassment that considers the frequency of the offensive conduct; the severity of the conduct; whether it is physically intimidating, humiliating, or merely offensive; and whether it unreasonably interferes with work performance.

ROMANTIC RELATIONSHIPS AT WORK

Romantic, consensual relationships at work are a problem for supervisors. Should supervisors monitor these relationships to protect against legal complaints or ignore them as private matters? It is clear that a romantic relationship between a supervisor and subordinate in the chain of command is not advisable and is fraught with potential problems. Corporations generally have specific policies in this area that serve as behavioral templates. When a romantic relationship ends, there are also potential influences on workplace performance. It is possible for consensual workplace romances to be considered as contributing to a hostile work environment. The advice in this area is to know the company policy, be aware of the organizational culture regarding these relationships, and, as a supervisor, tread lightly in this area.

WORKPLACE VIOLENCE

Companies have a duty to provide a safe workplace environment that is derived from the Occupational Safety and Health Act of 1970. Workplace violence takes many forms, including intimidation, threats, physical attacks, domestic violence, and property damage. It includes acts by other employees, clients, customers, strangers, relatives, and acquaintances. Supervisors need to be alert to the warning signs of potential workplace violence. Indicators of potential violence are sudden changes in behavior, claims of unfair treatment, blaming others, obsessing about other coworkers, alcohol or drug use, instability in family relationships, previous threats, sudden mood swings or depression, financial problems, and outbursts of rage. Workplace violence is minimized by effective design of the workplace environment (controlling access, security devices, and so on); administrative oversight involving distribution of workplace violence policies; documenting incidences of workplace violence; and certain behavioral strategies involving training and enforcement of established workplace violence policies.

DISCIPLINE

Most employees are governed by the doctrine of employment at will. Under this doctrine, an employee can be terminated for any reason or no reason at all with or without notice, and an employee can leave at any time with or without notice for any or no reason at all. However, many organizations, in order to treat their employees fairly and avoid any claims of discrimination, will engage in a progressive disciplinary process. Progressive discipline begins with coaching and counseling, typically for minor infractions that a supervisor believes can be corrected by an informal verbal meeting. If necessary, retraining is the next step if it is believed that the employee simply does not know how to do a job and will comply once retrained. A verbal warning follows next; it gives guidance as to corrective steps to take and serves as a warning that disciplinary action will follow if the behavior is not corrected. A written warning follows and details the employee's future status if the corrections are not made. A warning letter should clearly state the rule that was violated, state the reason for the rule, demonstrate how the rule was communicated (e.g., employee handbook), describe the previous counseling or discipline, and state future expectations and consequences. Next, many companies will suspend an employee to indicate to an employee that his or her job clearly is in jeopardy. Having moved through the steps of progressive discipline without correcting the required behavior, an employee can be considered to have terminated him- or herself.

APPLIED

A chapter such as this conveys the ethical world of supervisors and managers as a neatly written and pristine business case, a multiple-choice test where the answers are provided and one of the choices is right and the others are wrong. Some choices are easy; don't steal, bribe, or abuse; anyone would understand what is right and what is wrong. The truth is that the ethical choices that supervisors are required to make are seldom this obvious. They are often a choice between right and right. It is appropriate to terminate employees who are deficient in their job performance as a way of preserving the organization and reinforcing a principle of equity for all employees. But what if the deficient employee is a single mother with a special-needs child who needs the job and the health care coverage? And what if the performance, while deficient compared to the other staff, is not egregiously substandard? Moreover, the offending employee is a good corporate citizen, pleasant to work with, civil, and punctual. The famous management thinker Peter Drucker captures this dilemma by writing, "A decision is a judgment. It is a choice between alternatives. It is rarely a choice between right and wrong. It is at best a choice between 'almost right' and 'probably wrong'—but much more often a choice between two courses of action neither of which is probably more nearly right than the other" (1973, 470).

It is impossible to supervise or manage a department and a group of people without getting your hands dirty. For guidance, supervisors can turn to corporate mission statements, corporate codes of ethics and conduct, legal precedent, and the principles detailed in this chapter. Applying any or each of these is not likely to aid a manager in knowing which "right" choice to make. These standards are simply too vague and emanate from the noble but sterile offices of writers, attorneys, and philosophers. That is not to say that these frameworks should not be utilized; they should, but they are not likely to resolve the dilemma. An applied framework is this—having made a choice, can I, as the supervisor with the power to decide, sleep soundly? President Harry Truman reportedly declared that he lost no sleep over the decision to use the atomic bombs on Hiroshima and Nagasaki to end World War II. There is a danger in using the self as a reference for ethical behavior. However, a thoughtful, mature, reflective supervisor of reasonable character and moral development, following due deliberation and consultation, has, using the sleep test standard, a mechanism for deciding. Remember, no decision is inherently right; both choices are almost right. Also, organizations are not ethical tribunals; they are constituted to accomplish tasks while generating financial returns. A corollary to the sleep test standard is this: Can you tell the most important person in your life what you decided? If so, then you have most likely made the best choice possible, at least one that you can live with, and while your hands might be dirtied by the reality of practice, they remain as clean as possible.

SUMMARY

This chapter in no way was a comprehensive review of employment law or the nuances of sophisticated philosophical reasoning. The effort was to provide novice supervisors with a "sense" or "feel" for their responsibilities in this area and the constraints under which they must operate. The chapter presented several ethical frameworks, a discussion of corporate social responsibility and stakeholder theory, legal issues regarding employment and job interviews, the issues of sexual harassment, workplace violence, romantic relationships at work, and progressive discipline, and it concluded with the sleep test standard for ethical supervisory behavior.

EXERCISES

Summarizing
Write a one-page executive summary of the chapter.
Discuss with your classmates how you would teach this material.
Write a two-page case from your experience on this topic that would be instructional for other students.
Develop a mental model for this chapter based on the mind mapping technique.

What's Important to You in the Chapter?
With several of your classmates, discuss the most important ideas from the chapter. Which ideas do you think will be most useful to you in your career? Which ideas do you think you will remember in 6 months?

What Do the Practitioners/Others Say?
Discuss with your colleagues or someone at work any of the ideas in the chapter. Alternatively, read an article from any source on law, ethics, and stakeholders and be prepared to summarize its message.

   What would you advise Alex to do in the story at the beginning of the chapter? What criteria would you use to make the decision? How will your choice impact morale at work?

Do parents with children deserve special consideration if overtime hours are required to complete a project and they will be forced to incur extra day care expenses if they are required to stay extra? What would you say to a single mother who tells you that her child will now have to let himself in the house alone and fix his own dinner.

How would you handle it if an employee progressively over time put on so much weight that he or she could no longer meet some of the demands of the job? What if other staff had to pick up the slack? Would the source of the weight gain impact your decision?

In the battle over budget, is it ethical to ask for much more than is required knowing that the request will be cut somewhat?

Is it ethical to offer employees less that they deserve to make the financials for the department look better and thus increase your bonus?

Consider the following case; how would you handle it? Does it meet the test of a hostile work environment? Who do you talk to? What do you say?

You and your business partner had a wonderful working relationship for over ten years. Most decisions were made and all issues were resolved through open give and take in informal meetings. Each of you had taken pains to be respectful of differing points of view. As you came to work, the senior technician in the operation asked for a few moments of your time in private. The senior technician had worked there for over eight years and was a solid, dependable employee who was always on time, proficient at her job, and had the best interests of the business in mind. Not only that, but she was academically overqualified for the position, having a master's degree. She liked this job because she had six children and wanted flexible hours that would allow her to meet her family responsibilities.

The technician revealed that last night at closing time, the other partner's wife had made uncomfortable suggestions to her. The suggestions were not overt, more of an innuendo, but they were there nevertheless—at least, the technician felt so. The senior technician was very uncomfortable about what happened and said she felt badly about bringing it up and did not want to cause any trouble.

REFERENCES AND WORKS CONSULTED

Badaracco, J.L., Jr. 1997. *Defining Moments*. Boston: Harvard Business School Press.

Drucker, P. 1973. *Management*. New York: Harper and Row.

Haanaes, K., D. Michael, J. Jurgens, and S. Rangan. 2013. "Making Sustainability Profitable." *Harvard Business Review* (March): 110–14.

Kuehn, K., L. McIntire. 2014. "Sustainability a CFO Can Love." *Harvard Business Review* (April): 66–74.

Lawrence, A.T., and J. Weber, J. 2008. *Business and Society*. Boston: McGraw-Hill Irwin.

Lubin, D., and D.C. Esty. 2010. "The Sustainability Imperative." *Harvard Business Review* (May): 2–9.

Mathis, R.L., and J.H. Jackson. 2011. *Human Resource Management*. Mason, OH: South-Western.

Mitchell, B., and C. Gamlem. 2012. *The Big Book of HR*. Wayne, NJ: Career Press.

Muller, M. 2013. *The Manager's Guide to HR*. New York: American Management Association.

Weiss, J.W. 2014. *Business Ethics*. San Francisco: Berrett-Koehler.

THINGS TO BE MANAGED

Best Ideas

Best ideas are defined as those ideas from the chapters in this section that you believe will be the most influential in your practice and that you will retain over time. Take a few moments to compile your ten best ideas. Consider these as the residue of the effort and time put into these readings and discussion. In other words, what did you learn?

IDEA ONE

IDEA TWO

IDEA THREE

IDEA FOUR

IDEA FIVE

IDEA SIX

IDEA SEVEN

IDEA EIGHT

IDEA NINE

IDEA TEN

CONCLUSION

Gather all the electronic devices that you possess—phones, iPads, Nooks, Kindles, computers, and so on. Now acquire enough different devices and systems to equal about fifteen in number. Some may be of foreign origin, some vintage 1986; others may have been dropped, neglected, or never updated. None of the operating systems are the same, some are version 1.0 or 2.0 or something later. The task is to get all up and running in synchronous harmony focused on a specific application that needs to start and end at the same time and yield the desired information and outcome. Which buttons to push, in what order? How do I change the operating systems? Do they need to be changed?

One last thing: what if you couldn't see which buttons to push or know which buttons do what?

Supervision and management is hard.

- It is hard because unlike the electronic systems described in the first paragraph, you are working with people. Silicon-based systems are much more malleable than carbon-based systems. Supervision is as described above; to get everyone's operating system to sync up and produce the desired outcome on time.
- It is hard because you are human with your personal agendas, issues, problems, and neurotic accommodations to life and its stress—it's why you line up all your pencils in a row or avoid unpleasant situations as long as possible or procrastinate before tests.
- It is hard because what is most important changes from moment to moment. Sometimes sensitivity to human feelings is the most important thing, while at other times strict adherence to schedules and output is the priority.

- It is hard because there are always more problems and issues to deal with than time or energy to fix them. Once a problem is fixed, another one emerges; it is an immutable truth.
- It is hard because with humans and human systems, stuff happens, generally most of it negative. This is a pessimistic view, but supervisors and managers are not allowed to be Pollyannaish. It always costs more, takes longer, and is usually just slightly below standard.
- It is hard because supervisors are in the middle, upper management wants results, colleagues at the same level want you to make their jobs easier, and those below you want their workday smoothed out.
- It is hard because the problems you deal with are ill structured. The issues are buried under layers of confounding, confusing, and irrelevant information.
- It is hard because it is lonely; you have no one else to blame. It is your job to make it work. There are no excuses. People depend on you.

Each chapter began with a vignette describing an issue that the character Alex had to deal with. The italicized "thoughts" that followed tried to convey the sense that this was a real person with feelings, fears, and aspirations—as you will be when confronted with the challenge of management. Each chapter then presented ideas, theories, and concepts that would be helpful to a new supervisor, one who is professionally educated in some other discipline but now has to make a department work. Book chapters are tidy; they are meant to be. They are edited and pruned for ease of understanding and clarity; hence, they don't reflect reality. The process for dealing with conflict is fairly straightforward, but if you have a visceral aversion to it because your father was an abusive alcoholic, or if you are being pressured to cut corners to meet the numbers by senior executives, a chapter is inadequate preparation. Unfortunately, most professional programs don't offer practicums or rotations in supervision.

The chapters are useful however, in that they provide a beginning mental model, or schema, of how to proceed if the world were tidy and supervision could be done "by the book." Book chapters are a necessary first step to supervisory success, but not sufficient. Supervision is a blood sport; you have to get your hands dirty, hurt people's feelings, confront personal inadequacies, live with your failures, and then come back the next day for more punishment because you are a professional. It is your job to take care of the patients, design the building, reconcile the financials, write the brief, and manage the classroom. Support staff, technicians, and paraprofessionals are necessary to accomplish these objectives. **Viewed this way, supervision is a professional mandate.**

Thumb through the chapters and pick any three vignettes involving Alex and that will be the to-do list for Monday. If you are lucky, you might solve one of the issues, get started on the second issue, and have no idea about the third. On Tuesday pick one of the remaining vignettes and add that to the to-do list. Wednesday nothing pops up, but on Thursday pick three more issues. By Friday another issue has been completely resolved, leaving approximately four issues to be dealt with. The reasons for not being able to resolve the issue vary; approval is needed from human resources, finance won't approve the budget, your boss wants you to rethink the solution, your proposal to the staff was less than enthusiastically received, you don't know what to do, you know what to do but are afraid of doing it, you tried something and it didn't work, you didn't have enough time, you had the right solution but did not execute it properly, you did everything perfectly and something changed at the last minute, you did everything perfectly and it still didn't work. Of course, it starts over again the next Monday.

Though supervision and management is hard, it is not impossible. It takes practice and reflection. At the end of the day ask yourself, what worked, what didn't, why not, what should I have done differently, what were my emotions, what was I thinking, what were my assumptions? And then correct and try again.

Over time, as you practice the art of supervision, you will develop your personal rules that work for you. They will be learned by trial and error—mostly error. What follows are some thoughts gleaned from over twenty years managing pharmacies and almost twenty-five years teaching, reading, and writing about management. Pick and choose, modify and discard, but gradually develop your own personal Ten Commandments.

THOUGHTS

It's not about me: You are not a supervisor or a manager to fill in some void in your soul or to prove something to someone else. You are a supervisor with the influence and authority to make other people's lives better. This includes staff, coworkers, and customers. Let the sun shine on them and you can bask in their reflected accomplishment. The moon with no source of energy is still the brightest object in the night sky due to reflected light.

Things get better when I get better: You are in charge. For the most part you hired, trained, coached, motivated, and promoted your staff. If they are deficient or the department is deficient, take a look in the mirror. The source of improvement begins with you. Avoid thinking, "If only these people would do this." Instead, think, "It gets better when I get better."

Just fix it: A lot of decisions will be at best ineffective and at worst just wrong. Don't beat yourself up. Just fix it and move on. The writer Maya Angelou got it right when she wrote, "You did what you knew how to do. And when you knew better you did better."

Don't confuse simple with easy: A lot of supervision is conceptually easy to understand and straightforward; for example, focus on the task, craft a vision, be positive, think strategically. It is the execution that is hard. The rules for weight loss are simple; exercise more or eat less in the amount of 3,500 calories and you lose a pound. Easier said than done.

Stop whining: Everyone has problems with their job and their personal life. No one else wants to hear it.

Luck: Sometimes you may get lucky, but the only thing that ensures performance is preparation, work, and dedication—mostly work.

Keep things in perspective: Work is serious business; it just doesn't need to be taken seriously. Most work situations do not have life-and-death consequences. It is not likely anything you do will stop the planet from spinning.

Look for the simplest solution: Don't overcomplicate. Just thank people for their good work. It is likely to be more effective than developing a new performance evaluation metric.

Keep things private as long as you can: The best way to handle most situations at work is in private. Once a situation moves into the public sphere, the organizational gears, often clumsy and heavy handed, will start to crank.

Never go over anyone else's head: Consider how you would feel if your position were bypassed in dealing with a problem. The only exceptions are for legal and ethical violations.

Organizations are not rational, nor are they democracies: And as a corollary, people are not rational, including you. People and organizations do stupid and self-handicapping things routinely. It is the terrain.

Take the high road: When you don't know what to do, are being bombarded by circumstances and people that don't seem fair, and your inclination is to retaliate—DON'T. Take the high road; be professional. It is the winning hand over a career.

FINAL ASSIGNMENT

In three pages or less, describe what you believe is necessary to be a successful supervisor.